M000307453

Edouard Glissant is an accomplished and influential novelist and poet, and has recently emerged as a major theorist in Caribbean studies and post-colonial literature. In this first full-length study of Glissant's creative and theoretical work J. Michael Dash examines his poems, novels, plays and essays in the context of modern French literary movements and the post-negritude Caribbean situation, providing both a useful introduction to, and a challenging assessment of, Glissant's work to date. Dash shows how Glissant has focused in an unprecedented way on the Caribbean in terms of the diverse and hybrid culture that has been created in the region, and how his ideas on a cross-cultural poetics are the shaping force in the francophone Caribbean 'Creolite' movement.

EDOUARD GLISSANT

CAMBRIDGE STUDIES IN AFRICAN AND CARIBBEAN LITERATURE

Series editor: Professor Abiola Irele, Ohio State University

Each volume in this unique new series of critical studies will offer a comprehensive and in-depth account of the whole *oeuvre* of one individual writer from Africa or the Caribbean, in such a way that the book may be considered a complete coverage of the writer's expression up to the time the study is undertaken. Attention will be devoted primarily to the works themselves – their significant themes, governing ideas and formal procedures; biographical and other background information will thus be employed secondarily, to illuminate these aspects of the writer's work where necessary.

The emergence in the twentieth century of black literature in the United States, the Caribbean and Africa as a distinct corpus of imaginative work represents one of the most notable developments in world literature in modern times. This series has been established to meet the needs of this growing area of study. It is hoped that it will not only contribute to a wider understanding of the humanistic significance of modern literature from Africa and the Caribbean through the scholarly presentation of the work of major writers, but also offer a wider framework for the ongoing debates about the problems of interpretation within the disciplines concerned.

Already published
Chinua Achebe, by C. L. Innes
Nadine Gordimer, by Dominic Head
Edouard Glissant, by J. Michael Dash

EDOUARD GLISSANT

J. MICHAEL DASH

Reader in Francophone Literature
University of the West Indies
Mona, Kingston, Jamaica

CAMBRIDGE
UNIVERSITY PRESS

Published by the Press Syndicate of the University of Cambridge
The Pitt Building, Trumpington Street, Cambridge CB2 1RP
40 West 20th Street, New York, NY 10011–4211, USA
10 Stamford Road, Oakleigh, Melbourne 3166, Australia

First published 1995

Printed in Great Britain at the University Press, Cambridge

A catalogue record for this book is available from the British Library

Library of Congress cataloguing in publication data

Dash, J. Michael.
Edouard Glissant/J. Michael Dash.
p. cm. – (Cambridge studies in African and Caribbean literature)
Includes bibliographical references and index.
ISBN 0 521 40273 5 (hardback)
ISBN 0 521 47550 3 (paperback)
1. Glissant, Edouard, 1928 – Criticism and interpretation.
2. West Indies, French – In literature.   3. Caribbean Area – In literature.
I. Title.   II. Series.
PQ3949.2.G53Z63   1995
841′.914–dc20   94-878621   CIP

ISBN 0 521 40273 5 hardback
ISBN 0 521 47550 3 paperback

For Elise

Contents

Acknowledgements

I would like to thank Abiola Irele who first proposed a book on Edouard Glissant in this series and read the first version of the manuscript with great care. I must also acknowledge a debt of gratitude to Edouard Glissant himself who was always helpful and encouraging. In a general sense, I think I must acknowledge all those at the University of the West Indies who have worked on Edouard Glissant: Beverley Ormerod, Richard Burton, Bridget Jones and Vere Knight. I should also mention the helpfulness of Pat Dunn and her staff at the West Indies Collection of the University Library. I would like to thank Linda Bree for her careful copyediting of the typescript. Last but by no means least, I must acknowledge a debt of gratitude to Cynthia Nangle who typed the first version of the text, and Elsa Ettrick who produced the final typescript.

Chronology

1928	Edouard Glissant born 21 September in Sainte-Marie, Martinique.
1939–45	Attends the Lycée Schoelcher in Fort-de-France.
1941	André Breton visits Martinique.
1945	Participates in the election campaign of Aimé Césaire.
1946	Martinique becomes an Overseas Department of France.
1946–53	Successfully completes a licence in philosophy at the Sorbonne in Paris and studies ethnology at the Musée de l'homme.
1953	Publishes first poems *Un champ d'îles*.
1953–59	Active in the Société Africaine de Culture, co-founds with Paul Niger the Front Antillo-Guyanais pour l'Indépendence and a regular contributor to *Les lettres nouvelles*.
1954	Publishes book of poems *La terre inquiète*.
1956	Publishes epic poem *Les Indes* and first volume of essays *Soleil de la conscience*.
1958	Publishes first novel *La Lézarde* which is awarded the Prix Renaudot.
1959	Publishes poem *Le sel noir*.
1959–60	Travel ban placed on Glissant by French Government.
1961	Publishes collection of poems *Le sang rivé* with Présence Africaine.
1961	Publishes play *Monsieur Toussaint*. Death of Frantz Fanon.

1963   Writes play *Rêve de ce qui fut la tragédie d'Askia*.

1964   Publishes novel *Le quatrième siècle* which is awarded the Prix Charles Veillon.

1965   Glissant returns to Martinique to take up a post as professor of philosophy at the Lycée des Jeunes Filles in Fort-de-France.

1967–70 Founds the Institut Martiniquais d'Etudes.

1969   Publishes book of essays *L'intention poétique*.

1971   The review *Acoma* appears and will have three more numbers over the next three years.

1974   Banana workers killed in strike at Chalvet plantation in the north of Martinique.

1975   Publishes novel *Malemort*.

1976   Attends Carifesta in Kingston, Jamaica. The appearance of the play *Parabole d'un moulin de la Martinique* announced.

1979   Publishes poem *Boises* in Martinique.

1980   Leaves for Paris to work as editor of the UNESCO *Courrier*.

1981   Publishes novel *La case du commandeur* and book of essays *Le discours antillais*.

1985   Publishes poem *Pays rêvé, pays réel*.

1987   Publishes novel *Mahagony*.

1988   Becomes Distinguished Professor at Louisiana State University, Baton Rouge.

1989   Honoured with the twelfth Puterbaugh Award at the University of Oklahoma. Honorary doctorate conferred by Glendon College, York University, Toronto.

1989   *Eloge de la Créolité* by Patrick Chamoiseau, Raphael Confiant and Jean Bernabé appears.

1990   Publishes book of essays *Poétique de la relation*.

1992   Patrick Chamoiseau awarded the Prix Goncourt for the novel *Texaco* and Derek Walcott wins the Nobel Prize. Glissant publishes the collection of poems *Fastes* in Toronto.

Introduction

At present, Edouard Glissant's eminence not only in French Caribbean literature but in Caribbean literature as a whole is undisputed. There is also evidence of his emerging status as a theorist whose concepts and terminology have gained widespread acceptance. The use of such terms as *opacité*, *détour* and *relation* is increasing as these notions have become the investigative tools of literary critics as well as of those whose concerns are anthropological, sociological and linguistic. Since one of the distinctive features of Glissant's work is the fusion of the imaginative and the theoretical, it comes as no surprise that his influence should transcend the narrowly literary. This is especially so given the present theoretical context of postmodernism and the general interest in cultural diversity that Glissant's ideas seem to have anticipated.

No one initially seemed to know quite what to make of Glissant and his work. He offered a bewildering range of ideas at a time when surrealism, negritude and *francophonie* were the dominant movements. He was neither exclusively poet, novelist, dramatist nor essayist but creatively combined all categories, often simultaneously. This at least partly accounts for the early difficulty in assessing Glissant's significance and in establishing his literary and ideological credentials. For instance, Gaëton Picon in his *Panorama de la nouvelle littérature francaise* (1960) presents Glissant as a Marxist because of the latter's apparent criticism of European expansion and his sympathy with the dominated peoples of the Caribbean in his epic poem *Les Indes* (1956). Later, Jacques Nantet, given the ideological orientation towards negritude of his *Panorama de la littérature noire d'expression francaise* (1972), would offer Glissant a place in black *francophonie* as Aimé Césaire's successor in French Caribbean negritude. To Nantet, Glissant's work showed evidence of a late surrealism, very much in the vein of Aimé Césaire. Nantet's conclusion was no different from that of Léonard Sainville's *Anthologie négro-africaine* (1963) and Jacques Chévrier's *Littérature nègre* (1974).

The success of Glissant's first novel *La Lézarde*, which won the Prix Renaudot in 1958, established him as an important post-war writer. The Bordas *Histoire de la littérature francaise* (1972) commends him for his meditation on history in the wake of World War II. His place was equally secure in anthologies of black writing, such as the well-known *Anthologie négro-africaine* (1967) by Lilyan Kesteloot who includes him in the category 'une négritude militante'. Kesteloot's reservations about his inclusion are, however, very revealing. She confesses that Glissant's novel *La Lézarde* pleased French more than African readers. She goes on to say that French West Indians hardly recognise Martinique in Glissant's characters and the language they utter. The usual panegyrics in reference to Glissant's prose barely conceal the problems posed by trying to fit Glissant into a Procrustean bed of predetermined literary and ideological categories.

Some of the difficulties presented by Glissant's work were, perhaps, unique at the time. What does one make of a writer whose literary ancestors do not appear to come from his own cultural past? In particular, what does one do with a black francophone writer who invokes neither Marx, Breton, Sartre nor Césaire? Glissant professed an attachment to writers as diverse and puzzling as the novelist from the American South, William Faulkner; Saint-John Perse, born in Guadeloupe but destined to be a poet wandering across cultures; and the little-known French travel writer Victor Segalen, whose meditations on cultural displacement and diversity have deeply influenced Glissant. It was not until the 1970s that the nature of Glissant's literary enterprise was understood, and it was no coincidence that an accurate grasp of Glissant's ideas would emerge within the context of Caribbean writing as distinct from negritude or *francophonie*.

In the 1980s, Martinique's literary politics notwithstanding, appreciation of Glissant's impressive undertakings by French Caribbean critics has been increasingly insightful. In *Caraïbales* (1981) Jacques André uses a Freudian methodology to analyse Glissant's work. In 1982 Daniel Radford devoted one book in the series 'Poètes d'aujourd'hui' to Glissant. The power of Glissant's ideas in the French West Indies has, perhaps, been most dramatically apparent in the essay *Eloge de la Créolité* by Jean Bernabé, Raphael Confiant and Patrick Chamoiseau published in 1989. Both Confiant and Chamoiseau represent a new literary generation, steeped in Glissant's language and ideas. As Glissant's reputation as a major Caribbean writer becomes more recognised, special issues of journals such as *CARE*, *World Literature Today* and *Carbet* have been devoted to him.

With an oeuvre comprising six novels, seven books of poetry and four books of essays by 1993, Glissant is now the major writer and theorist from the French West Indies. This is no small achievement since the francophone Caribbean has produced such influential literary figures as Jean Price-Mars, Jacques Stephen Alexis, Jacques Roumain, Aimé Césaire and Frantz Fanon. Perhaps, more than any of his predecessors, Glissant's ideas and his writing are centred on the Caribbean and the socio-cultural dynamism of the archipelago. In a region characterised by impermanence, instability and hybrid forms, Glissant undertakes the daunting task of tracing each 'fold' of Caribbean reality, of establishing hidden continuities and creating a 'neo-baroque' form of expression in his works. Most importantly, the major thrust of his ideas is the conceptualising of a Caribbean identity within the Americas. It is precisely this impulse that informs the strength and originality of Glissant's all-encompassing literary endeavour.

CHAPTER I

Contexts

Dans le monde où je m'achemine,
je me crée interminablement.

Frantz Fanon

It is difficult to write unselfconsciously about Edouard Glissant's life, if only for the simple reason that modern literary theories have fiercely questioned the use of biography and the notion of author as a useful way of approaching the literary text. This problem, however, is further complicated in Glissant's case by the fact that he himself is acutely aware of the danger in seeing the individual as sole agent or originating source of the work. As he states in his essay 'Le roman des Amériques':

L'auteur doit être démythifié; oui parce qu'il doit être integré à une décision commune. Le nous devient le lieu du système génératif, et le vrai sujet.[1]

(The author must be demythified, certainly, because he must be integrated into a common resolve. The collective 'we' becomes the site of the generative system, and the true subject.)

Given Glissant's awareness of the need to 'demythify' the author, it is problematic to resort to a biographical centre, the authorial self, as an ordering principle for explaining the evolution of his literary production.

The acute selfconsciousness and the attendant need to replace the idea of self as origin with the ideal of a collective identity point to both the literary tradition which Glissant criticizes and the nature of the community he inhabits. On one hand, Glissant is reacting against the solipsistic authorial self

which is central to early attempts at self-affirmation in Carib-
bean writing. Such an idea is easily demonstrated in Aimé
Césaire's well-known 'profession de foi' from his *Cahier d'un
retour au pays natal*: 'ma bouche sera la bouche des malheurs qui
n'ont point de bouche' ('my mouth will be the mouth of those
calamities that have no mouth'). The heroics of self permeate
Caribbean writing, whatever its ideological persuasion, and
point to its origins in nineteenth-century Romanticism. For
Glissant, this demiurgic impulse reveals a certain blindness on
the part of the artist or intellectual who thinks he alone can
give coherent and full representation to those who are
voiceless. If anything, Glissant, as he admits in *L'intention
poétique*, attempts to dramatise a range of voices from the past
and present, even to have his narrator marginalised by this
polyphony of voices.[2] This, then, raises the second issue in
Glissant's sceptical treatment of the totalizing powers of the
individual self, the need to assert a community, to write the
'we' into existence.

In his rewriting and recreation of Martiniquan history,
Glissant is attempting to assert a creolised collective presence
in defiance of the amnesia and repression produced by
departmentalisation. In the face of centuries of unbroken
metropolitan dominance, to assert such a collectivity is an
act of defiance, with clear political implications. Officially
Martinique, as an Overseas Department of France, is a
simple extension of the metropole, identical, as Richard
Burton puts it, 'in theory if not in fact to the Tarn-et-
Garonne, the Hautes-Pyrénées, or the Ardèche'.[3] The
extreme nature of this policy of officially integrating the
French Overseas Department into the metropolitan system
has provoked an acerbic observation by V. S. Naipaul in his
early book *The Middle Passage*.

Martinique is France, a legally constituted department of France, so
assimilated and integrated that France, or what is widely supposed to
be that country, is officially seldom mentioned by name. 'M. Césaire
est en metropole,' the 'chef de Cabinet' said to one as though
M. Césaire had simply motored down to the country for a long week-
end and hadn't flown 3,000 miles to Paris.[4]

It is this myth of non-separation from France that makes the Departments of Martinique, Guadeloupe and the former prison colony of French Guyana so unique in the Caribbean. They are as different from their English-speaking and French-speaking neighbours as they are from that other country which is included under the term 'French West Indies', Haiti. Haiti, independent since 1804, is as different as one can possibly imagine from the Overseas Departments whose relations with France go back to the seventeenth century.

For Naipaul, Martinique is just another of the half-made, shipwrecked communities of the New World. Glissant, however, does not share this bleak view of the Caribbean. His sense of the positive continuities with the past may well point to Glissant's own origins, far from the alienating world of the plains, with their sugar cane plantations and urban centres. He was born in 1928 in the hilly commune of Sainte-Marie noted for its retention of local traditions from both the pre-Columbian and African past. Glissant, nevertheless, does not dwell excessively on these beginnings. The notion of unique origins, or establishing historical and cultural bearings in some unviolated space, is continuously resisted by him. We know little about his father except that he was a plantation manager. Glissant tends to refer rather to his mother to whom *La Lézarde* is dedicated. He would later write an essay on his mother in the collection 'Soixante écrivains parlent de leur mère' (1988). The autobiographical impulse, which is deeply rooted in the post-colonial preoccupation with writing the self into existence, is clearly resisted in Glissant's work.

Glissant has aimed much of his criticism of French West Indian society at the latter's fascination with fathers or forceful patriarchs. Whether in the form of Schoelcher, the maroon as primogenitor, Columbus or even Césaire himself, the problem of the father figure is constantly raised as part of the pathology of the dependency complex among the French Departments. Indeed, Glissant is not even tempted to deal with his origins in an idyllic fashion. A clue to Glissant's biography is, perhaps, more easily derived from the characters in his novels through whom his experiences are diffracted. For instance, much of the author's self-consciousness is projected into the character of Mathieu who is marked by wandering, self-exploration and fragility. Glissant is equally present in the character of Mycéa, who incarnates the relationship between negation and acquiescence, past and present. Certainly, he can be compared to the character Thael in *La Lézarde* as the latter shakes himself free from the paralyzing beauty of his mountain landscape and follows the river down to the plains of Lamentin.

It is important to note here that Glissant's evocation of landscape is never in terms of static sense of belonging but rather in terms of movement and metamorphosis. It seems to be a conscious rejection of the agoraphobic tendencies of the colonial mentality. In *La Lézarde* he suggests an intense dialectic between mountain and sea, closed and open.

Etre montagnard, dans ces pays de toute montagne qu'allèche toujours et de partout, la tentation de la mer, suppose une suprème vocation du refus.[5]

(To be a mountain dweller, in this land where every mountain is licked perpetually by the seductive sea, depends on a capacity for unflinching defiance.)

In *Soleil de la conscience* the same phenomenon emerges as the traveller confesses:

Maintenant, je ne vais pas sur la Montagne-attendez, attendez; la Mer grandit par moi.
  J'écris enfin près de la Mer[6]

(Now I do not return to the Mountain-wait, wait; the Sea grows with me.
  At last I am writing close to the sea)

Again in his recent work *Poétique de la relation* Glissant returns to the ideal of the 'unhoused' poet facing the exemplary, elusive sea at the beach of Diamant.

He entered the Lycée Schoelcher in 1939 in Fort-de-France and spent the next six years in Martinique's best-known educational institution. From these years he retains memories of the francophile excesses of various teachers and the suppression of the Creole language and local culture. One of the peculiarities of the cultural politics of French colonialism is its emphasis on the elitist and hierarchical notion of culture. The French language and its acquisition by a select few, tellingly categorised as 'évolués', meant entry into an enlightened culture, a universal civilization that stood in stark contrast to the unenlightened, folk culture of the native population. Consequently, to belong to the 'francophone' world, the gift of *francophonie*, meant admission to a superior culture. The Lycée Schoelcher signified Glissant's first intense contact with this process. Many of his later polemical utterances are aimed at the culturally repressive thrust of acculturation that this rigid policy of assimilation promoted. The roots of his passionate defence of diversity, creolisation and multilingualism were formed at this time.

In 1939 Aimé Césaire returned to Martinique and was appointed to a post in Modern Languages at the Lycée Schoelcher. Glissant, who was twelve years old at the time, was too young to be actually taught by Césaire. However Frantz Fanon, who was three years older, attests to the impact of Césaire's ideas and the power of the creative imagination at this time. Fanon, indeed, was so deeply affected by Césaire that the language of his first major work *Peau noire masques blancs* in 1956 is inextricable from Césaire's earlier texts. The presence of Césaire in parochial Martinique has been admiringly described by Fanon, who was more deeply affected than Glissant by Césaire's presence.[7] Glissant was consequently indirectly exposed to a number of radically new ideas on poetry and poetic theory introduced by Césaire and disseminated in his review *Tropiques*.

This early initiation into literary modernism in the 1940s was further reinforced in 1941 by the arrival of André Breton. These were years of great hardship for Martinique and the French Caribbean colonies because of German control of France through the Vichy regime. As a consequence, the islands were blockaded by the Allied fleet for four years. Nevertheless this was a time of great intellectual and artistic effervescence. This period is even viewed with nostalgia among younger writers today as it represents a kind of forced indepen-

dence and self-sufficiency that have been lost since departmen-
talisation.

Glissant had his first experience of political activity through
his involvement with the movement 'Franc-Jeu' formed by his
fellow students at this time. This group, which had neither
political nor ideological affiliation, played an active role in
Césaire's electoral campaign of 1945. 'Franc-Jeu' provides
material for the characters who are central to the action of the
novel *La Lézarde*. Its resistance to an ideological orientation sets
the pattern for a refusal of rigid political loyalties, consistently
seen in Glissant's career. Césaire was overwhelmingly elected
mayor of Fort-de-France as a member of the French Commun-
ist Party. In the heady days that followed Césaire's victory and
the end of the Second World War, Martinique shed its iso-
lation and parochialism. Glissant and his generation acquired
a greater sense than had existed in the past of links with the
other islands of the Caribbean. Contacts with the Cuban
painter Wifredo Lam and the Haitian poet René Depestre
reinforced this regional consciousness. Just as the young people
at the end of *La Lézarde* go their separate ways, Glissant's
student group did not survive the political activism of the 1940s
and he left for France on a scholarship in 1946.

The years that followed World War II in France were tur-
bulent ones – the defeat of the French in Vietnam in 1954, the
beginning of hostilities of the Islamic Front for National Liber-
ation (FLN) in Algeria and the increasing agitation for
independence in West Africa and Madagascar. As opposed to
an earlier generation which was affected by Sartrean existentia-
lism, Glissant was exposed to the phenomenological movement
in Paris and the 'new novelists'. Many ideas about literary
activity, politics and language itself were being rethought at this
time. Sartrean dualism, opposing mind and world, was now
replaced by an emphasis on links between individual and
reality, even to the extent of seeing the subject as acted on by
reality. In the company of Roland Barthes, Philippe Sollers and
the avant-garde circles of Paris, Glissant began to rethink the
ideals of authority, comprehension and totalization in terms of
participation, involvement and interdependence.

In this regard, the differences between Glissant and other
French Caribbean writers, like Frantz Fanon and René Depes-
tre, were becoming increasingly apparent. Fanon in all his
major work showed the deep influence of Sartre's political
prescriptions and Depestre, in the 1950s, had fallen under the
sway of Aragon's promotion of a new 'realism' in committed
verse. Many others of Glissant's contemporaries showed an
allegiance to negritude. Although Glissant was linked to the
'Société Africaine de Culture' in Paris, he could not be called a
devotee of the *Présence Africaine* movement. An early article, 'Le
romancier noir et son peuple', published in *Présence Africaine* in
1957, already points to his reservations about the new militant
black novelists. He gently deplores the unrelieved denun-
ciation of colonialism in their works and advocates as an idea
for the novel a complex approach to socio-political realities
which was impossible at the time.

Il semble qu'un roman qui se donne pour but de 'révéler' une réalité,
doit aborder cette réalité de tous les côtés à la fois, en ce qu'elle a de
positif et de négatif.[8]

(To my mind a novel whose aim is to 'expose' reality must approach
this reality from all sides simultaneously, in terms of both the positive
and the negative.)

Indeed, in his inventory of novels by black writers provided in
this article, the only two successes for him are Jacques
Roumain and Richard Wright, whose works are not a thinly
disguised anti-colonial polemic. Glissant goes so far as to say
that the genre of the novel displays an apparent inferiority to
that of poetry because of its inability to reach beyond anti-
colonial protest.

The reviews written by Glissant for *Les lettres nouvelles* in the
mid to late fifties provide evidence of a wide range of interests.
It was at this time that he became acquainted with the work of
Victor Segalen, Djuna Barnes and the Chilean painter Roberto
Matta. An early essay on Shakespeare's *Hamlet* (1954) reveals
his interest in the question of paternity and filiation. He also
published three collections of poetry – *Un champ d'îles* (1953),
La terre inquiète (1954), and *Les Indes: poème de l'une et l'autre terre*

(1954) – and a book of essays entitled *Soleil de la conscience* in 1956. Given his comments in 'Le romancier noir et son peuple', it is not surprising that Glissant's early work should concentrate on poetry. His early interest in the poetry of Saint-John Perse is in part responsible for this emphasis. Both Bernadette Cailler and Daniel Radford have pointed to the importance of Perse to Glissant's early poetry. Perhaps it would be truer to say that Glissant had become aware of Perse's importance as part of a poetic tradition which increasingly favoured themes of travel and the encounter with foreign cultures. Such a tradition would include Segalen, Claudel, Perse and many of the Surrealists. A number of French poets of no particular ideological orientation were close to Glissant at that time. The most important of these is Henri Pichette whose *Apoèmes* and *Epiphanies* are fondly remembered by Glissant. Pichette's observation that 'la littérature n'est belle que dans le lit du monde' ('literature is beautiful only in the bed of the world') shows the nature of the affinity that he shared with Glissant. Both Gaëton Picon and Jean Paris in their anthologies are sensitive to Glissant's relationship to these French poets.[9]

From the outset poetry was seen by Glissant as an investigative system, a creative probing that forces the underside of a lived experience to the light. Coming of age artistically when negritude was at its height, Glissant felt some impatience with the symbolic mapping of the Caribbean that had taken place. The dualities that characterised the poetic discourse of negritude, opposing master and slave, hill and plain, vertical defiance and horizontal passivity, were essentially an extension of political rhetoric. Glissant's early poetry suggests that nature does not bear meaning in a clear and legible way. He concentrates on the teeming estuary, the raging ocean, which convey a sense of uncharted profusion rather than fixed symmetries. This early verse reveals an enormous appetite for language. It is as if an earlier ideological reductiveness had created a deficient diet of words for the Caribbean poet. It is no coincidence that one of the dominant images of *La Lézarde* should be that of a slow savouring of the complex and elusive flavour of a

ripening fruit. His entire oeuvre would be concerned with the
sensuous complexity of experience.

This sense of an opaque and elusive world, which emerges in
the early verse, is explored in a more discursive and narrative
fashion in *Soleil de la conscience*. This is a sustained reflection on
exile and *errance*, not in terms of the Romantic cliché of rootless-
ness but of self-discovery. It is as if Glissant was proposing the
importance of the unfamiliar in the whole project of self-
scrutiny. This work is not only thematically significant to the
development of Glissant's ideas but also stylistically combines
exposition and lyricism, essay and poem in a form which defies
categorisation according to traditional genres. As Glissant
himself says in this work, he is 'l'ethnologue de moi-même'
('performing ethnology on myself'), as he scrutinizes himself
and the Caribbean from the perspective of exile. It is within
this phase of creative dislocation that self-awareness becomes
more acute. The subject then for Glissant can become the
object of intense investigation. Frantz Fanon himself noted, in
Peau noire, masques blancs, the intensification of racial self-
consciousness in the West Indian when he was in France. The
'sun of consciousness' sheds light for Glissant on what might
constitute a Caribbean and by extension a New World sensibi-
lity. The orderliness of European landscape, the rhythmic
measure of changing seasons, create for Glissant a kind of
psychic unease because it is so different from his world of excess
and profusion.

Mon paysage est emportement, la symétrie du planté me gêne. Mon
temps n'est pas une succession d'espérances saisonnières, il est encore
de jaillissements et de trouées d'arbres.[10]

(My landscape is passion, the symmetry of cultivation makes me
uneasy. Time for me is not a sequence of seasonal expectations, it is
still explosive and torn by surging trees.)

In this link between landscapes and self-possession, Glissant
echoes the Claudelian idea of *co-naissance* as individual
consciousness grows with the discovery of external reality. This
sensuous approach to the Caribbean as an unregimented and
agitated landscape would become not only the hallmark of

Glissant's own creative imagination but also the basis for this aesthetic theory, creating, in his own words, the need for a 'chaos d'écriture'.

It would be a distortion to treat Glissant's concerns at this time as exclusively literary. He makes the importance of politics to this decade clear in *Soleil de conscience* when he writes:

On peut dire aussi que le problème premier de notre temps est celui du choix politique. Mais je ne veux ici que suivre la trace de mon voyage, et non proposer des leçons ou des programmes.[11]

(One can also say that the major issue of our time is that of political choice. But I now wish only to follow the path of my journey and not to teach or to establish programmes.)

In the late fifties Glissant, like his contemporary Frantz Fanon, became increasingly involved in political concerns. His poem *Les Indes* had already established his interest in the historico-social implications of Columbus's voyage of discovery. It is Glissant's first attempt to evoke the unwritten history of resistance and sacrifice in the New World and already anticipates his later play based on the experience of Toussaint L'Ouverture. The increasing criticism of Marxism and the Communist Party in 1956, as well as the intensifying debate on decolonisation, produced a response in Glissant. After riots in 1959 in Fort-de-France, he founded the 'Front-Antillo-Guyanais' with his friend Paul Niger. This group called for the decolonisation of the French Departments and their integration into the Caribbean region. At this point his political position was radically different from that of Aimé Césaire who had chosen the route of departmentalisation. The group was disbanded in 1961 by General de Gaulle and Glissant forbidden to leave France. The Algerian crisis also forced him to take a stand in favour of the FLN war for independence from France. These are years of great political turbulence for Glissant and his activism marks a break with a previous generation which favoured the restraint of the traditional Caribbean man of letters. In this regard Fanon, Glissant, Alexis and Depestre revealed a younger generation's desire to go beyond the strictly literary and to opt for personal involvement, no matter what the risks were.

The two significant features of the next phase of Glissant's
career are his return to Martinique in 1965 and an increasing
interest in the novel form. This return to Martinique
reinforced the link between individual activism and collective
destiny already evident in Paris. As Glissant was later to say in
Le discours antillais, return is a vital phase of the dialectical
process involving a turning away and a turning back, diversion
and reversion: 'Il faut revenir au lieu. Le Détour n'est ruse
profitable que si le Retour le féconde; non pas retour au rêve
d'origine . . . mais retour au point d'intrication' ('One must
return to one's place. Diversion is not a useful ploy unless it is
nourished by Reversion; not a return to the longing for origins
. . . but a return to the point of entanglement').[12] Too often, as
Glissant himself has noted, Caribbean artists and intellectuals
have taken leading roles in other people's revolutions and
neglected their own societies. Fanon in Algeria, Padmore in
Ghana, Garvey in the United States and even Césaire's
importance to African decolonisation are some of the major
examples of this pattern. Just as 'Détour' can lead to a dead
end, 'Retour' can be tragic. Attempts to bring radical change
to Caribbean societies can have disastrous consequences as in
the case of Jacques Stephen Alexis, who was executed by the
Duvalier regime in 1961 after a clandestine landing in
northern Haiti.

Glissant spent the next fifteen years in Martinique. This
period saw the founding of IME (Institut Martiniquais
d'Etudes) by Glissant in an effort to break the cultural stran-
glehold of France on Martinique.[13] Even though he was not
politically aligned to any particular group or ideology, his
position could be broadly described as *indépendantiste* and he
strongly favoured the integration of the French Departments
into the Caribbean region. In political terms, Glissant's
rupture was now complete with Aimé Césaire who had insti-
tuted the departmentalisation of Martinique in 1946 and
whose Parti Progressiste Martiniquais dominated local politics.
Apart from his educational and research institute, Glissant in
1971 launched the journal *Acoma* to disseminate the ideas of
a research group attached to IME. Unlike Césaire's journal

Tropiques in the forties, Glissant's publication did not concentrate on a revaluation of Martinique's African past but on the problems of psychological and cultural dispossession that followed in the wake of departmentalisation. Also in *Acoma*, we see an elaboration of a poetics of the American imagination through investigations of the work of William Faulkner, Alejo Carpentier, Nicolas Guillen and Pablo Neruda.

Glissant had already begun to turn his attention to prose fiction, towards the end of his stay in Paris. In this regard he had had enormous success. His first novel *La Lézarde* had won the prestigious Prix Renaudot in 1958 and his second work of fiction, *Le quatrième siècle*, the Prix Charles Veillon in 1964. Both these works are linked not only by characters but by an elaboration of ideas of landscape and history that first emerged in his early poetry. They represent a remapping of hill and plain, forest and sea, as well as an effort to establish new continuities between normally opposed areas of Martiniquan experience. The relation between maroon and house slave, journeys inward and journeys outward, negation and acquiescence, were given an original treatment by Glissant. From the formal perspective, these works of fiction were unprecedented in Caribbean writing, in eschewing documentary realism and the rhetoric of protest in favour of a dense and digressive style that probes beneath individual consciousness and encompasses both negative and positive areas of Caribbean experience. The novels that follow Glissant's return to Martinique in 1965 are less accessible in some ways and represent thoroughgoing attempts to articulate the collective unconscious of what Glissant called the 'pays réel'.

Whereas Glissant's two previous novels dealt with the immediate past of Martinique, *Malemort*, published in 1975, is about contemporary Martiniquan reality. The very title of this novel indicates a bleaker phase in Glissant's writing. The term *malemort* – the undead or the living dead – points to the corrosive power of the phenomenon of successful colonisation in the French West Indian Departments.[14] Glissant's despondency is reflected in the fact that the Lézarde river has now become a stagnant and polluted trickle. The sense of collective impotence, cultural dispossession and official corruption is depressingly different from the evocation of sensory plenitude so characteristic of his earlier writing. This mood would persist through much of the writing of Glissant's fifteen-year stay in Martinique. For instance, a short book of poetry, *Boises* (1979), which refers to the wooden collars worn by slaves, is subtitled 'histoire naturelle d'une aridité' ('natural history of aridity').

The capacity of IME and *Acoma* to counteract the officially sponsored onslaught on Martinique as a political, cultural and economic entity was inevitably limited. Departmentalisation had created a passive, consumer-culture in Martinique. The various articles in *Acoma* pointing to the erosion of Martinique's economic base, the absence of self-supporting productivity and the belief in the disinterested generosity of the metropolis could do little to halt the process that makes of Martinique a community ignorant of its past, resentful of its impotence and yet fearful of future change.

Some of the crucial political questions of this period of Glissant's stay in Martinique are reflected in his only published play *Monsieur Toussaint*, the first version of which appeared in 1961. As in all his other literary works, Glissant in this play steers clear of didacticism and a simplistic glorification of Haiti's revolutionary leader. Instead, the play is charged with tragic ambiguities, and Glissant concentrates on the ironies and paradoxes thrown up by the complications of a given political situation. At the centre of this drama are two antagonists. The action of the play turns on a debate between Toussaint and Makandal, neither of whom brought the Haitian revolution to a successful conclusion. However, their positions in Haiti's revolutionary process were extremely important and furthermore had clear relevance to contemporary politics in Martinique. Past and present continuously interact in the play which opposes the liberal leader with the radical maroon, the compromises of acquiescence with the negation of revolt.

Makandal is the incarnation of the dream of *marronnage* or the rejection of servitude, of the people's conscience, and the complete opposition of Toussaint's accommodation of the white world. Toussaint is very much the product of the ideas of

the French Revolution of 1789, and increasingly cut off from
the values of his people. Neither the abstract ideas of the latter
nor the fiery rebelliousness of the former are in themselves
capable of producing revolutionary change. The parallels
between Césaire's politics and Toussaint's liberal policies in
pre-Independence Haiti are irresistible. It is left to Dessalines
to achieve the ideal of independence. He is prepared to see
Toussaint arrested and feels that it is by reviving the ideals of
Makandal that success can be realised. Yet Glissant does not
provide us with a blind celebration of *marronnage*. Both Makan-
dal and Toussaint are parts of a process of change. By impli-
cation Martinique, still trapped in departmentalisation, awaits
its Dessalines. As Toussaint says:

Il y eut Makandal pour annoncer le combat et la douleur du combat,
puis il y eut Toussaint pour prendre la victoire et la douleur de la
victoire. Ne sommes-nous pas comme deux journées qui se suivent
avec logique, sans que jamais tout autour de la terre elles se recon-
trent?[15]

(There was Makandal to announce the battle and the suffering of
battle; then there was Toussaint to take the victory and the suffering
of victory. Are we not like two days following one after the other
logically, without ever meeting all around the earth?)

Even when turning to theatre Glissant avoids making clear
political statements and ventilating local quarrels. Such a
theatre which eschews agitation and propaganda received a
very limited response from the local Martiniquan public.
Glissant has always been impatient with the simplifications of
militant art. In his drama he remains consistent, as the central
argument of Monsieur Toussaint demands patience and atten-
tiveness from an audience which must also be prepared for no
happy resolution of the conflict. Indeed, this flirtation with the
theatre produced some interesting and original thoughts from
Glissant on the problem of theatre and community in Martini-
que. In the second issue of *Acoma* in July 1971, Glissant
published his essay, 'Théâtre, conscience du peuple' which
establishes a parallel between the emergence of drama and the
community's awareness of itself. Theatre is the concrete real-

isation of a collective self-consciousness: 'Le théâtre est l'acte
par lequel la conscience collective se voit, et par conséquent se
dépasse' ('Theatre is the act through which the collective
consciousness sees itself and consequently moves forward').[16]
Therefore, theatre is not capable of flourishing in a community
where there is little reflection or self-consciousness. This is
Glissant's dismaying conclusion about the Martiniquan situ-
ation. He would leave Martinique in 1980 when invited by the
newly re-elected director of UNESCO, Amadou-Mahtar
M'Bow, to come to Paris as the editor of the magazine, *Le
Courrier de l'UNESCO*.

In the 1980s and once again in Paris, Glissant applied many
of the ideas that had evolved within the specific cultural and
linguistic space of the Caribbean, on a global scale. His poetics
of creolisation and multilingualism were elaborated to encom-
pass an international phenomenon which he called a poetics of
relating. The interpenetration of cultures, the interference of
languages with each other, the continuous movement of
peoples are all reflected in his work as editor of the *Courrier*.
Under Glissant the magazine appeared in more than thirty
languages and there was even a Creole edition. Glissant's work
in this international organization was facilitated by the policy
of the director, Amadou-Mahtar M'Bow. M'Bow was equally
sensitive to the issue of multilingualism and the risks of pri-
vileging one language over another. He shared with Glissant a
sense of the importance of culture in notions of development
and the collection of his speeches, *Les temps des peuples* (1982),
with its emphasis on cultural diversity, seems closely in accord-
ance with Glissant's views on cultural and linguistic plurali-
ty.[17] From as early as 1972 Glissant had spoken out on the
question of the need to conceive of a new linguistic order, at a
meeting of French teaching Departments in Montreal. His
opening speech, 'Langue et multilinguisme dans l'expression
des nations modernes', speaks of abandoning the categories of
spoken as against written language, and the importance of
rejecting the notion of a universal language.

These ideas were shared by other writers who were close to
Glissant at the time and also working at UNESCO, such as

Tchicaya U Tam'si, the Congolese poet, and the Haitian writer, René Depestre. Depestre's intervention on the question of exile in the July–August issue of *Magazine littéraire* in 1985 reveals the extent to which old notions of cultural wholeness and identity were being radically redefined. What Depestre called the present 'ubiquité culturelle de la planète',[18] in reference to the unceasing process of global change, was the subject of some of Glissant's most original thinking at this time. As he admitted in a 1984 interview, his work at UNESCO was an intensification and acceleration of interests he had had during his entire career. His job as editor put him at the centre of a vast field of cultural and linguistic relationships, a multinational crossroads.

Je suis directement en contact avec cent cinquant-huit pays et vingt-six langues, j'apprends beaucoup sur les relations culturelles entre peuples, j'essaie de mettre ce que j'apprends au service de la collaboration culturelle entre peuples[19]

(I am directly in contact with 158 countries and 26 languages, I am learning a lot about cultural relations between peoples, I am trying to apply what I learn to collaboration between peoples on the cultural level)

The eight years spent in Paris with UNESCO represented for Glissant a period of great personal satisfaction. Not only was he satisfied with the official policy of UNESCO, but his own reputation grew enormously at this time because of the appearance of *La case du commandeur* and *Le discours antillais* in 1981. The latter was described by the literary critic for *Le Monde* as one of the three most important works of the decade. Just as critical interest in his work intensified in the late fifties and early sixties because of the success of his two first novels and the prestige of the Prix Renaudot, so in the eighties Glissant was rediscovered by literary critics. In 1981 alone, four interviews with him were published. By 1984, the number had grown to eleven, indicating the level of interest in the ideas expressed in his work at this time. His earlier works were reprinted and many of his texts were published in English, Spanish and German translations. In 1982, he appeared in the 'Poètes d'aujourd'hui' series published by Seghers.

Glissant also published two further new works during the eighties. As in the past, poetry and prose are closely intertwined in his literary projects. *Pays rêvé, pays réel*, a poem, appeared in 1985 and the novel *Mahagony* in 1987. The former returns to the characters who had been given special attention in earlier novels. To some extent *La Lézarde* could be said to be Thael's novel, *Le quatrième siècle* Mathieu's novel, and *La case du commandeur* that of Mycéa. These three characters return in *Pays rêvé, pays réel* to voice the author's poetic concerns. This work reveals how misleading it is to see Glissant's oeuvre as a sequence of steps or a logical evolution towards some ultimate, perfect or definitive work. It would be far more accurate to visualize his literary production as a series of probings which move back and forth in time, between landscapes and personae. This pattern is clear from the outset as *La Lézarde* precedes *Le quatrième siècle* which is situated chronologically before the earlier work. It could be said that *La Lézarde* made the writing of the second work possible. There is a sense in which each work is a provisional utterance elaborating earlier themes and anticipating future ideas. As Glissant himself asserted, his work is relatively unprovoked by accidental occurrences or external circumstance. Rather, it is a question of an uninterrupted internal debate which erupts as it were into conscious articulation.

Un projet de littérature ou, ce qui revient au même, de connaissance, se maintient flexiblement autour d'un axe irréductible . . . Pour ma part, je n'écris pas d'article de circonstance ni de livre occasionnel: ce que j'écris est le plus souvent, du moins je m'y efforce, centré.[20]

(The project of literary creation or, what comes down to the same thing, that of knowing, is flexibly sustained around a fixed axis . . . In my case, I do not write essays or books occasioned by circumstance: what I write is most often, at least I strive for this, centrally focused.)

Pays rêvé, pays réel can be read as an oratorio which gives dramatic expression to a series of voices. The polyphonic element in Glissant's work, evident in earlier texts, becomes even more emphatic at this stage. In formal terms, this poem recalls *Monsieur Toussaint*, which is a static drama of voices and echoes, and anticipates the single most important feature of the novel *Mahagony*. The theme of this novel is suggested in the title – the agony of a people destined for happy oblivion. The real threat to Martinique in particular, and the French Caribbean Departments as a whole, is that they are cut off from the process of cultural interrelationship. Glissant's nightmare vision of Martinique is represented in this text as a hermetically-sealed world which has become a harmless curiosity for tourists, no longer even a haven for thrill-seekers.

The global dimension of the phenomenon of cultural relationships in a post-plantation society was of growing importance to Glissant at this time. Already in *Mahagony* there are indications of a theory of cultural relativity, of dynamic global change that characterises Glissant's most recent writing. It had also become overwhelmingly clear that Glissant's work represented an epistemological break with earlier theories of universality and difference that have dominated Caribbean thought. For Glissant Martinique, or the Caribbean for that matter, was not just a homeland to which one returned. From the very beginning he seemed uneasy with the idea of an original heartland. Even as he launched the term *Antillanité*, in *Le discours antillais* he seemed to hesitate for fear of turning it into another monolithic idea, becoming in the process yet another ideological founding father.[21] The ideal of Martinique as home, 'the navel of the world', had already been brilliantly charted by Aimé Césaire whose work can be regarded as a thoroughgoing cadastral survey of this unique space. Martinique became for Glissant his point of insertion in the world. The impulse to move outwards and not back intensifies in later work as he explores relations between Martinique and the Caribbean, Martinique and the Americas, Martinique and 'le tout monde'. It is perhaps not surprising that Glissant's audience should emerge among those who could no longer resort to the consoling notions of racial difference and cultural uniqueness, in particular Haiti's exiled community in Canada.[22]

In 1988 Glissant retired from UNESCO. In any case the director's term in office had come to an end and there was strong opposition to his policies, in particular his efforts to

promote the views of the developing world in his New Infor-
mation Order, from most of the large western donor nations to
UNESCO. At this time Glissant was offered a distinguished
professorship at Louisiana State University in Baton Rouge.
His move to Louisiana can be seen as the latest phase of a
career of *errance*, of the writer as wanderer, 'vagabond', across
cultures. Glissant had become, by his own admission, marginal
within France and French literature; Louisiana, with its own
very Caribbean blend of plantation past and cultural *métissage*
(the creolisation that results from cultural or racial encounter),
opened up for him in a very concrete way the possibility of
exploring the American dimension of a Caribbean identity. As
he declares in a recent special issue of *Le nouvel observateur*:

les paysages des Amériques, de la plus petite île au plus vertigineux
canyon, 'communiquent' une ouverture, une démesure, une manière
d'irruption dans l'espace, qui influencent profondément nos façons
de sentir et de penser. C'est de là que je partirai, pour y revenir
encore et toujours.[23]

(the landscapes of the Americas, from the smallest island to the most
staggering canyon, 'communicate' openness, an excess, a violent
entry into space, which deeply influence our ways of feeling and
thinking. It is from there that I start, only to return again and
always.)

Forever the ethnologist of his own experience, Glissant's recent
formulations draw heavily on chaos theory. His notion of *le
chaos-monde* is used to describe the creative unpredictability of
the explosive archipelago of cultures represented by the
Caribbean.

　　Glissant's recent thinking is summed up in his latest book of
essays *Poétique de la relation*. As has been the case in the past,
Glissant tries to avoid incarnating the voice of the master or
intellectual authority.[24] The perspective of the literary patri-
arch, the *maître*, is consistently undercut by a looser, more
imaginative approach which is well suited to Glissant's elusive
subject. *Relation* ('relating', in all senses of the word) is opposed
to *difference* and, more than in his previous essays, Glissant
ranges beyond the Caribbean to describe a global condition.

Indeed, one could say that he sees the entire world in terms of a Caribbean or New World condition. The world, for Glissant, is increasingly made up of archipelagos of culture. The Caribbean has become exemplary in this creative global 'chaos' which proliferates everywhere.

Broad and non-reductionist in their thrust, Glissant's most recent essays grapple with a major and complex issue in Caribbean writing – the temptation of cultural difference and intellectual containment on one hand and the impulse towards relativity and interdependence. There has been, however, an almost predictable tendency to turn Glissant's ideas into ideological dogma. The recent essay *Eloge de la Créolité*, by Jean Bernabé, Patrick Chamoiseau and Raphael Confiant, situates its argument in a post-negritude context and sets out to define *créolité* and *Antillanité* in terms that are suggestively reductionist:

Nous declarons que la créolité est le ciment de notre culture et qu'elle doit régir les fondations de notre antillanité. La créolité c'est *l'agrégat interactionnel ou transactionnel* des éléments culturels caraïbes, européens, africains, asiatiques et levantins, que le joug de l'Histoire a réunis sur le même sol.[25]

(We declare that *créolité* is the cement in our culture and that it must determine the foundations of our *Antillanité*. *Créolité* is the interacting and transacting aggregate of the cultural elements which are Carib, European, African, Asian and Levantine, put together by History on the same terrain.)

Words like *agrégat*, *ciment* and *foundations* suggest an approved hierarchy of value which emerge from a new ideological iconoclasm. *Créolité* is tempted to produce its own rhetoric, its own approved texts, its own hierarchy of intellectuals and a new heroics of *marronnage*, orality and popular discourse. It lacks the ironic self-scrutiny, the insistence on process ('creolisation' and not *créolité*) that is characteristic of Glissant's thought. Indeed, despite its avowed debt to Glissant, *Eloge de la Créolité* risks undoing the epistemological break with essentialist thinking that he has always striven to conceptualise.

Maryse Condé in 1977 notices that 'l'Antillanité n'a pas

suscité un courant littéraire analogue à la Négritude' ('*Antill-anité* has not promoted a literary movement anything like negritude').[26] However, there have been remarkable changes in the last decade or so. A new generation of novelists from Martinique in particular has emerged and the influence of Glissant on their ideas, subjects and literary technique is pervasive. The novelist Patrick Chamoiseau, winner of the Prix Goncourt in 1992, attests to the importance of Glissant's influence. He claims that he could not find a creative voice: 'Jusqu'au jour où je lus, ou plus exactement relus *Malemort*. Alors, commença entre Glissant et moi, une aventure que je pense éternelle (c'est dire toujours féconde)' ('Until the day I read, or rather reread, *Malemort*. Then began between Glissant and myself, an adventure that I think is eternal (meaning always fertile)').[27] Chamoiseau openly and disarmingly admits to the effect of Glissant as a catalyst for his own writing – even to the point of saying that in order to begin writing he would read one of Glissant's works. It is now through a younger generation that Glissant will be rediscovered. In his 1991 review article in *The New York Review of Books* Milan Kundera praises the work of Patrick Chamoiseau because the latter 'takes liberties with French which not one of his French contemporaries could even imagine taking'. With no apparent awareness of Edouard Glissant or his ideas, Kundera locates the strength of the Martiniquan literary imagination in its cultural multiplicity.

I will say this: the strength and richness of Martinique culture seem to be to be owing precisely to the multiplicity of the mediating contexts within which it moves. Martinique: plural intersection: crossroads of the continents.[28]

Thus Kundera discovers in 1991, through the novels of Chamoiseau, ideas expressed by Glissant decades earlier.

The political thrust of earlier ideologies such as cultural universality, negritude, indigenism, Marxism was clear. It would however be impossible to derive a systematic politics from Glissant's poetic and generously open-ended ideal of irreducible plurality and diversity for the Caribbean. This at once explains his having been somewhat neglected in the past, as well as his present importance. His vision of opacity, disorder, chaos and infinite profusion, so confusing before, now seems to offer new insights into the elusive complexity of the Caribbean experience.[29] The strength of Glissant's entire oeuvre lies in the self-consciousness that prevents him from resisting the Mallarméan ideal of turning the world into a book, a theory or an idea. As he writes in his first book of essays:

Qui n'a rêvé du poème qui tout explique, de la philosophie dont le dernier mot illumine l'univers, du roman qui organise toutes les vérités, toutes les passions, et les conduit et les éclaire?[30]

(Who has not dreamt of the poem that explains everything, of the philosophy whose last word clarifies the universe, of the novel that organizes all truths, all passions, and orients and deciphers them?)

Those who have yielded to this temptation of ultimate explanations have produced one of two ideologies in Glissant's view – either the notion of universal humanism ('l'Universel généralisant') or irreducible singularity ('l'identité-racine'). Both of these ideologies are typified by uniformity and intolerance. They have also both been dominant in the Caribbean since the nineteenth century. Driven by the dream of total, systematic predictability these views tend to distort the complex, dynamic nature of human experience. Glissant has consistently emphasised chance, error and unpredictability in all his ideas. In his poetics of interrelating and his recent theories of chaos, this emphasis has become full-blown. As is evident in his entire oeuvre, Glissant continues to use the imaginative impulse, his 'poetic intention', to release potential for reflection and theoretical formulation. Despite the hagiographic tendency of this assertion, Patrick Chamoiseau does signal Glissant's formative influence among a newer generation of writers when he describes him as 'père d'une littérature future' ('father of a future literature').[31]

CHAPTER 2

The poetic intention

UN CHAMP D'ILES, LA TERRE INQUIETE, LES INDES,
SOLEIL DE LA CONSCIENCE

celui, dans le sommeil, dont le souffle est relié au souffle de
la mer

Saint-John Perse, *Exil*

Edouard Glissant's literary reputation rests primarily on his
novels and essays. There is also strong evidence of his interest in
the novel form in his reference to the work of other novelists
such as Alejo Carpentier, Gabriel García Márquez, Djuna
Barnes and William Faulkner. Nevertheless, Glissant began his
career as a poet and continues to produce books of poetry in
conjunction with his fictional narratives and theoretical dis-
courses. This sustained refusal on his part to abandon poetry,
or even to recognise the conceptual boundary that tradi-
tionally exists between poetry and prose, creative and critical
writing, is central to the understanding of Glissant's entire
literary enterprise. In introducing Glissant in his *Anthologie de la
littérature négro-africaine* in 1963, Léonard Sainville shrewdly
observes:

C'est un poète dans toute l'acception du mot. En devenant roman-
cier, il reste plus que jamais poète.[1]

(He is a poet in the fullest sense of the word. In becoming a novelist,
he remains more than ever a poet.)

In this comment Sainville points to a vital and problematic
area of Glissant's work and invites us to examine what is meant
by 'a poet in the fullest sense of the word'.

Since Glissant's oeuvre does not evolve in the normal sense – in terms of either theme or genre – his major preoccupations are apparent from his earliest writing and return obsessively throughout the various phases of his work. One of these pre-occupations – perhaps even the major one – is tied to the issue of language itself and Glissant's challenge, very much in the modernist vein, mounted against language as transparent communication. As he himself says, expression is inextricably related to the unsayable, to a subconscious imaginative thrust.

Il n'est pas d'intention qui résiste à la poussée de l'imaginé. Mais il n'est pas d'oeuvre qui, s'élaborant, ne s'arme d'une seule inaltérable et souvent incommunicable intention. Celle-ci, à s'accomplir, aussi-tôt se masque; ce centre, éclairé, s'étoile. Dans le même temps le projet, d'être diffus et bientôt diffusé, se ramasse, se fortifie. Double volée: l'imaginé déporte le propos, le propos fixe peu à peu l'imaginaire et le somme.[2]

(There is no intention that can withstand the thrust of the imagined. But there is no work which, as it unfolds, is not fortified by a single unchanging and often incommunicable intention. The latter, in order to be fulfilled, immediately conceals itself; this centre, once illuminated, shines like a star. At the same time the project, from being diffuse and soon diffused, is pulled together and fortified. A double trajectory: the imagined undermines intention, intention orients little by little the imaginary and directs it.)

From the outset this complex relationship between conscious intention and the surge of the unconscious, between premeditated prose and spontaneous improvisation, has a shaping force on Glissant's approach to the Caribbean. Indeed, this ever-changing, creatively unstable relationship between intention and imagination can be seen as the model for investigating all areas of human experience.

It is not that Glissant was the first to propose this particular linguistic model – even though he may be the only Caribbean writer who is so explicitly obsessed with the slippery nature of language. In fact this awareness firmly places him within the tradition of twentieth-century modernism and establishes a literary affinity with the poet Stéphane Mallarmé. It was Mallarmé, after all, who made the provocative comment, in an

1891 interview, that 'en vérité, il n'y a pas de prose'. In so doing, he emphasized the nature of the mystery of language, the problem of formal control and the uncertain identity of the author. A no less famous dictum of Mallarmé's is the assertion that a creative work necessitates 'la disparition élocutoire du poète qui cède l'initiative aux mots'. If words take the initiative for the nineteenth-century French poet, Glissant is no less sensitive to the precarious nature of the writer and of literary intention: 'L'écrivain est toujours le fantôme de l'écrivain qu'il veut être' ('The writer is always the phantom of the writer he wants to be').[3]

The fragility of the literary vision as well as the intractable nature of external reality are acutely sensed by Glissant from his earliest work. He, perhaps provokingly, alludes to Mallarmé in *Soleil de la conscience* which begins with a suggestion of seductive impotence: 'L'hiver a ses séductions redoutables' ('Winter has its daunting forms of seduction'). But whereas Mallarmé's ideas allow us to situate one of Glissant's major poetic concerns, it would be wrong to see Glissant as magnificently trapped in one of Mallarmé's icy prisons of language. It is the difference that separates Glissant from Mallarmé that permits an understanding of the former's view of the literary act. What Glissant objects to in his French predecessor is his poetic hubris, the belief dear to the Symbolist movement in France, that the poet could provide the 'orphic explanation of the world'. For Glissant neither does the world exist to become a book, nor can reality be trapped in a net of words. There would inevitably be a great difference between the nineteenth-century French poet's view of nature as infinitely manipulable, of the referent as helplessly docile, and Glissant's sense of the elusive nature of external reality. As Barbara Johnson persuasively argues, Symbolist aesthetics can be seen as the product of a specific historical moment.[4] The fact is that the world and the individual's relation to the world is inscribed differently in Glissant's work, written in the second half of the twentieth century and from a Caribbean perspective.

For Glissant the world is neither menacingly inscrutable in a Kafkaesque sense nor able to be eliminated in a Mallarméan sense. He defines his relationship with Mallarméan aesthetics in the following fashion:

L'ouvrage d'un poète paraît (à ce poète) dérisoire, au regard de ce qu'il a rêvé: ce n'est jamais que l'écume de cet océan d'où il veut arracher une cathédrale, une architecture définitive. Mallarmé est un des rares à admettre ce manque, à cultiver cette absence; jusqu'à faire de l'absence une présence, et en quelque sorte du défaut de poésie l'objet et la fin de la poésie.[5]

(The finished work of a poet seems (to this poet) ridiculous, in the light of his dream: it can never be anything more than the foam from that ocean from which he wants to force a cathedral, some definitive architecture. Mallarmé is one of the few to acknowledge this failing, to cultivate this absence: to the point of making this absence a presence and, in a way, the weakness of poetry the ultimate goal of poetry.)

Mallarmé's refined suppression of reference, reality and history itself creates for Glissant a formalist excess that produces a false separation of poetry and reality. It is rather poetry's failure to give full expression to reality that haunts Glissant's poetics. Human experience is tellingly evoked as 'cet océan' which can neither be avoided nor controlled.

The problem of the docile referent, of nature's literary inscription as consoling, bountiful and defining space is a major one in Caribbean writing. For Glissant the freeing of the referent from a narrow ideological or moral grid is a major preoccupation. The revenge of the referent, or the elusive nature of reality, is a pervasive theme in this work. This is evident, whether we are dealing with Columbus's futile reduction of the New World to his dream in *Les Indes* or Glissant's other characters precariously poised between the inscrutable ocean and the obscure force of the *morne*, of the problematical relationship between 'pays rêvé' and 'pays réel'. This troubling interdependence between subject and reality, self and other, is one of the major themes of western modernism and for Glissant represents a vital link with what he calls the 'modernité vécue' ('lived modernity') of New World writing. As he would later conclude in his essay 'Le roman des Amériques':

la littérature 'américaine' se présente dans un système de modernité soudaine et non pas consécutive ni 'évoluée' . . . La question est pourtant que cette modernité, vécue totalement dans les 'nouveaux mondes', rejoint les axes de modernité 'maturée' dans d'autres zones de culture et de réflexion.[6]

('American' literature is the product of a system of modernity that is sudden and not sustained or 'evolved' . . . The idea however is that modernity, lived to the fullest in the 'new worlds', overlaps with the preoccupations of 'matured' modernity in other zones of culture and thought.)

Consequently, Glissant begins his career not only as a poet but as one who is acutely conscious of the legacy of an 'American' modernism. It is within such a context that we need to examine Glissant's early relationship to the poetry of Saint-John Perse. He, after all, has continuously felt a greater affinity with Perse than with French Caribbean poets such as René Depestre and Aimé Césaire. He has even gone so far as to describe Perse as 'le plus essentiel poète vivant' ('the most essential living poet'), and to admit that Perse is 'souvent présent dans la clairière de mes mots' ('often present in the clearings of my words').[7] These are important admissions in the context of the whole debate on poetic form in the 1950s provoked by René Depestre's endorsement of Aragon's rec-ommendation of the sonnet form.[8] Glissant's attraction to Perse's poetry, generally seen at the time as neither authentic-ally Caribbean nor politically committed, was highly unusual in the heyday of negritude and the pervasive influence of Césaire's poetry on young black writers.

In attempting in the fifties to settle the troubling question of poetic form, what he would call 'la juste mesure de mon chaos primordial' ('the true measure of my primal chaos'), Glissant reacted strongly against the organization of space and time he sensed in Europe, the predictable rhythm of the seasons, the symmetrical organization of cultivated land, and the pastoral vision of harmony and order.[9] As he asserts in one of his early essays in *Soleil de la conscience*:

J'aime ces champs, leur ordre, leur patience; cependant je n'en participe pas. N'ayant jamais disposé de ma terre, je n'ai point cet atavisme d'épargne du sol, d'organisation. Mon paysage est encore emportement; la symétrie du planté me gêne. Mon temps n'est pas une succession d'espérances saisonnières, il est encore de jaillissements et de trouées d'arbres.[10]

(I love these fields, their order, their patience; however they are not part of me. Never having had control over my land, I do not experience this reflex of managing the land, of organization. My landscape is still convulsive; the symmetry of planted fields makes me uncomfortable. My time is not a succession of seasonal hopes, but it is still explosive and torn by surging trees.)

This statement establishes a clear link between poetics and landscape. In attempting to respond to the linguistic and aesthetic problem posed by Mallarmé, Glissant seeks an answer within an 'American' tradition, that is within a New World sensibility shaped by an 'American' landscape.

Poetically Glissant identifies two responses in 'American' modernism. They are the poetic forms established by two French Caribbean poets – Aimé Césaire and Saint-John Perse. Glissant has from the outset seemed ill at ease with Césaire's poetic temperament. He describes Césaire's poetry as a 'cri de conscience', as an important phase in Caribbean self-affirmation.

Dans le langage de notre temps, *le Cahier d'un retour au pays natal* est un 'moment': la retournée flamboyante d'une conscience, l'élévation vers tous de la volonté neuve de quelques uns. C'est aussi un cri: plongée aux noires volutes de la terre.[11]

(In the language of our time, *the Notebook of a return to my native land* is a 'moment': the flaming reversal of a consciousness, the raising to everyone of the new will of a few. It is also a cry: plunging into the dark spirals of the earth.)

For Glissant, however, the need exists to transcend this 'cri', the Rimbaldian explosiveness of Césaire's sensibility, and 'muer le cri en parole devant la mer' ('to transform the shriek into language before the sea'). Césaire himself, in describing his sensibility as 'Péléen', in reference to the volcano Mt Pélée admits to this explosive tendency.[12] Glissant is drawn away from this *fulgurance*, the systematic derangement of the senses:

'Sinon, notre délire nous submerge' ('If not, we will be drowned in our delirium'). It is within this struggle to establish his own poetic voice that Glissant is attracted to the work of Saint-John Perse.

If Césaire's sensibility is 'Péléen', then Perse's is marine. If Césaire emphasises the liberation of the subject, the romantic celebration of the 'nègre fondamental', Perse's subject tends to be overpowered by the continuously surging sea. In approaching Perse's work through Glissant, we must keep in mind the place occupied by Perse in modern poetry. One of the increasingly important aspects of post-Romantic and post-surrealist verse is the attempt made by widely diverse poets to come to terms with, or establish some kind of cosmic order for, a world of interacting and conflicting cultures. In a useful survey of this tendency within French writing, Christophe Campos writes:

As the frontiers of knowledge explode they must, if they are to perpetuate the romantic ideal of leadership, attempt first an encyclopaedic, then a synthetic survey, similar to the 'descriptions of the world' written after the great voyages of discovery of the fifteenth and sixteenth centuries. Claudel's special interest in Columbus the mapmaker is significant; like Saint-John Perse, he is attempting to encompass our world within a system of poetry.[13]

The need for the encyclopaedic survey and the synthetic vision is not peculiar to French poetry. Gerald Moore sees this attempt by the modern poet to create a poetic cosmos 'from the conflicting and incoherent diversity around him' as characteristic of poetry from Senghor of Senegal to Walt Whitman of the United States.[14] Rootless in a world of bewildering diversity, poets within this tradition take on a central ordering or demiurgic role in an effort to establish new continuities and to produce a new synthesis or what Senghor would call the 'civilisation de l'universel'.

This relationship between poetry and collective experience is what draws Glissant to Perse and establishes the basic affinity between them. Yet Glissant is uneasy with the demiurgic persona of the poet within this tradition. He feels that the pull of diversity is so powerful that it is false to establish any notion of poetic authority or of sameness, universality or a grand supranational vision in order to contain it. Indeed, one could say that he is trying to combine the Mallarméan view of the author overpowered by language with a poetry of collective cultural diversity. Octavio Paz, the Mexican poet and essayist, is equally sensitive to Mallarmé's undermining of the ideal of poetic genius:

Mallarmé's method, creative destruction or transposition, but above all surrealism, destroyed forever the idea of the poet as an exceptional being. Surrealism did not deny inspiration, an exceptional state: it affirmed it was common property . . . Language creates the poet, and only in proportion as words are born, die and are reborn within him is he in turn a creator.[15]

Glissant is drawn to Perse, partly because of the latter's Caribbean origins, but also, or perhaps more importantly, because of his also very 'American' role within this modern poetry of cultural diversity.

Roger Little, in attempting to situate Perse's literary influence outside France, makes the following comment:

Perse's Caribbean origins may go some way to explaining the appeal he has for poets in former French colonies: *Eloges* in particular provides them with a familiar and attractive introduction to the exploration of their own world.[16]

Not surprisingly, Little finds strong evidence of Perse's poetry in that of Senghor and Glissant. Despite the fact that Perse is said to come from Guadeloupe and to express a brand of 'Caribbean negritude', Little is right in situating the importance of Perse's Guadeloupean origins to other writers from the region. What Glissant values in Perse is an essentially Caribbean sensibility:

Perse est antillais par la croissance primitive et entrecroisée de [son] style; la nature parle d'abord en nous. Sa nature, c'est le mot comme végétation; mais son histoire, c'est l'errance comme pur projet.[17]

(Perse is Caribbean in the primitive tangled growth of [his] style; landscape speaks first in us. His landscape is the word as vegetation; but his history is wandering as pure intention.)

It is not this aspect of Perse's work that Glissant emphasizes, and not what he calls Perse's longing to be housed ('la nostalgie de l'impossible maison'), nor his celebration of a totalizing vision of the world ('le monde-en-système'). Glissant makes a difference between Perse's openness to the 'movement of the world' in the early verse and the demiurgic Perse of later writings.

Les porosités chaudes d'*Eloges*, les opacités en strates d'*Anabase*, l'espace liquide d'*Exil* prévalent sur le bruissement totalisateur de *Vents*.[18]

(The porous warmth of *Eloges*, the layered opacity of *Anabase*, the liquid space of *Exil* overpower the totalizing rustle of *Vents*.)

The point being made here by Glissant about Perse's poetry from *Eloges* (1911) to *Exil* (1944) is echoed by a fellow Caribbean poet Derek Walcott who speaks admiringly of 'the elation in presences which exists in *Eloges* and 'Pour fêter une enfance' and 'the possibility of a man and his language waking to wonder here'.[19] The language of Perse's later poetry Walcott rejects as 'hammered and artificial'.

There are four aspects of Perse's early poetry – that is up to 1944 and the publication of *Exil* – that have deeply influenced Glissant and shaped his work aesthetically and thematically. First, Perse's use of the poetic persona. His self-consciousness concerning his poetic function seems so intense that only by using a *nom de plume* can he differentiate between the biographical self and the poetic self. Also, in a related way, Perse's predilection for a diversity of voices and personae in his work seems to undercut the notion of a coherent, identifiable poetic self and emphasize the collective experience through the manipulation of a series of masks. Whether this mask is that of a forlorn Crusoe or the dialogue of voices in *Exil*, the author in Perse's work could be seen as a site facilitating the interplay and reanimation of other voices. From the very outset, Glissant would seize the importance of this polyphonic element in the creation of poetic discourse: 'Ainsi l'homme court-il à la rencontre du monde; et se débarrasse dans la course, comme d'un fardeau inutile, du poids de son être' ('Thus man races forward to meet the world; and in so doing sheds, like a useless burden, the weight of his being').[20]

Secondly, Perse's conception of the text itself as precarious and erasable as opposed to immutable and enduring is entirely compatible with Glissant's concept of the ambiguous, elusive, fissured nature of literary discourse. As Perse himself would say, the poem born of nothingness ('poème fait de rien', *Exil*) is always threatened by the wind, sea, rain and snow. Perse's legacy would be a system of images based on the notion of the 'poème délébile' ('the erasable poem') where ideal utterance is unattainable and writing, itself threatened by erasure, is not privileged over dream or speech. Poetry, then, is created out of fragile presences:

J'ai fondé sur l'abîme et l'embrun et la fumée des sables.

(I have built on emptiness and sea spray and smoke rising from the sands.)[21]

In this regard, the central image is of the sand as an exemplary space, neither land nor sea, neither pure nor impure, but an ideal image of the mediating threshold, a zone of interrelating presences. As Perse exclaims in 'Chant II' of *Exil*: 'Ma gloire est sur les sables! ma gloire est sur les sables!'

Thirdly, Perse's use of the sea as a metaphor of history, experience, consciousness itself provides another clear link with Glissant's poetic endeavour. 'La commune mer', which for Perse becomes the source of poetic expression, is for Glissant an objective correlative both for the movement of the world and for the rhythms of thought itself.

D'un même mouvement s'abandonne pour s'imposer, s'impose pour s'abandonner encore, mer immobile et en marée vers la myriade et son armure.[22]

(In one and the same movement it releases itself to thrust forward, it thrusts forward in order to release itself again, this still sea and its tidal surge towards profusion and yet finding a form.)

Glissant's refusal to be 'Péléen' in Césaire's terms is part of a larger rejection of the associations of being *montagnard*, the mountain being consistently associated in his work with blind negation, the defiant cry, indeed diametrically opposed to the sea. As he writes in *Le soleil de la conscience*, the mountain connotes winter:

La mer était le contraire de l'hiver, comme la montagne en était l'homonyme.[23]

(The sea was the opposite of winter, just as the mountain was its homonym.)

The sea represents the unstable referent, that zone of inter-relationship and polyphony which provides an insight into Caribbean history. Perse's sense of the sea as central to poetic vision tellingly overlaps with that of Glissant. One sometimes has a sense that it is difficult to distinguish Perse's words from Glissant's when it comes to the imagery of the sea. 'O mer sans âge ni raison, ô mer sans hâte ni saison' – the timeless, unchanging, inscrutable sea evoked here by Perse in *Amers* is essential to Glissant's notions of *métissage*, creolisation, *relation*, *Antillanité* and *errance*.

Finally, at a moment when protest poetry, the radical invec-tive of negritude writers, dominated the literary scene, Perse provided for Glissant an alternative poetics, as Glissant himself would never cease repeating, a poetics of 'l'accumulation' as opposed to that of 'la fulguration', of 'la durée' as opposed to 'l'instant'.

La fulguration est l'art de bloquer l'obscur dans sa lumière révélée; l'accumulation, celui de consacrer l'évident sur sa durée enfin perçue. La fulguration est de soi, l'accumulation est de tous.[24]

(Fulguration is the art of containing obscurity with its blast of illumination; accumulation is that of consecrating the obvious in terms of ultimately accumulated duration. Fulguration pertains to the individual, accumulation to the collective.)

Glissant in the fifties associated the poetics of negritude with that of *fulguration*, 'un combat bref et flamboyant'. Perse offered a conceptual and ultimately ideological breakthrough by steering clear of a Rimbaldian flash of illumination. The critic Jean-Pierre Richard has noted this element in Perse's work.

Chez Rimbaud, dit à peu près Sartre, la sensation est comme un oeuf qui serrerait la main et dont le contenu giclerait soudain aux quatre coins du monde. Rien de tel chez le Perse d'*Eloges*: quelque chose de lourd, d'un peu huileux lie le bonheur sensible et l'empêche de s'égarer en un lointain.[25]

(In Rimbaud, Sartre more or less says, sensation is like an egg which pressed in the hand suddenly explodes to the four corners of the world. Nothing of the sort in the Perse of *Eloges*: something heavy, slightly slippery binds a palpable happiness and prevents it from drifting away in the distance.)

For Glissant such a poetics allows the writer to transcend the rigid binary categories that are pervasive in Caribbean thought – master/slave, negation/acquiescence, self/other, elite/people. Rather it is the relationship, the contact between these categories, which for Glissant provides a special insight into the complexities of the New World experience. In literary terms, it means that Glissant would avoid the protest poem, the 'poème de circonstance', the aesthetics of committed verse, for forms that undermine the dramatic monologue of free verse so characteristic of much negritude poetry. Instead, the poetics of 'la durée' and 'l'accumulation' favours more indeterminate forms – in particular, the prose poem which blurs the division not only between poetry and prose but also between the lyrical subject and the collective experience, between expression and investigative analysis.

Glissant's first published books of poetry in the mid-fifties might be more appropriately called poetic experiments than straightforward or conventional poems. He himself uses words like *épure* (diagram) and *barême* (graph) to describe these works. They are visibly hybrid forms that are characterised by a pervasive indeterminacy. This is as apparent in the form of these works as in the subjects treated. The traditional polarisation of prose as opposed to poetry is broken down by Glissant as both expository and expressive forms seem freely to intermingle in the space of the text. The subject is equally indeterminate as Glissant avoids the predictable themes of race, anticolonial polemic and the problem of cultural assimilation to concentrate on the process of imagining or rather to reflect on the nature of the poetic experience. It is as if these early works, in particular *Un champ d'îles* (1953) and *La terre inquiète* (1954), enact what Glissant called 'la poussée de l'imaginé'; they should be read in close association with the section 'Le cours du poème' of *Soleil de la conscience*. These texts are characterised by images whose meanings are accumulated in the course of the poem and convey a sense of wandering and drifting that establishes a clear aesthetic distance from the Manichean combativeness of negritude. Already one has the feeling in Glissant's work that negritude would one day be little more than a period style.

One of the notable features of these works is the fact that the first editions all come with illustrations. They were unceremoniously dropped from the republished versions which simply list the names of the artists: Wolfgang Paalen, Wifredo Lam and Enrique Zañartu. This loss is particularly disturbing because Glissant would later pay greater attention to the non-verbal medium of painting and the plastic arts, particularly in the Americas. Indeed, he analyses in some detail the pictorial discourse of Lam and Zañartu, from Cuba and Chile respectively, in *Le discours antillais*.[26] Not only does this relationship between graphic sign and poetic language further enhance the indeterminacy and intertextuality of Glissant's work, it seems to touch the question of the relationship between both the written poem and the graphic drawing and reality. That is, the drawings are not mere illustrations but may be complementary or alternative ways of designating reality. This seems to be particularly true of the illustration by Wifredo Lam which contains birdlike forms and has all the associations of space animated by the freed imagination, by flight beyond confining space.

The little critical commentary that has been published on these early works is less than helpful. They are dismissed by Jean Paris in his anthology as 'entachées de preciosité' ('flawed by affectation').[27] Beverley Ormerod is far more sensitive to their importance, especially as far as images of the sea are concerned. However, even for her, this early writing is 'intensely stylized and cerebral'.[28] Yet words like 'preciosité' and 'stylized' do not accurately describe these meditations on poetic expression. Stylization, as a false aesthetic coherence imposed on the imagination, is explicitly rejected in Glissant's

Soleil de la conscience: 'Mais l'art n'est pas . . . la fin de la poésie'
('But art is not the goal of poetry.')[29] He clearly values process
over product, the risks of the journey over the promise of
landfall. The very first images of *Un champ d'îles* convey pri-
mordial chaos, a painful gestation, 'Tourmentes, feu marin,
étendues sans pitié' ('Torment, marine fire, pitiless wastes'). If
anything, Glissant is attempting to remain as faithful as pos-
sible to the act of poetic creation. Indeed, the central idea of
these poems turns on the difficulty in resolving the question of
organization and form. All three early works (*Un champ d'îles*,
La terre inquiète and *Les Indes*) contain in their titles references to
land and the relationship to matter, as a metaphor of poetic
form.

In *Soleil de la conscience* Glissant expresses a disquiet with the
patience and order of the fields and by extension the world view
of Europe. What he calls 'cet atavisme d'épargne de sol' is not
his but belongs to a culture that jealously guards private
property and treasures individualism. His writing is an attempt
to find expression for the chaos of his world and for his vision of
a collective aesthetic. So the imaginative spaces of Glissant's
poem alternate between the terrestrial – field of islands, anxious
earth, the Indies – and the liquid world of the sea, the poetic
world of the voyage of the drifting towards language and
meaning. Perhaps one should bear in mind the events of the
fifties – the revelations of Stalin's concentration camps, the
recent experience of World War II and the rise of technology –
in order to appreciate fully Glissant's concern with the politics
and the poetics of possessiveness, domination and conquest. It is
precisely this theme that forms the link between the somewhat
obscure first poems and the evocation of Columbus's journey in
Les Indes, between the poetic ravishing of the obscure object of
desire and the historical conquest of the desired Indies.

The exemplary nature of Columbus's dream of the Indies is
clarified in the prose passage introducing the section 'La Rela-
tion' of *Les Indes*:

La poème s'achève lorsque la rive est en vue, d'où s'éloignèrent jadis
les Découvreurs. Retour à ce rivage, où l'amarre est toujours fixée.
Quelle richesse a grandi, durant ce cycle? Qui revient? Et celui-là,

que conçoit-il à son tour? Mais peut-être enfin l'homme n'a-t-il que
même désir et même ardeur, n'importe soit-il? et d'où qu'il vienne,
même souffrance connaissable?[30]

(The poem ends when the shore is in sight, the one formerly left
behind by the Discoverers. Return to this shore whose mooring never
shifts. What riches have accumulated during this cycle? Who makes
the journey back? And what does the one returning, in his turn,
desire? But perhaps ultimately all men share the same desires and the
same passion whoever they are? And wherever they come from, the
same knowable suffering?)

Glissant here avoids the stereotype of Columbus as genocidal
imperialist. Instead, the eternal pursuit of a dream, of imagin-
ative fantasy, is proposed by Glissant as the point of departure
for all poetic and human activity, whether the dreamer pursues
the conquest of the Muse, of territory or of truth. For Glissant,
the objective always remains elusive and the journey inevitably
begins again. As he writes in *Soleil de la conscience*, 'toute vérité
est la consommation dialectique' ('all truth is a dialectic con-
summation'), the one thing that is certain is the journey
towards truth and truth is the function of this process. It is the
sea, stretching between dreamer and dream, that is eternal.

   These early poems can be seen, then, as various evocations of
'crossings' (*traversées*) in which a central and obsessive drama is
enacted between the dreamer, the sea and the shore. What is
unusual about these poetic crossings is that the self is objectified
by Glissant. Because of his insistence on being the 'ethnologist
of himself' the texts cannot be conventionally self-centred but
the subject is open to examination as the other element in the
drama. When the self does emerge as a first-person voice, it is
hesitant and vulnerable to self-doubt.

Alors, forçant l'écume, j'irai par les plages où meurt le mot . . .
cependant je cherche, lourd et brûlant.[31]

(Then forcing my way through the surf I will journey along the
beaches where the word dies . . . However I continue searching,
heavy and burning.)

These lines which bring *Un champ d'îles* to a close show that
Glissant's work does not provide a triumphant denouement.
The wintry space from which the poem emerges, with the

clumsy poet searching as it closes, indicate the extent to which this crossing is framed by failure. As he confesses, it is impossible to maintain the rhythm of his oars as he crosses the sea of the unknown: 'En vain dans le courant veut-il garder the rythme des pagaies.'

The 'crossing' evoked in *Un champ d'îles* takes place as if in conformity with the unity of time and place, in one revolution of the sun. The text begins at dawn in the poet's room, 'l'aurore fourvoyée dans cette chambre' ('dawn gone astray in this room'), 'le soleil entrant encore dans cette chambre' ('the sun re-entering this room'), and the first section ends with evening in the room ('chambre du soir'). The text traces the emergence and the illumination of this light of consciousness on the poetic subject immured in solitude in his room. The images expand outwards across the vast stretch of sea ('étendues sans pitié') towards the sunlit world of memory. The object of this transcendence of the material, of the corporeal, is the island, the absent woman: 'O poème qui naît de vous' ('O poem born from you'), 'Votre absence . . . ouvre la lumière' ('Your absence . . . opens the light'). As he comments in *Soleil de la conscience*, the aim is to chart the 'Etranges noces de la terre et du coeur, sous le signe et la poussée de la mer souveraine' ('strange union of the earth and the heart, under the sign and the surge of the sovereign sea').[32]

In dramatising the relationship between 'terre' and 'mer souveraine' Glissant is not merely repeating the theme of nostalgia for home and belonging so pervasive in Caribbean writing. It is significant that his work does not contain an obsessive listing, naming or invoking of Caribbean flora and fauna. As he declares in *L'intention poétique*, 'Je répugne à sérier les noms des arbres, des oiseaux, des fleurs' ('I am loath to produce a series of names of trees, birds, flowers').[33] Rather the land vibrates at a more symbolic level with the accumulated meanings of language, poetry, knowledge, otherness and desire itself: 'je me sentirai solidaire de cette "parcelle de terre" non par quelque régionalisme sentimental, mais parce que pour moi cette terre a lentement pris figure de symbole' ('I will feel solidarity with this "piece of earth" not through some regionalist sentimentality, but because this land has slowly acquired symbolic values').[34] These values are a function of the sovereign sea in which the subject is immersed.

The pattern of images in *Un champ d'îles* is dominated by the subject's loss of physicality, weight and self-mastery in the dense medium of the imagination. Glissant describes the process in *Soleil de la conscience* in terms of 'shedding the weight of one's being'[35] and this determines image patterns in *Un champ d'îles*. For instance, the text is studded with images of birds – sea birds ('oiseau des bords de mer', 'pluviers', 'flamants', 'martins-pêcheurs', 'oiseaux marins'), nocturnal birds ('paradisiers') – and bird metaphors: 'l'oiseau de son regard' ('the bird of his look'), 'l'oiseau guide le ciel vers une source' ('the bird guides the sky to a spring') and 'le vent . . . surprend le coeur et l'empanache' ('the wind . . . surprises the heart and ruffles its feathers'). Birds function as images of transcendence, as material representations of thought, luminous images of movement. The space they cross is not a vacuum but they are at the mercy of the winds – arbitrary and unpredictable – which batter them.

Just as birds represent luminous ascent, so images of trees function as representations of vegetable forces akin to the animal flight of birds. Trees seem also to have the capacity to be projected across space. They become, for Glissant, a centre of confusing, contradictory forces. Unlike the Césairean image of the tree that represents an explosive plunging shaft, the tree here seems to fade into air and light. Again, this image can be seen as a rehearsal for the later novels which use in a more focused and clearer way the symbolic values of trees as a way of organizing time and space, of establishing an unceasing vision of interrelating forces. Glissant in *L'intention poétique* clarifies the image of the tree in terms that return almost verbatim in the later novel *Mahagony*.

Quand je dis: arbre, et quand je pense à l'arbre je ne ressens jamais l'unique, le tronc, le mât de sève . . . Mais l'arbre est ici l'élan, le Tout, la densité bouillante. Que j'essaie, maladroit, de dessiner un arbre: j'aboutirai à un pan de végétation, où seul le ciel de la page mettra un terme à la croissance indéterminée. L'unique se perd dans ce Tout.[36]

(When I say: tree, and when I think of the tree, I never feel a sense of the singularity, of the trunk, the mast of sap . . . But the tree here is impulse outwards, the whole, a seething density. When I clumsily attempt to draw a tree: I end up with a mass of vegetation for which only the ceiling of the page can cut off its unpredictable luxuriance. The singular gets lost in this collective mass.)

Trees in *Un champ d'îles* introduce us to the act of poetic creation. There are frequent references to parts of trees ('racine', 'frondaisons', 'feuille') and actual trees ('acacias', 'araucaria') and they are invariably associated with the act of creating a poetic language or moulding an artistic form from memory and experience. The identification between poet and tree is clear in the passage:

Durant que vous dormez dans cette plaine, le souvenir encourt les tournoiements de l'arbre, et plus haut son sang. Toute prose devient feuille et accumule dans l'obscur ses éblouies. Faites-le feuille de vos mains, faites-le prose de l'obscur, et l'ébloui de vos brisures.[37]

(While you are sleeping in this plain, memory entwines the revolving tree, and its blood mounts. All prose becomes leaf and accumulates its dazzling brilliance in the dark. Make it leaf of your hands, make it the prose of obscurity, and the dazzle of your fissures.)

Or in the following section:

cet arbre hésite au bord de vous . . . Comme un poème hésite au bord de l'eau.[38]

(this tree hesitates at your edge . . . Like a poem hesitates at the water's edge.)

The tree's growth is like that of the poem feeding on the surrounding space. Indeed, the symbolic values of trees suggest the field in the poem's title. The field or the earth represents raw experience and even language itself, which is the life force of the tree/poem. The tree's searching root in the following image is akin to the poet as peasant tilling the soil, 'un labour-eur, guettant sous le soc les lèvres de la terre' ('a peasant on the lookout for the lips of the earth under the plough').[39]

> Toute parole est une terre
> Il est de fouiller son sous-sol
> Où un espace meuble est gardé
> Brûlant, pour ce que l'arbre dit.[40]

(All language is land
Its sub-soil must be explored
There loose soil awaits
Burning for what the tree says.)

This particular use of trees as images of a coalescing of languages, of poetic visions moulded in space, would recur throughout Glissant's novels whether in the form of the silk cotton tree, the mahogany or the banyan.

The relationships established in this early text between bird and space, tree and earth, sea and land, are essential to the poetic sensibility that provokes and facilitates the later prose texts. Just as the sky contains the bird, as the land projects the tree outwards, the self for Glissant becomes a kind of womblike space, amniotic fluid where the poet dreams 'Je me fais mer où l'enfant va rêver' ('I turn myself into a sea where the child will dream'). Poetry is here dissociated from conscious intention, from a demiurgic impulse or a false synthesis. Poetry is a means of understanding for Glissant, but one which is not a conscious search or deliberate enquiry. Rather the poet makes room for impressions that emerge and proliferate.

J'attends la plénitude de la parole qui est donnée. Je ne cherche pas en elle, sachant que la fouiller c'est ici l'appauvrir. Je bêche à côté. Et la Maison s'ouvre sur l'éclat de la parole.[41]

(I await the full force the word conveys. I do not search within it, aware that to explore in this manner is to impoverish. I dig to the side. And the House opens as the word explodes.)

It is in the uncertain light of consciousness offered by the poetic imagination that 'Celui que trouble l'opacité, celui qui devine l'enfance' ('He who is troubled by opacity, he who guesses at childhood') fumbles as he reaches out for the 'plénitudes de la terre' ('the fulfilment of the land').

Glissant's second poetic work, *La terre inquiète*, continues his meditation on the theme of an imaginative understanding of the land. As in the previous work 'terre' has multiple associations of earth, native land, motherland and language itself. The key to this work can be traced to the image of the woman who suckles a snake, which is elaborated in *Soleil de la conscience*.

It is a complex and ambiguous image of painful inter-
dependence, of the necessity of suffering and the birth of
consciousness. The image is inextricably bound up with the
title of the book of essays. It is the snake's bite that brings
knowledge and consciousness. The snake itself is likened to the
sun's circle of illumination, with its hiss of truth.

Et quand un serpent tête une femme immobile il lui parle silenc-
ieusement, c'est-à-dire dans son langage de suceur: 'Ne te plains pas,
je t'apporte le sens et la gloire de mon ordre, le cercle parfait.'[42]

(And when the snake suckles an immobile woman, it speaks to her
silently, that is in its language of sucking: 'Do not feel sorry for
yourself, I bring you the meaning and the glory of my order, the
perfect circle.')

The petrified victim, the painful gift of awareness, the deadly
nature of the encounter with wisdom and the importance of a
threatening force in the process of self-discovery are all sug-
gested in this image and form the basic message that underlies
Glissant's entire oeuvre.

The link between *La terre inquiète* and the image of the
woman suckling a snake is suggested in *Soleil de la conscience*:

Je fais de cette terre la face de toute femme violée en son lait tendre;
de cette femme l'image de toute terre secouée pour que pleure son
lait, comme d'un prunier.[43]

(I see in this land the face of any woman raped for her tender
suckling; in this woman the image of any land shaken until it weeps
its sap, like a plum tree.)

And in the text of the poem 'Promenoir de la mort seule'
('Walkway of lonely death'), we find the lines 'Un cri de femme
labourée/A la limite des jachères' ('A woman's ploughed-up
shriek/As far as her fallow fields'). Glissant makes no attempt
to flatten the complexity and the ambiguity of this nightmarish
encounter. His treatment of the image ranges from the his-
torical, the violation of Africa in the slave trade, and the
predicament of Martinique as a French Department, to the
personal, his own encounter with alienating otherness in Paris
and the seductive force of the light of consciousness. However,

for him this encounter is presented as an important 'rivage' –
both threshold and riveting attachment. The night of the
earth/woman's silent suffering is called fertile and vital to the
victim's 'prise de conscience'. Out of this alienating encounter
a new order, a new dawn emerges as the poet identifies closely
with the violated land.

Dans ta nuit lourde voici pousser le matin, ses hautes feuilles qui sont
lutte. Entre deux soutirements de lait, tu ne sais plus si tu acquiesces
où tu mords . . . De cette nuit à cette beauté, le chemin sera naturel.[44]

(Out of the weight of your night grows the morning struggling
through its high leaves. Between two sucks of milk, you no longer
know if you are yielding or you are biting . . . From this night to this
beauty, the path will be natural.)

In this regard, Glissant seems to echo a recurrent image in
Saint-John Perse's *Exil*, in which the poetic persona exiled on
the shoreline is drawn to the alienating force of the ocean:

Je vous connais, ô monstre! Nous voici de nouveau face à face. Nous
reprenons ce long debat où nous l'avions laissé.[45]

(I know you, o monster! Here we are once more face to face. We
begin again the long struggle where we left off.)

Perse, on the New Jersey shore facing the ocean that separates
him from his homeland, and Glissant, facing the Atlantic that
cuts him off from Martinique, share the same sensibility. They
do not turn to self-pity or express anger at being uprooted but
see their exile as fertile wandering. *Errance*, a term that will
increasingly be used by Glissant to restore the positive connota-
tion of uprooting, is closely associated with Perse's sense of
exile as a gateway to a new beginning. Perse in *Exil* finds glory
on the sands of the American shoreline. Glissant sees the beach
as that threshold of pain and consciousness, 'le sable d'azure
serré de sable noir' ('the sand of the heavens studded with
black sand').

There is frequent reference in *La terre inquiète* to suffering and
sacrifice as a precondition for knowledge. The serpent of know-
ledge leaves its mark, hieroglyphs of its painful truth, on its
petrified victim's flesh. Often, the serpent's undulating form
seems related in Glissant's poem to the waves of the sea and the

wisdom of the deep. The dynamic hiss of the surf constantly
gnawing away at the shoreline suggests furrows where new
seeds can grow.

> Mort beauté gloire éternité! labours
> Du semeur en l'espace étincelant, pour qui
> Le Sel vient à douleur et s'efface toujours.[46]

> (Death, beauty glory eternity! furrows
> Of the sower in glittering space, for whom
> The Salt comes with grief and always goes away.)

The suckling force of the sea on the land and the wounds
inflicted on the land in this encounter are clearly suggested in
such phrases as 'l'eau bifide', 'femme labourée', 'rivages nus
guettant quelles vagues', 'la plaie muette des rochers', 'viol
sacré de la lumière' ('the bifid water', 'ploughed woman',
'naked shoreline watchful for what waves', 'the dumb wound
of the rocks', 'the light's sacred violation'). The light of
consciousness is related to the wisdom of the ocean, a repository
of patient understanding, memory and the ambiguities of
history. The ocean waits constantly and inscrutably. It epito-
mises the complexities of experience: 'L'océan est patience, sa
sagesse est l'ivraie du temps' ('the ocean is patience, its wisdom
is the chaff of time'). In confronting its past, Martinique and
the Caribbean can have only one ancestor, the sea: 'L'ancêtre
parle, c'est l'océan'.

The confrontation in *La terre inquiète* between woman and
serpent, land and sea is not a simple one of cleansing and
redemption. It cannot be transcended but constantly lures the
poet back, as the two sections of the work suggest. They are
entitled 'Le mouvement, loin de rivages' ('The movement, far
from the riveting shore') and 'Le retour à la mer' ('The return
to the sea'). The original edition of this book of poetry made
this pattern even clearer with an opening and concluding prose
text which was omitted in the republished version. The 1955
edition begins

> Ce qui inquiète la Terre devient présence
> et mouvement de l'Océan.
> Courtisan lassé, il sommeille sur son
> obscure vérité: la Terre est sombre.[47]

> (The Earth's anxiety becomes the presence and
> movement of the Ocean.
> World weary flatterer, he dozes on his
> obscure truth: the Earth is dark.)

It ends with the same site where a mutual interdependence is established, on the threshold between land and sea.

> L'un cherche l'énigme l'énigme
> Dont les champs ferment la clarté
> L'autre ne fait que paraître
> Sans ordre, sur la grève, ni beauté![48]

> (One seeks the enigma the enigma
> Whose revelation is blocked by the fields,
> The other simply appears
> Without form, on the beach, or beauty!)

Glissant's subjects vary with the changes in his life. However, the perspective would invariably be the same: this crucial intersection of experiences, between land and sea.

The possibility of vision is imagined in this space as the tree (of knowledge) rising abruptly from the barren terrain.

> J'étreignais le sable, j'attendais entre les roches
> j'embrassais
> L'eau puis le sable, les rochers – ce coeur
> des choses rêches – puis un arbre! M'écriant
> Que le langage se dénoue.[49]

> (I hugged the sand, I waited between the rocks
> I kissed
> The water then the sand, the rocks – this heart
> of coarse-grained things – then a tree! Shouting
> That the knot of language is loosened.)

The tree of words feeding on this wounded shore, on the horrors of this nightmare, can be read as a paradigm for all of Glissant's oeuvre, what he calls in 'Le champ aride', another poem not represented in the later edition, 'un arbre de splendeur nu sur l'immensité' ('a tree of glory naked against infinite space'). *La terre inquiète* closes with a short poem which evokes the Sun's zenith and the moment of knowing. 'Sacre' ('Consecration') sums up the dramatic, solemn sense of the stripped-down truth that rises from the fiery heat.

Délicieuse dangereuse approche de Midi. L'ombre de l'arbre est vertige de l'âme nue qui en soi consulte et décide. Puis, les triomphes aveugles.[50]

(Tempting menacing approach of Midday. The shadow of the tree is the vertigo of the naked soul which examines itself and comes to a decision. Then moments of blind triumph.)

The overhead sun centres the tree on its shadow, the poet on his inner truth. As in *Un champ d'îles* the tree is established here as a repository of experience and knowing to which human beings need to pay attention.

The third book of poetry from the fifties differs from the other two in that it is less abstract and more obviously composed within a Caribbean tradition of rewriting the journey of discovery. The prose introductions that precede the six 'Chants' ('Cantos') refer to historical figures, actual events and dates which give rise to an imaginative response in the poetry. Columbus, Genoa, Cortez, Pizarro, the slave trade, Delgrès, Toussaint are all part of this drama held together by the 'knowing sea'. The Indies undergo transformation from the desired land to the Indies of suffering, the market of flesh and the violated space. These strange multiple associations are the stuff from which the New World is made.

Il est une Inde qui finit quand le réel brosse son poil ardu; terre de rêve.
Elle cède à ce qui vient souffrance et joie, qui est multiple sur l'argîle
. . . Terre née d'elle même, pluie des Indes assumées.[51]

(There is an Indies which ends when reality brushes its dishevelled hair; land of dream.
It yields to what follows, suffering and joy which is manifold on the clay . . . Land born of itself, precipitation of the acknowledged Indies.)

In *Soleil de la conscience* Glissant observes that awareness of history and politics inevitably intrudes on the process of literary creation. We simply know too much about the world to be innocent of its more disturbing features.

L'immense broiement des découvertes, des analyses (allant du rêve
exotique au travail de l'ethnographe en passant par le livre d'aven-
tures) a déplacé les mobiles de la sensibilité. Nous ne pouvons plus
rêver des villes secrètes de l'Amérique du sud, sans évoquer la
condition actuelle des *peones*.[52]

(The great crushing force of discoveries, of classification (ranging
from the exotic dream to the ethnographer's work by way of adven-
ture stories) has altered our sensibility. We can no longer dream of
secret cities in South America without referring to the present *labour-
ers* there.)

The earth, the island do not resonate on a political or artistic
level exclusively. Inevitably, our conscience demands that his-
torical reality be included, that solidarity be felt with experi-
ences of diverse communities. Nevertheless, Glissant's perspec-
tive on history and politics is a poetic one and the originality of
Les Indes, the reconstruction of Columbus's voyage of discovery
and conquest, lies in its treatment of the ambiguous relation-
ship between sea and island, as well as on the grip of the dream
of possession on the discoverer's fevered imagination. The
desire to possess provokes in *Les Indes* writing that is uncharac-
teristically erotic.[53] Gaëton Picon, while being too insistent on
the Marxist dialectic in *Les Indes*, nevertheless makes the point
that Glissant does not allow political considerations to compro-
mise his imaginative treatment of the consequences of 1492.[54]
Les Indes is important for precisely this reason. It demonstrates
the poet's insistence on manipulating historical and political
reality imaginatively. Consequently, while *Les Indes* deals with
Columbus's voyage, the conquest of the New World, the exter-
mination of the indigenous peoples, the slave trade, slave
resistance and the inevitable transformation of the would-be
conquerors, its ultimate meaning transcends both the historical
and the narrowly political. The 'Indies' – which are tellingly
not called the Caribbean – are presented as human fantasy.
They are destined to recur constantly in human history
because of the longing for a prelapsarian Eden, a primordial,
untouched space. Equally inevitable is the deterioration of this
dream, the inexorable debasement after the romance of adven-
ture. Whether the dream is that of a Genoese sailor in 1492 or

the more contemporary Caribbean fantasy of the unspoilt,
primordial world of Africa, the longing for the 'pays rêvé' is the
same. In this regard, Glissant's Columbus is no different from
Saint-John Perse's Crusoe, whose dream is the deserted island
and total power. Perse's *Images à Crusoé* (1909) presents the
shipwrecked protagonist's longing for his lost paradise after his
return to civilisation.[55] Glissant's epic poem ends with the
return to Europe and the longing for otherness and purity that
would provoke the voyages of Marco Polo, Vasco da Gama
and Henry Magellan.

Mais peut-être enfin l'homme n'a-t-il que même ardeur, n'importe
soit-il? Et d'où qu'il vienne, même souffrance connaissable? Quelles
Indes l'appellent? Ou, si son rêve n'est déjà qu'une passionnée raison,
quel océan pourtant s'impose entre elle et lui? – Nul ne peut dire en
certitude; mais chacun tente la nouvelle traversée! La mer est éter-
nelle.[56]

(But perhaps man after all, whoever he is, has the same desire and the
same passion. And wherever he comes from, the same familiar suffer-
ing? What Indies beckon to him? Or, if his dream is already nothing
but reality shaped by passion, what ocean nevertheless stretches
between it and him? – No one can say with certainty; but each one
attempts the new crossing! The sea is eternal.)

The Indies are eternal. So is the sea. Of course, so is Genoa –
the place from which we begin, the familiar world which is
constantly threatened by the dream and desire.

Le blé mouvant, le douve, et le quai de bois mort, la plaine où sont les
villes, toutes Gênes sur leurs ports.
Et une Inde, laquelle? en qui le rêvé a son limon.[57]

(The waving wheat, the moat, and the pier of rotten wood, the plain
where the towns are, all Genoas with their ports.
And an Indies, which one? From whose mud the dream takes shape.)

The poet's answer to this question seems to be man's conquest
of space in the contemporary period, 'la dernière étoile con-
voitée au coin de la lune l'oasis de l'infini' ('the last coveted star
in the corner of the moon, the oasis of the infinite').[58]
Les Indes is not anti-colonial polemic nor ideological carica-
ture but rather a major text of the post-negritude period in

Caribbean and New World writing. It proposes nothing less than a new way of viewing New World history. Already, we sense that Glissant has located the Caribbean historically and imaginatively within the western hemisphere and in terms of contemporary concerns of the fifties. What he would later call his 'prophetic vision of the past'[59] is already apparent in this early poem. The vision of history he proposes here is not tied to events (inevitably these would be events in European history) but organised in terms that are more imaginative, cyclical and less narrowly chronological. For instance, the imaginative phases suggested in *Les Indes* evoke the lure of the 'other', the adventure, conquest, The Middle Passage, The Night of Resistance and the inextricable bonds between Old and New World. The vision would later be elaborated in *Le quatrième siècle* but already Glissant was suggesting that a new conceptual order was needed to understand fully the New World and by extension the Caribbean experience. To this extent we can again see the parallels between Glissant and other twentieth-century artists of cultural diversity such as Victor Segalen, Paul Claudel, Saint-John Perse and Glissant's Caribbean contemporary Derek Walcott. From the carnage of history and the conflicting diversity of the past, new correspondences emerge, making the link between an imaginative system and the real world a vital one for Glissant. The New World past is conceived as a 'féconde Tragédie' ('Tragedy filled with promise') and a sense of this cannot be found in historical detail but in the imaginative grasp of continuities. As he says in *L'intention poétique*, 'le rapport minutieux des dates et des faits nous masque le mouvement continu . . . de notre passé' ('the scrupulous reporting of dates and events conceals from us the continuities . . . in our past').

The dense poetic meditations that comprise Glissant's early publications clearly convey a sense of the importance he ascribes to an imaginative and reflective approach to even the most vexed and disturbing political questions. His later rejection of realist technique and moral prescriptiveness in the novel is not surprising given the nature of these poetic works. Glissant, however, does not go to the other extreme and suggest

that the poet's vision provides a complete and total expla-
nation. Poetic 'discoveries' are, after all, likely to suffer the
same fate as historical discoveries. Consciousness is a slow,
patient and painful process. It is one that is also destined to be
repeated with predictable regularity. Poetry, an essential part
of this process, offers at best provisional answers. As he admits
at the end of *Soleil de la conscience*:

Et s'il résout pas de problèmes, du moins aide-t-il aussi à les poser
dans la lumière trop diffuse, quand la connaissance est possible et
toujours future.[60]

(And if it does not resolve problems, at least it also helps to pose them
in the too-unfocused light, when knowing is possible and always
incomplete.)

CHAPTER 3

Novels of time and space

LA LEZARDE, LE QUATRIEME SIECLE

Je me suis toujours efforcé d'aller dans l'âme des choses
. . . Pas de monstres et pas de héros!

Gustave Flaubert, 31 December 1875

Nothing is perhaps more fascinating than to observe the way in which, in some artists, a certain mental disposition, tendencies in sensibility, a repertoire of images, begin to acquire a kind of definitive realization. The next phase of Glissant's literary development is of great importance because we sense that the governing impulses in the early writing are beginning to produce highly original work. His tendency to penetrate, to use the words of Gustave Flaubert, 'into the soul of things', to move from graphic detail to an intense concentration on associations that go beyond the realm of appearances, lead to spectacular success with prose fiction in the late fifties and early sixties.

These years saw Glissant produce two moving and original meditations in prose on Caribbean landscape and history. His first novel, *La Lézarde* ('The Ripening'), won the prestigious Prix Renaudot in 1958 and his second work of fiction, *Le quatrième siècle* ('The Fourth Century'), the Prix Charles Veillon in 1964. These major works concentrate on Martinique and the fates of a group of characters, more specifically of two families through whom the diverse aspects of a community's experience could be probed and articulated. Given the official silence in departmentalised Martinique about the past, and the self-inflicted amnesia among the Martiniquan people, these novels proposed new and disturbing insights into the perception of space and the importance of memory in that community. Indeed, they would eventually become a matrix from which later works of prose and poetry would be derived.

It would be misleading, however, to disregard completely other works that appeared during this period. If nothing else, they attest to the restlessness of Glissant's creative imagination and a reluctance on his part to abandon his early poetic impulses. This creative dispersion of energies would be consistent throughout his career and form part of a poetics that challenges repeatedly the traditional divisions that separate reflective and imaginative activity, narrative, dramatic and poetic forms. The shift to the novel form at this time does not represent a definitive break with the past or a new blind loyalty to prose. If anything, it signifies an openness to forms that would be apparent in his entire oeuvre.

One should also bear in mind the pressures put on Caribbean writers at this time to conform with the reformist politics of negritude or Marxism. Art was essentially seen as moral utterance. This literature of revenge, conversion or moral uplift left Glissant, as we have seen, with serious misgivings.[1] This may have been a time of intense political activism for Glissant, but his prose narratives seem less politically purposeful, less ideologically focused, than those of his contemporaries. In this regard, his two books of poems and two plays written in the early sixties are very revealing, in that they were not typical of the committed black writing of the sixties. They represent somewhat different directions and concerns from those of the two novels.

The two plays, *Monsieur Toussaint*, first published in 1961, and *Rêve de ce qui fut la tragédie d'Askia* ('Dream of what was the Tragedy of Askia'), written in 1963 but never published, take us away from Martinique and the experiences of the descendants of the Béluse and Longoué families. The first deals with the Haitian War of Independence and is neither 'politically inspired' as the preface says nor tailored to the practicalities of theatrical production. The importance of this play would be more apparent after Glissant's return to Martinique and the appearance of a definitive version in 1978. The author's impulse in the early version of *Monsieur Toussaint* is to confront what was seen as the absence of history in the Caribbean. The second play is also historical, and also concerns itself with an imaginative investigation of the past. This time, however, the text deals with the origins in Africa of the tensions between the families that appear in the prose narratives.

The book of poems *Le sel noir* ('Black Salt'), which appeared in 1959, and the collection of poems *Le sang rivé* ('Riveted Blood'), published in 1960, take us even further away from the island space of Martinique. The former recalls the epic poem *Les Indes*. It can be seen as a historical journey, a wandering through histories, peoples, encounters, languages. The paradoxical title suggests the nature of the direction taken on this journey. 'Black' here suggested not only Africa and the suffering of the Diaspora, but the unknown, the hidden, the unconscious and the colour of melancholy. 'Salt' connotes that which is life-giving as well as sterile, that which is human and mortal as well as enduring and preserving. Ultimately, it is all summed up in the paradoxical and elusive nature of the sea itself. As Jean-Pierre Richard observes in the work of Saint-John Perse, a strong poetic influence on Glissant at this time, Perse uses a complex pattern of images of salt in an attempt to 'poser la possibilité morale d'une sécheresse fertile, d'une aridité féconde, d'un vide qui soit créature d'être' ('raise the moral possibility of a fertile dryness, of a fecund aridity, of an emptiness out of which being could be created).[2]

Once again Glissant steers clear of a narrowly ideological text which would mean a departure from the epic poem devoted to black suffering which can be found in Jean Brierre's *Black Soul* (1945), Jacques Roumain's *Bois d'ébène* (1947) and René Depestre's *Minérai noir* (1956). The salt of Glissant's title refers often to the poem itself. The poetic text is here residue, an accumulation at the point where different elements encounter each other.

Il est – au delta – un fleuve où le mot s'amasse, le poème – et où le sel se purifie.[3]

(There is – at the delta – a river where the word accumulates, the poem – and where the salt is purified.)

In this regard, the connections with Glissant's first poems are obvious in these images of the power of the surge of the unconscious and the inscrutable gift of salt deposited on the shoreline. Another link with the early verse can be seen in Glissant's fascination in *Le sel noir* with pictorial discourse. Again an artist, this time the Chilean painter Matta, offers a complementary vision to enhance that of the poetic language.

While treating themes that are quite distinct from those of the early novels, Glissant in *Le sel noir* nevertheless demonstrates a tendency to drift towards narrative. Already his interest in the extended narrative form is apparent in *Les Indes*, and *Le sel noir* similarly contains a clear chronological pattern in its wandering through history and a descent towards knowledge. This odyssey begins with 'Temps anciens' and follows the sea through the adventures of Carthage whose ruins were covered with salt by the Romans, then takes in the salt trade in Africa, and ends with the cessation of wandering in 'mon noir pays' where the salt of the unconscious washes up dissolved in the sea. In *Le sel noir* these experiences which represent the diverse legacy of the past are set in motion by the figure of the *conteur* or storyteller. This figure, who is key to the narrative of *La Lézarde*, is imagined in the poetic text as:

Ce sage marin, mesuré diseur . . . Il vient, enfant, dans le premier matin. Il voit l'écume originelle, la première suée de sel. L'Histoire qui attend.[4]

(This wise man of the sea, unhurried teller of tales . . . He comes like a child into his first morning. He sees the pristine foam, the sweat of salt. History waiting.)

The element of paradox that pervades this work is epitomised in this persona who is both experienced and naive, a wanderer not a navigator who, standing before the sea and history, is poised to begin the adventure of knowing. At this point, one cannot but think of the character Thael in *La Lézarde* about to leave for his own adventure through the plains of Lambrianne and down to the sea.

What Glissant wishes to convey in *Le sel noir* is the taste of a paradoxical and diverse human past ('ce goût de terres

emmêlées'). The association of both knowledge and poetry
with accumulation, the poem as salt deposited on the shoreline
and the harsh yet liberating taste of reality, would become a
central pattern of imagery for his first novel. The other poetic
work of this time, *Le sang rivé*, is not, however, about accretion
of experience but rather about flashes, scatterings and frag-
ments. These poems can be seen as offshoots of work in progress
'tous, liés a quelque project qui bientôt les rejeta' ('all tied to
some project which soon rejected them').[5] Traces of *Un champ
d'îles* and *La terre inquiète*, as well as *Soleil de la conscience*, can be
found in these collected poems.[6] The company that Glissant
kept in the fifties can be traced in the dedications. Names like
Jean Laude, Roger Giroux and Jacques Charpier evoke the
literary circle he frequented. Words like 'Océanie' and
'Sampan' suggest the adventures of Segalen and Claudel whose
works about the East impressed Glissant deeply at this time.

However, it is the epigraph of this collection that really
provides a clue to deeper artistic preoccupations and internal
coherence. 'A toute géographie torturée' ('For tortured geo-
graphies everywhere') from the outset points to an interest in
landscape as well as the secretions, eruptions, deposits and
residues produced from the extremes of nature and, by exten-
sion, extreme states of feeling. The poems are studded with
words that refer to emanations from a natural order: *boue*
(mud), *brume* (mist), *fumée* (smoke), *écume* (foam), *cendres*
(ashes), *mousse* (moss), *lave* (lava), and *givre* (frost), among
others. The last two, *lave* and *givre*, are the titles of sections of
this collection. They suggest both the products of tortured
geographies as well as the creations of extreme heat and
extreme cold. The former is thick, molten, dark matter pro-
duced from volcanic eruptions whereas the latter is the hard
crystalline product of winter.

Glissant's short preface does mention 'l'effervescence de la
terre' ('the earth's effervescence'), and the various products of
this process of 'effervescence' point to the poet's interest in
metamorphosis, transformation and, possibly, instability.
Some of the most striking images in this work have to do with
altered states. As he declares in 'Train lent', 'à force de penser

terre j'éclate' ('by thinking earth I explode'),[7] or in 'L'air nourricier', 'Vers l'espace j'aspire j'irrue mondes mondes' ('Towards the open air I aspire I irrupt worlds').[8] Glissant focuses on violent metamorphosis, on the shattering or the erosion of that which is concentrated and hard. One is not surprised to find a sequence of images as those of 'Eléments' which suggest both openness and contraction, inner erosion and resistant exterior: 'C'est moi le fleuve la pierre impassible et dans son sein l'ardeur de la terre' ('It is I the river the unmoved stone and within its heart the burning of the earth').[9] The convulsions that abound in this text do not simply refer to the politics of the Caribbean or the political agitation of the post-war period, they are part of a larger, philosophical reflection on the nature of change and its inevitability.

These ideas are contained in the image of the stone. In the poem 'La pierre', the poet's identification with the stone is explicit: 'Moi la pierre je hèle' ('I the stone call out'). One of the closing poems, 'Abrupt', focuses on this image of animated stone, on the forces of decomposition and ferment, even perhaps on the subject of exile and fertile encounter:

> Mais cette pierre dans ta main où vient le vent
> Et rêvent des oiseaux blessés des fruits des mots
> Pendant que vive tu surprends
> Le sang rivé vivant dans la nuit sans autan.[10]

> (But this stone in your hand where the wind blows
> And wounded birds dream of the fruits of words
> While alive you come up on
> Riveted blood living in the windless night.)

This blood which contains the image of the title of the collection conveys the essential idea of these works. Poems like stones constantly shaped by external forces, unyielding yet offering the possibility of an opening, are the key to the 'riveted blood', alive despite its tortured state. Again the paradoxes so evident in Glissant's fiction appear – pain and fertility, aridity and tenderness, closed and open. Ultimately, these works are important as sensuous explorations of themes that would be more politically and philosophically focused in the early novels.

Glissant won the Prix Renaudot for *La Lézarde* in 1958, one year after Michel Butor's novel *La modification* had been awarded the same prestigious prize. To some, Glissant's novel was a kind of tropicalised 'new novel', conceived in the same experimental mode as that of Michel Butor. This attitude is hardly surprising given the attention devoted to what the theoretician of the 'new novel', Alain Robbe-Grillet, had proclaimed as the new aesthetic revolution in literature from the early 1950s. To complicate matters further there were superficial similarities between Glissant's work and the experimental French novel.

Early reviewers were struck by the strangeness of Glissant's novel. This is particularly true of those from the Caribbean who, while being respectful, were not quite sure what to make of the work. For instance, the venerable Haitian man of letters, Jean Price-Mars, declared the author to be an 'avant-garde writer' but was evasive on the question of the book's artistic merit.[11] Like the avant-garde novelists of the time, Glissant challenged the conventions of the traditional novel, emphasised the importance of consciousness and evoked a world of intense strangeness. As Beverley Ormerod observes, the novel is 'for the most part as bare of everyday domestic detail as a classical French tragedy. Few concrete events are described.'[12] However, these similarities are essentially circumstantial. *La Lézarde* departs in significant ways from the obsession with inanimate objects and the sense of the world's inscrutability such as we find in the work of France's 'new novelists'. But, most of all, Glissant's work bears the indelible stamp of his early poetic beginnings.

It would be more useful to see Glissant's fiction as an important generic crossroads in his oeuvre. The links between this novel and Glissant's earlier poetic works are undeniable. The novel is divided into four sections whose titles echo the universalising quality as well as the actual images of the early poetry: 'La flamme' ('The flame'), 'L'acte' ('The act'), 'L'élection' ('The election'), 'L'éclat' ('The explosion'). The initial sequence of the novel is an extended poetic meditation on the beginning of a journey, the consequences of leaving home, the

dawn of a new consciousness, the taste of the bitter-sweet fruit
of knowledge and the complex bonds between hill and plain,
forest and sea in the Caribbean. The opening words 'Thael
quitta sa maison' ('Thael left his house') echo through the
entire text as each character is forced, for one reason or
another, to abandon his or her old secure world and face the
challenge of growth and change.

The density of the pattern of images in Glissant's novel is
remarkable. The poetic power of his early texts remains undi-
minished in his prose narratives. However, simply to describe
La Lézarde as a 'poetic novel' would be to gloss over the radical
nature of Glissant's critique of the novel form, implied in this
text and made explicit in later theoretical writing. Certainly
one of the characters, Pablo, tells the narrator, 'Fais le comme
un poème' ('Write it like a poem'),[13] and Glissant himself in
L'intention poétique claims that the novel form can be seen as a
'dévoilement de l'opacité poétique' ('a stripping away of poetic
opacity').[14] From the 1950s Glissant is advocating funda-
mental changes in Caribbean prose fiction. His critique is
focused on the practice of the technique of realism. He would
later write in *Le discours antillais*,

L'une des premières difficultés qu'affronte un écrivain touche à la
manière dont il rend compte du réel. Or le réalisme, théorie et
technique de la reproduction littérale ou 'totale', n'est pas inscrit
dans le réflexe culturel des peuples africains ou américains . . . Le
réalisme occidental n'est pas une technique 'à plat', hors profondeur,
mais le devient quand il est adopté par nos écrivains.[15]

(One of the first difficulties facing a writer concerns the way in which
he deals with reality. Now realism, a theory and a technique of literal
or 'total' representation, is not inscribed in the cultural reflex of
African or American peoples . . . Western realism is not a dull or
shallow technique, but becomes like that when adopted by our
writers.)

If Caribbean literature were to play a role in the process of
self-discovery and were to be seen as a tool of scientific investi-
gation, then it would need to go beyond borrowed techniques.
In this same article Glissant would go so far as to say that 'Le
roman ni le poème ne sont . . . nos genres. Autre chose est

peut-être à venir' ('Neither the novel nor the poem are . . . our genres. Something else will perhaps emerge').[16]

Therefore we should be sensitive to the radical nature of Glissant's experimentation in this novel. Even though it is centred on specific political events in post-war Martinique, it is by no means a historical account of 1945. Such an approach would be less than useful. In a statement reminiscent of his concept of poetics of accumulation, of duration, he says in *L'intention poétique*, 'Le rapport minutieux des dates et des faits nous masque le mouvement continu . . . de notre passé' ('The meticulous reporting of dates and facts conceals from us the dynamic continuum of our past').[17] Perhaps we have a clue to Glissant's objective in *La Lézarde* in the expression 'naître au monde' ('to be born in or with the world') used early in *L'intention poétique*. If nothing else, this first novel is about the movement from self to other, from individual to collective, from solitude to new relationships.

Set in Martinique during the elections of 1945, the novel is about a group of young political activists led by Mathieu, who decide they need to eliminate a hired killer called Garin. The job is entrusted to Thael, a mountain-dweller, unknown to the people of the town. The narrative unfolds through a series of journeys across the landscape and intense contacts between various characters. Ultimately their experiences produce a ripening of individual awareness, whether political, emotional or spiritual. In this regard the novel is dominated by the Lézarde river, the chief 'protagonist' and symbol of an open and complete state of consciousness. In its course down from the mountains through the oppressive plains to fuse eventually with the open sea, the river represents a fertile insight into the continuum of Caribbean experience. In various ways the river's journey is repeated in the lives of the characters as they go from innocent beginnings to a painful state of knowing.

Such an objective has clear implications for the structure of the novel. A reader of this text is immediately struck by the deliberately naive nature of the narration. This experiment-ation with narrative voice would intensify in later novels, but already in this first work Glissant introduces an unstable narrator. Caught between a direct experience of rapidly changing events, and an imperfect recollection of the recent past, the narrator is tentative, reticent, apologetic. He confesses desperately to the desire both to remember and understand the past and to be a witness and participant.

Oui, je suis double, le temps m'étreint dans cette tenaille, j'entends les échos de la derniere fête, j'entends l'ivresse du temps passé. Ils crient. Ils crient tous: 'N'oublie pas, n'oublie pas. Souvenez vous.' Comme si les mots pouvaient être une rivière qui descend et qui à la fin s'étale et déborde. Comme si les mots pouvaient concentrer tout en éclair et le porter dans la terre propice (qu'il fructifie). Comme si dans la richesse et le lancinant monotone appel et la chaleur sans frein les mots pouvaient conduire leur part de boues, de racines, de limon, jusqu'au delta et à la mer: jusqu'à la précise réalité. (pp. 230–1)

(Yes, I am two people, a sensation frozen in time. I still hear echoes of the last celebration, I still hear the wild rejoicing of bygone days. They all call out to me. 'Don't forget, don't forget. Remember us.' As if words could be a river flowing down, which finally spreads out and overflows. As if words could become concentrated like a bolt of lightning and strike the waiting earth (and make it fertile). As if, in their richness and their acute yet ordinary appeal and their unrestrained heat, words could carry their share of mud, roots, silt down to the delta and the sea: down to the precise definitions of reality.)

The nature of Glissant's challenge to the conventions of narration is clear in this extract; the difficulty of being both a witness and recorder, the incompatibility of omniscience and direct experience, objectivity and subjectivity. This again indicates the combination of creative and critical invariably present in Glissant's work as well as the sense that the very medium of his craft, words, are unreliable and unpredictable. As Bernadette Cailler rightly declares in her discussion of his narrative devices, Glissant is a 'poète aussi puissamment donné au rêve qu'analyste vigilant du "réel"' ('poet as powerfully open to fantasy as vigilant analyst of the "real"').[18]

Not only does Glissant use the narrator in *La Lézarde* to raise questions of the transcription of reality and the reliability of memory, he also suggests crucial and inevitable relationships between the 'Je' and the 'Nous', self and community. This concern follows logically from his interest in the inextricable link between thinking and feeling. Inevitably, the subject in Glissant has a shaping effect on and is in turn shaped by the object of its attention. This tendency to lose subjective perspective is ever present in Glissant's narrative. The 'I' of *La Lézarde* is often in danger of becoming a 'we' or a 'you'. The sixth chapter of the third section of this novel is actually narrated in the second person singular, almost giving a sense of the older narrator's effort to reinsert himself in the collective memory of the election victory. This immersion in the crowd and the town's festivities is almost a parallel scene to an earlier reference to the child-narrator immersed in the Lézarde river (p. 31). The carnival atmosphere opens the door to communion between individual and group. In this situation the subject loses his sense of a distinctive individuality or self-consciousness and is bewildered, vulnerable, and thus becomes in Glissant's text the narrative site for the collective experience.

Such an interest in investigating or restoring the collective memory is crucial to Glissant's enterprise. As Mathieu himself suggests to the narrator at the end, the narrator should record the events but 'Pas l'histoire avec nous, ce n'est pas intéressant' ('Not our story, that is not interesting', p. 224). Indeed Mathieu, himself a historian, should not be concerned with details. What is required is not the 'hard evidence' of historical documentation, nor the melodrama of remorse and revenge to which the turbulent events of Caribbean history are susceptible. The narrator does mention the Westerns he had seen as a child at El Paraiso cinema (p. 210) and their passionate resolution of conflict. Perhaps the implication here is that, more than a Hollywood artefact, the Western, with its faded notion of heroism and honour and its simplification of history, would distort the complexity of the collective experience. Both ideological and sentimental appropriation of the past are seen by Glissant as narrow and distorting. The form that allows insight into the collective experience is the folktale. As he argues in *Le discours antillais*, 'Le conte nous a donné le Nous, en exprimant de manière implicite que nous avons à le conquérir' ('The tale has provided us with the collective, while expressing implicitly that we must master it').[19] Consequently, the storyteller in the novel becomes the ideal narrator, the narrator his inexpert literary manifestation.

The figure of the *conteur* telling his tale in the flickering circle of light is frequently repeated in the novel; the tale he relates is neither clear nor straightforward. It has the meandering elusiveness, the opaque unpredictability of the Lézarde river, which is the Lézarde text, an ambiguous, open-ended sign that dominates the language of Glissant's landscape, what he calls 'La parole du paysage'. A relationship between *conteur* and narrator is explicitly indicated.

En l'enfant que j'étais et l'homme que je suis ont ceci en commun: de confondre le conte et l'histoire; c'est parce que les flambeaux n'ont pas encore fini de brûler, que le cercle de la lumière est encore là, autour de la voix! (p. 105)

(And the child that I was and the man that I am have this in common: they confuse folktale and history. That is because the torches still burn, because the circle of light is still there, gathered around the voice of the storyteller.)

Towards the conclusion of the novel the image returns with great force at the end of the victory parade. The storyteller, the one who resists imaginatively and from within the community, is privileged over the figure of the maroon in this novel. The old maroon, Papa Longoué, dies in the story. It is the storyteller who endures.

Et les flambeaux étaient plus fantastiques encore; on pensait à des histoires, à des contes, à des sorciers. (p. 211)

(And the torches were even more eerie; they made you think of legends, folktales and witchcraft.)

Yet the tale as told in the novel is by no means one with a clear moral message. Beverley Ormerod quite accurately enumerates the archetypal motifs in this story – the mysterious wood, the magical spring, the quest, the sacrificial victim and the freeing of the river.[20] However, one needs to resist the temptation to see this as a conventional tale of damnation and redemption, of a successful quest for spiritual renewal.

What Richard Burton calls Glissant's 'determination to understand, espouse and assume the Martiniquan reality in all its multi-faceted contradictoriness',[21] is precisely what makes this story more complex than the traditional moral fable. It is not a novel of heroes and villains and in no way do characters progress towards an ideal self-sufficiency. The novel is not about closure but about explosion, a realization of incompleteness as is suggested in the title of the last section, 'L'éclat'. In this novel Glissant's concern is the crack or 'lézarde' in the Martiniquan experience of the past. This is the ideological and historical discontinuity that isolates hill from sea, arrival from flight, *marronnage* from submission. Glissant was well aware that the marvellous ambiguity of the title would at once suggest the meandering text that would allow twists and turns of the river in filling in the yawning, disorienting gap in Caribbean history. As the narrator declares, the whole story can be seen as 'Un effort absolu pour rejoindre le flamboyant, le fromager terrible, la barre resplendissante' ('A supreme effort to join together the flame tree, the terrible silk cotton tree and the shimmering sand bar', p. 216). The rupture or vacuum in the past haunts the main figures in this narrative – both victor and victim, intellectual and non-intellectual, male and female. Thael and Garin literally experience the complex hidden reality of Martiniquan history as they go down the Lézarde river together. Mathieu, the intellectual and activist, is haunted by the need to connect the discontinuous past: 'Il va du flamboyant à l'usine au flamboyant, et il n'a pas trouvé' ('He goes from the flame tree to the factory, from the factory to the flame tree, and he has not found', p. 82). He is equally puzzled by the actual events of 1788, in which year there was a slave revolt as well as a new arrival of slaves. As Mathieu confesses, these secrets of the past, fixed between hill and sea, are not the official history of the island and do not yield themselves to conventional methods of historical investigation (p. 213).

The novel is as much about the general problematic of knowledge of the ruptured past as it is about actual political events that took place in 1945. Glissant seems to have chosen this year because it represents the end of a short period of relative autonomy for Martinique (blockaded by the Allied fleet after Germany occupied France), the year in which Aimé Césaire was swept to power on a tide of nationalist self-affirmation and the year before departmentalisation produced a loss of control over local affairs, intensified consumerism and undermined productivity. The self-sufficiency created by Martinique's isolation during the war, now a popular theme among contemporary writers,[22] was undone by 1946. In *La Lézarde* we still see characters like the peasant Lomé who at the end proposes a farming project with Pablo and Tigamba. Lomé is, however, replaced in the later novel *Malemort* by the figure of the *djobeur*, forced from the countryside to do odd jobs around the town. Indeed, central to events of *La Lézarde* is the question of productivity and taking charge of one's space. The young activists in the novel are struggling against the cynical attitude of people like Garin, who declares:

C'est un trou, même pas, on ne peut pas dire que c'est un trou, c'est un assemblage, il y a la terre, mais on ne peut pas la cultiver, il y a les maisons mais elles tombent sous le vent, il y a les hommes! que font-ils? Ils ne travaillent pas la terre, ni le métal, ni la roche. C'est sale, mais c'est terreux, et il n y a pas d'outils. (p. 125)

(It's a hole, not even that, you cannot call it a hole, it's a hodge-podge, there is land but it cannot be worked, there are houses but they collapse in the wind, there are men, but what do they do? They do not work the land, nor metal nor rocks. It is dirty but filled with silt, and there are no tools.)

Throughout the novel one is continually aware of the poverty that is scarcely concealed by the luxuriant natural scenery. The picturesque calm is suddenly disrupted by the nightmarish appearance of a cane trailer (p. 171). The image of a four-year old child driving oxen across a barren field haunts the work as does the everpresent red earth, indelibly marked with the blood of the past. At the end Thael is forced to see the island as a world of leprosy, tuberculosis and malaria, and not an exotic vision of tropical beauty. It is within this context of dependency and the need for a new local self-supporting productivity that the novel's politics are inscribed.

This is not a novel about heroes. The novel belongs to Thael but one should not be tempted to construe him as the hero in the same way that Manuel is in Roumain's *Gouverneurs de la rosée*.[23] As the critic Jacques André observes, in Glissant's work the 'proud certitudes' of Roumain's heroes are absent.[24] What is interesting is the author's decision to choose Thael over Mathieu as the central point of focus. The beginning and end of the novel are devoted to Thael. The reader also discovers the land, politics and personalities of Lambrianne through Thael's descent from his mountain solitude. Both Mathieu and Thael share the revealing experience of fatherlessness, for Glissant the quintessential condition of the Caribbean. One is illegitimate and the other an orphan. Yet Mathieu is an intellectual who is provocatively drawn as frail, sickly and an excessive drinker. He seems to belong to those characters in Caribbean and Latin American fiction – surveyors, explorers, historians – who are overwhelmed by the world they attempt to order, discover or chart. Thael discovers the world sensuously and it is, perhaps, into his raw, physical descent into the realm of the senses that Glissant, isolated from the Caribbean while writing the novel in Paris, poured his memories of the Caribbean.

La Lézarde is an adventure in sensations, surfaces and textures. Beyond the cynicism of the treacherous Garin or the scholar's scepticism of Mathieu, Thael feels the elemental beauty of Lambrianne. The sense of elation he feels during his explorations is diametrically opposed to the vision of decay that dominates Aimé Césaire's epic poem *La cahier d'un retour au pays natal*. The narrator's voice in the text seems to take its cue from Thael's ecstatic state of mind. It is not retentive or minimalist but a Baroque, luxuriant flow like that of the river itself. In this regard, Thael is as distinct from the 'bien pensants' of the town, hidden behind their jalousied windows, as he is from the ancestral Papa Longoué who, having resolved to live his life in a world of shadows, as Mathieu says (p. 140), has literally lost touch with the rest of his landscape. In contrast to them, Thael is an exemplary figure, choosing to expose himself fully to the diversity of the land.

Leaving the distorting shadows of his world, Thael must

turn away from the shadows and like Plato's deluded cave dweller, face the light of direct sensation. This is not a gratuitous exercise since Glissant sees the freed imagination and heightened sensation as antidotes to the amnesia that haunts the Martiniquan psyche. This view of reality as the creation of sensation and memory recalls Glissant's poetic beginnings. There is constant reference in the text to reality apprehended through sensation – through taste, in particular. Taste becomes part of a process of initiation and understanding. The growth in individual consciousness is likened to a ripening fruit, from which the title of the English translation is drawn:

ce pays est comme un fruit nouveau, qui s'ouvre lentement (lentement) devoilant peu à peu (par-delà les épaisseurs et les obscurités de l'écorce) toute la richesse de sa pulpe . . . l'homme importe quand il connaît dans sa propre histoire (dans ses passions et dans ses joies) la saveur d'un pays. (pp. 31–2)

(this country is like a new fruit, slowly (slowly) opening, gradually revealing (under a thick and mysterious skin) the full richness of the pulp . . . a man only fulfils himself when he savours the meaning of a country in his own story (in its moments of passion and joy).)

The relation of taste to consciousness is repeated throughout the story. Thael's very journey down to the plain begins with his defiant bite of the fruit of the hog plum tree, a symbolic act of willed damnation for having tasted of the forbidden fruit of knowledge. As he is drawn further into the sun-bleached world of the plain, he swallows the harsh product of the cane fields, molasses.

je suis comme un touriste, pensait-il, on lui montre les machines, on lui fait boire un peu de mélasse, il s'étrangle, il tousse et dit merci, les ouvriers rient doucement, tout baigne dans la suffocation du sucre, les yeux pleurent . . . pourtant c'est mon pays et je ne le connais pas. (p. 72)

(I am like a tourist, he thought, they show him the machinery, they offer him a little molasses, he chokes on it, he coughs and says 'Thanks', the workers laugh gently, the fumes of the burning sugar are suffocating, his eyes stream . . . yet this is my country and I do not know it.)

The final phase of his initiation into the world of the plain is sealed with the meal at Valérie's house. It is a ceremonial rite that signifies Thael's final and total acceptance of the unfamiliar plantation world (p. 184).

The intimate relation between taste and knowing is constantly repeated in the novel:

Les mots prenaient dans ces bouches une saveur toute neuve. (p. 17)

(Words took on in these mouths a totally new taste.)

C'est l'effort d'un seul homme . . . content de se sentir plus neuf que la première caîmite (avec son goût âcre de colle). (p. 53)

(It is the effort of a single individual . . . happy to feel a renewed vigour like the first star-apple (with its tart, cloying taste).)

Celui qui découvre la mer a soudain un goût de pain noir dans la bouche. Il veut aussitôt boire un lait de fruit. (p. 143)

(He who discovers the sea suddenly has a taste of black bread in his mouth. He immediately feels the urge to drink the milk of some fruit.)

Les enfants faisaient . . . la pulpe légère et changeante de ce fruit dont les hommes et les femmes étaient le noyau hurlant. (p. 211)

(Children were . . . the soft, ever-changing pulp of this fruit whose core was formed by the clamour of men and women.)

Glissant, who in *Le sel noir* had alluded to the importance of the sense of taste, now equates the slow, painful emergence of awareness with a carnival of sensation, an omnivorous, hedonistic feeling of the sense of taste as well as touch, vision and smell. Thael's awakened responses are so acute after his experience of the plain that when he returns to the hills in search of Garin, it is as if he is overwhelmed by an orgy of sensation. All his senses are affected in this shadowy world of heightened *jouissance*.

As the novel comes to a close, at a moment of human and sensuous plenitude, the river has come down and flooded the plain and an inclusive and vital embrace of the diverse areas of the island space ensues. It is not coincidence that the last meeting of the group of activists should break into rhythmic

song and dance.[25] Not so much ideologically constrained as
corporally overwhelmed, the group displays a common spon-
taneous, rhythmic unity. The identification between indi-
viduals and landscape is complete.

Ce fut la dernière fête du groupe. Nous étions un torrent. Nous étions
une montagne avec des forêts. Nous étions un soleil de rhum . . . le
chant avait vaincu le crépuscule. (pp. 229–30)

(This was the group's last celebration. We became like a rushing
river, like a mountain with thick forests, like intoxicating sunlight . . .
the singing had won out over the twilight.)

La Lézarde ultimately deals with the individual's sensory
responsiveness to the stimuli of his or her landscape. Those who
are out of touch like Papa Longoué, who hesitate like Valérie,
who are insensitive like Garin, are destined for death.
However, the ideal state for Glissant is not one of suspended
jouissance. If anything, nature is the locus of sacrifice and not a
zone of pleasure. The last section of the novel is explosive and
tragic. It is ultimately about Thael's longing for home, for a
prelapsarian innocence before his fall down to the plains. At
the end of his harsh initiation in the world of political activity,
heat, struggle, he chooses to withdraw. He takes Valérie back
to the sanctuary of his home on the hill. Having defied the
pastoral seclusion of his world of protective shadows for what is
called the 'carrefour d'espaces' ('crossroads of spaces'), Thael
is now tempted by his love for Valérie to insulate himself from
the realm of heat and struggle. Thael does not get his wish as
his dogs savagely attack Valérie and kill her.[26] Through the
violent act of his dogs, themselves products of the plantation,
Thael is forced to confront reality and its unknown daunting
complexity. Having faced the test of the unknown on the
outside – the sea – he now faces the test of the unknown inside –
the forest – with its deadly shadows. The novel ends with
Thael's spiritual awakening. He must now retrace his journey
back down to the plain, leaving behind his blood-spattered
paradise.

For Glissant, Martiniquan history is a series of missed oppor-
tunities. Written in 1958, *La Lézarde* is marked by the awareness

that 1945 was one such instance in the island's recent history. The act of electing the 'representative', as Césaire is called, like the act of getting rid of Garin, is not enough to guarantee freedom. Paradoxically, 1945 led to a deeper and potentially more debilitating relationship with the 'centre' or metropole. This realization seems to be suggested in the observation that

Les lendemains de fête sont nostalgiques, mais combien triste et désespérée la place de fête sous le soleil, quand la fête est pour le lendemain. (p. 164)

(The day after a holiday is filled with nostalgia, but how sad and desperate this square looks in the sunlight when celebrations are yet to take place.)

Awareness of the failure of the promise of 1945 hovers over this novel. But one also realizes that failure and death in the text are a form of knowledge. The three deaths in the story are telling. The old maroon Longoué, the young sheltered Valérie and the cynical Garin share a common refusal or inability to grasp the significance of the changes taking place around them or of the values of the Lézarde river. Their deaths are not arbitrary and those who survive do realize the link between grief and knowledge as well as death's capacity to facilitate growth and maturation.

After his evocation of the rupture in Caribbean history in *La Lézarde*, Glissant attempts not so much to reconstruct but to re-imagine the contacts, intersections and hostilities that abound in Martiniquan history through the incomplete family histories of the Longoués and the Béluses. *Le quatrième siècle* is not historical fiction in the conventional sense nor is it a family saga about dynasties, descendants and patriarchs. As in the first novel, *Le quatrième siècle* tries to avoid a simple polarisation of Martiniquan history, to dismantle the view of 'a straight-forward Manichean struggle between "noble savages" and collaborators', as Richard Burton observes.[27] Rather we have in this work a dialectical relationship between hill and plan-tation, maroon and field slaves, planters and enslaved, which are the basic human components that produced, in the Carib-bean, creole communities.

If Glissant's first novel gave us an insight into Martiniquan space, his second work tackles time and history. The plot is centred on the confrontation of two attitudes to time. One is epitomised by Papa Longoué who has an intuitive sense of time and the other by the young Mathieu whose schooling makes him want an ordered sense of history. The latter goes to the old storyteller hoping for a clear account of the past. The stories he is told are very complex and turn on a love/hate relationship between two families, the Béluses and the Longoués, whose primogenitors arrived on the same slave ship. One escaped almost immediately into the hills while the other was sold to a plantation. The paths of these families constantly cross over time. The encounter between Mathieu and Papa Longoué is the last encounter between these clans since Longoué is the last of the maroon line and Mathieu, the youngest Béluse, will endure as the spiritual heir to the Longoués.

It would be tempting to see in *Le quatrième siècle* an attempt to retrieve Martinique's lost past by inventing a family saga that fills in the gaps in French colonial history and that compensates for the distortions of prolonged metropolitan dominance. To do so, however, would be to turn Glissant's novel into a kind of tropical *Comédie Humaine* which uses recurring characters to give a documentary account of the whole of Martiniquan society. No fiction by Glissant, despite his interest in the evolution of characters and families, can be seen as a coherent representation of society in the tradition of Balzac. Indeed, Glissant has indirectly voiced his dissatisfaction with any such undertaking in the Caribbean by his comment on Alex Haley's *Roots*. Haley's genealogical enterprise is bluntly criticized for its 'filiation trop assurée' ('overly certain sense of filiation') which Glissant sees as a falsification of the complexities of New World history.[28]

The open-endedness of Glissant's fiction makes any fixed definitive view of the past, any vision of a clear, linear and unambiguous line of descent, impossible. For Glissant, the Caribbean past is not one of epic accumulation but rather of 'negative plenitude'. In *Le quatrième siècle*, Mathieu Béluse, this time more archivist than activist, must recognise the opaque, ironic and bewildering nature of the past. Mathieu in this novel is the incarnation of the Caribbean's desperate longing for a clear genealogy, an idealized notion of history. In the novel he must recognise the problematic nature of the past and the extent to which his wishful vision of filiation simplifies New World history.

In this regard, the importance of the work and ideas of the American novelist of the plantation South, William Faulkner, is crucial. Glissant credits Faulkner with destroying 'the sacred notion of filiation' which dominates the western imagination.[29] Glissant has frequently referred to Faulkner as one of the major influences on his work, as important for his fiction as Saint-John Perse is for his early poetry. Every major book of essays contains some discussion of Faulkner, of *Absalom, Absalom!* in particular. Glissant is drawn to Faulkner, as the novelist of a plantation society with a sense of the way in which half-truths and self-serving myths create a legendary past in the New World. It is no coincidence that the Colombian novelist Gabriel García Márquez who produced in his *One Hundred Years of Solitude* a mock epic of the New World, also acknowledges a debt to the American novelist of the deep South.

Faulkner's work had been available in French since the 1930s and in 1939 Jean-Paul Sartre had produced an oustanding essay on time in Faulkner. Glissant's own writing on Faulker goes back to the articles written for *Les lettres nouvelles* in the mid-fifties. Faulkner is useful to Glissant in the latter's conscious subversion and dismantling of the traditional historical novel. *Le quatrième siècle* is as much a deconstruction of historical fiction as *La Lézarde* is a sustained interrogation of the politically-committed novel. It is not that Martinique simply becomes Yoknapatawpha country. Glissant does not highlight the gloom, decadence and fatalism that pervade Faulkner's literary universe. There is generally a resilience and creativity in Glissant's characters that make them very different from Faulkner's doomed protagonists. The real affinity with Faulkner has to do with techniques and most importantly the themes of miscegenation and family conflict.

It is easy enough to draw parallels between Faulkner's use of the interior monologue, his switching back and forth in time and his interest in the disintegration of plantation society, and similar preoccupations in Glissant's fiction. In one of his earlier essays on Faulkner, Glissant indicated that the attachment of the former's characters to the land, to the curse of their inherit- ance, makes them truer than the creations of the violent melo- drama of the Western.[30] The element of time in Faulkner, which has always had a special fascination for French readers, equally intrigues Glissant. The present or, as Sartre called it, 'the irrational present' in Faulkner always at the mercy of a flickering elusive but nevertheless invasive past, is also echoed in Glissant as his characters are themselves caught between memory, unconscious impulses and the dramatic nature of their present situation.

The most important single aspect of Faulkner's work for Glissant, however, seems to be the issue of legitimacy and filiation. Bernadette Cailler touches on this question when she refers to the way in which Glissant transcends stereotypes in dealing with characters, whether white or black, and high- lights the strange complexities and the genealogical maze that mark Caribbean history. This 'quasi-Faulknerian dimension' is not given sufficient attention by Cailler and she tends to focus singlemindedly on the element of fatalism and decadence that is evident in the Senglis household and in particular in the neurotic condition of Marie-Nathalie.[31] The question of inter- racial contact is the crucial point of contact between Glissant and Faulkner. In the latter, miscegenation represents the curse of the past that dooms the characters in the immediate present. This is why the novel *Absalom, Absalom!* is so frequently men- tioned by Glissant. It is Faulkner's most obvious treatment of an infringed moral code, family tragedy and fratricidal conflict.

Glissant's comments on Faulkner's novel of miscegenation and incest could easily apply to what he is attempting to do in *Le quatrième siècle*. Faulkner's novel demonstrates the tragic ironies of a longing for history and legitimacy in the Americas. Consequently, the reader is forced to confront what Glissant calls the 'perversion of an original filiation' in the New World context. The longing for pure origins and a clear line of descent is an impossible dream because:

La linéarité s'y perd. Le désiré historique et son impossible se nouent alors dans un inextricable lacis d'alliances, apparentements et procréations, dont l'analogue répétitive et vertigineuse constitue un de principes . . . l'homme ici se perd et tourne dans sa trace.[32]

(Linearity gets lost. The longed for history and its nonfulfilment are knotted up in an inextricable tangle of relationships, alliances and progeny, whose principle is one of bewildering repetition . . . here man has lost his way and turns in circles.)

The words used by Glissant to describe the paradoxes and ambiguities of family relationships are very telling. For instance, 'lacis d'alliances' suggests a tangled network, an impenetrable density, and provides an insight into the relationship between landscape and character in the Americas.

The link between Faulkner and the writers of the 'other' America (that is, the Caribbean and South America) is the dimension of 'opacity' and the symbolic forest that reappears in writers as diverse as Carpentier, Faulkner, Márquez and Glissant himself. In *L'intention poétique* Glissant evokes the relationships between density of vegetation and inextricability of characters among themselves and within themselves.

L'inextricable et chaotique logique des personnages *décrit* la forêt. Autrement dit, les personnages de Faulkner ne sont pas denses de psychologie, mais d'attache à leur glèbe.[33]

(The inextricable and chaotic logic of the characters *describes* the forest. In other words, Faulkner's characters are not dense in psychology but in the bonding with their land.)

Faulkner is credited with creating a new vision of genealogy, of tragedy, of history in the New World. Faulkner's tragic world view represents a rupture with the Greek vision of tragedy as sacrifice, expiation and restoration of equilibrium. The prospective of linear filiation and legitimacy is impossible in *Absalom, Absalom!* where Faulkner 'détruit hérétiquement le sacré de la filiation' ('heretically destroys the sacred sense of filiation').[34]

While recognising the fundamental importance of Faulkner's world view to the Caribbean in particular, and the Americas as a whole, Glissant has reservations about the doomed nature of the Faulknerian hero. Cut off in time and space, he or she simply succumbs to fate. Faulkner had no sense of the rest of the Americas and their relationship to his views of the post-plantation South.

Ainsi Faulkner, qui partage l'obsession du passé propre aux ressortiss-ants du Nouveau Monde, ignore en absolu le reste du continent américain . . . l'Amérique du sud est décidément une 'réserve'. Voici la faiblesse. Installé dans sa solitude, le héros faulknérien (témoin et victime) est coupé du monde.[35]

(Thus Faulkner, who shares with other people of the New World an obsession with the past, ignores totally the rest of the American continent . . . South America is decidedly a 'reservation'. This is a weakness. Fixed in his isolation, the Faulknerian hero (witness and victim) is cut off from the world.)

Glissant's open-ended universe produces characters of greater resilience and flexibility. Indeed, those characters in Glissant's work that can be described as 'cut off from the world' suffer the fate of the Faulknerian hero.

Another reservation that Glissant expresses about Faulkner's work concerns the latter's treatment of non-white characters. Black characters for Faulkner represent an impenetrable opacity. They can only be evaluated from the outside. As Glissant points out in *L'intention poétique*, even the retarded Benjy in *The Sound and the Fury* is allowed an interior mono-logue. However, 'Le monologue intérieur ne sera jamais propre au personnage noir' ('The interior monologue will never be accorded to the black character').[36] Lucas, the main character in *Intruder in the Dust*, is described, as Glissant points out, in terms of postures and gestures, nothing but a silhouette profiled against the horizon. To this extent Glissant sets out to com-plete and expand Faulkner's vision. Central to his imagination, as it is to Faulkner's, is the reality of the plantation, that 'tragédie féconde' that produces cultures in spite of itself. Hence, Glissant in *Le quatrième siècle* sets out to demonstrate the

limitless human possibilities that coexist within plantation
slavery and that make the plantation 'un des ventres du
monde' ('one of the wombs of the world').[37]

Central to the construction of *Le quatrième siècle* is the matrix
of the plantation. It is evident that from these early years
Glissant had begun to reconsider the plantation in terms of its
powerful (and not necessarily negative) shaping force on
French Caribbean society. The centrality of the plantation or
habitation to the evolution of Martiniquan society and culture is
emphasized by Patrick Chamoiseau and Raphael Confiant in
their recent study of French Caribbean literature; the proxi-
mity that existed in the smaller *habitation* between master and
slave, maroon and enslaved, 'amplifia, bien plus que sur les
grandes plantations des pays de Faulkner, les interactions de la
créolisation' ('intensifies, much more than on the large plan-
tations of Faulkner's world, the interactions of creolisation').[38]
Despite the fact that the *habitation* was meant to be a productive
machine, it functioned as an important zone of acculturation.
Chamoiseau and Confiant highlight within this privileged
space the role of the *conteur* or storyteller who represents the
leading edge of the interculturative process.

Le quatrième siècle avoids being either an epic of maroon
resistance or a nightmarish account of plantation slavery. It
places great emphasis on the figure of the storyteller and
attempts to reanimate the process by which memories and
experiences are passed down through this figure who was
neither maroon nor slave and who within the plantation could
maintain some measure of imaginative and psychological
independence. As Chamoiseau and Confiant put it, the story-
teller is not 'un créateur en suspension, mais bien le délégué
d'un imaginaire collectif' ('an artist in isolation but rather the
representative of a collective imagination').[39] The storyteller
takes centre stage in *Le quatrième siècle*. His language is neither
the shrill cry of freedom of the maroon nor the resentful silence
of the plantation slave. His speech is digressive, ambiguous and
carries within it the complexities of the group's lived experi-
ence. Outside of the town, the world of official, written culture,
far from the metropolitan centre and its estranging view of the

island, the *conteur* Papa Longoué offers his memories of the past to the young Mathieu who seeks a version of the past that is a clear, linear chronicle of events. However, Mathieu's desire for clarity comes up against a vision of the past that can only be described as a symbolic forest, an inextricable tangle of lives and events where the unexplained and the explainable intersect.

Glissant's observations on the narrator in Faulkner's *Absalom, Absalom!* are pertinent in understanding the figure of Papa Longoué in *Le quatrième siècle*. The person who reports events in Faulkner's novel is also 'contaminated' by these events.

La *contamination* est réservée au rapporteur: à celui qui répercute l'histoire; celui-ci est le véritable témoin. Presque toujours un enfant, ou un adolescent, envahi, contrôlé, agi par la mécanique du dévoilement.[40]

(*Contamination* is reserved for the bearer of the tale: for the one who echoes the story; the latter is the true witness. Almost always a child or an adolescent overwhelmed by and subject to the control of the mechanics of revelation.)

The involvement of the narrator in his story, which we have seen before in *La Lézarde*, now becomes a fundamental aspect of the second novel. Mathieu earnestly seeks a truth-bearing figure, a kind of native informant who could satisfy his quest for origins by providing a chronicle of founding, naming, engendering, of inexorable 'filiation'.

Papa Longoué cannot oblige. He himself, although a direct descendant of the maroon ancestor, is no longer a maroon. His very title 'Papa' suggests creole 'contamination'. He has become a healer, a wise man, a storyteller, and not a very good one at that, as the forces of creolisation take effect over time.[41] By implication, Glissant's emphasis on the fallibility of his relator provides an assault on authorial omniscience, or a single dominant consciousness. Rather, as the representative of collective memory, Papa Longoué's voice is the vehicle for a polyphony of other voices. If Longoué is a dense character it is not because of his psychological composition but because of the

dialogic connections that exist between him as an individual
and voices from the past, between him as storyteller and his
audience, between him as consciousness and his unconscious.
The vision of the past that emerges is not a doctrinaire one or
one that can neatly fit into any theory or ideology. Irreducibly
opaque and unpredictable at times, it is a chronicle of rupture,
metamorphosis, impermanence and inconclusiveness.

Mathieu comes to Papa Longoué with a rigid concept of the
past. The year in which the first session with the storyteller
takes place is 1935 which marks three centuries of French
dominance over the island. Mathieu's mind is shaped by the
official version of the island's history. For him the schoolbooks
have dictated the following schematic version of history: 'la
Découverte, les Pionniers, le Rattachment, la lutte contre les
Anglais, le Bon naturel des natifs, la Mère ou la Grande Patrie'
('Discovery, Pioneers, Attachment, struggle against the
English, the natural Goodness of the natives, the Mother or the
Great Fatherland', p. 225). Mathieu is not happy with this
ideological strait-jacket that has been placed on the past. What
Longoué offers is a startlingly different alternative. His story
begins in 1788, a year before the French Revolution where
there are important revolts on the island and a shipload of
slaves arrive.

Critics tend to approach *Le quatrième siècle* as the first novel
written by Glissant and as a preface to his fictional oeuvre.
Indeed, the events of 1946 which form the main story of *La
Lézarde* are summed up towards the end of *Le quatrième siècle*. In
this way, Glissant undermines any attempt to establish a neat
chronology and demonstrates the importance of the present in
the discovery and reconstruction of the past. Mathieu, in this
novel driven by his desire to get a clear picture of the past from
Papa Longoué, is cast in the role of the protagonist who tries to
make his way futilely through a real or imaginary forest. Here
the forest of interwoven relationships, fragmented time and a
constantly shifting landscape makes easy penetration impos-
sible. The ultimate response is awe at its daunting luxuriance.

Mathieu learns that despite the fact that the tricentenary of
attachment to the metropole is being officially celebrated the

lived history of the 'pays réel' ('the real country') is not determined by dates and events. As the title states, it is really the fourth century for the people who have come to Martinique after the establishment of plantation slavery. The true chronology that is proposed by Glissant is an emotional juxtaposition of space and time.

'Ce nègre-là, c'est un siècle!' – mais aucun d'eux n'avait encore dit, la main en visière devant les yeux: 'La mer qu'on traverse, c'est un siècle.' Oui, un siècle. Et la côte où tu débarques, aveuglé, sans âme ni voix, est un siècle. Et la forêt, entretenue dans sa force jusqu'à ce jour de ton marronnage, simplement pour qu'elle s'ouvre devant toi et se referme sur toi . . . est un siècle. Et la terre, peu à peu aplatie, dénudée, ou celui qui descendait des hauts et celui qui patientait dans les fonds se rencontrèrent pour un même sarclage, est un siècle. (pp. 268–9)

(That black man is a century! – but neither of them had yet said anything, his hand as a shade over his eyes: 'The sea you cross is a century.' Yes, a century. And the coast where you get off, blinded, with no soul and no voice, is a century. And the forest, its power sustained until the day you escaped, simply in order to open before you and to close behind you . . . is a century. And the earth, little by little flattened, stripped bare, where he who came down from the heights and he who endured patiently in the depths met for the same task of weeding, is a century.)

What is proposed here is a view of the past based on duration and not on event. It stands in opposition not only to the official metropolitan view of history but to any attempt to produce a schematic version of the past. The lack of a consciousness of this past not only leaves the Martiniquan at the mercy of the official version of his history but creates a calendar of the past related to a sequence of natural disasters ('l'histoire obscurcie s'est souvent réduite pour nous au calendrier des événements naturels' ('obscured history is often reduced for us to a calendar of natural events')).[42]

The *conteur*'s vision of the past is, however, hesitant and restrained and given to emphasizing each sensuous detail. Mathieu seeks order, clarity and coherence in the old man's words that originate in an oral tradition and are subject to fitful recollection.

A travers les onomatopées, les réticences, les incertitudes du vieil homme, Mathieu égaré tentait d'avancer l'histoire, de mettre en ordre les événements. (p. 30)

(Through the onomatopoeia, the reticence, the uncertainty of the old man, Mathieu bewildered tried to advance the story, to put order into events.)

The image most associated with the concept of the past offered to Mathieu is that of the wind. This image dominates *Le quatrième siècle* just as the image of water is everywhere present in *La Lézarde*. Indeed, Glissant associated both these images from the very first lines of his second novel, suggesting the elusive, inscrutable and overpowering nature of the past and memory.

— Tout ce vent, dit Papa Longoué, tout ce vent qui va pour monter, tu ne peux rien, tu attends qu'il monte jusqu'à tes mains, et puis la bouche, les yeux, la tête. Comme si un homme n'était que pour attendre le vent, pour se noyer, oui tu entends, pour se noyer une bonne fois dans tout ce vent comme la mer sans fin. (p. 11)

(— All this wind, said Papa Longoué, all this wind which keeps climbing, you cannot stop it, you wait till it climbs up to your hands, and then your mouth, eyes, head. As if a man was meant to wait for the wind, to drown himself, yes you hear me, to drown himself once and for all in this wind like the endless sea.)

Later memory of the past is stirred through sensation in the present. The wind presses itself against the marks of the past indelibly stamped on Longoué's body: 'Et il sentit le vent: non pas autour de lui ni sur tout le corps indistinctment, mais qui suivait comme une rivière les sillons des coups de fouet' ('And he felt the wind: not around him nor vaguely over his entire body but following like a river the furrows of whip lashes', pp. 44–5). The past emerges with a shapelessness that defies categorisation, that refuses to congeal into simple dichotomies, 'Parce que le passé n'est pas dans ce que tu connais par certitude, il est aussi dans tout ce qui passe comme le vent et que personne n'arrête dans ses mains fermées' ('Because the past is not in what you know for certain, it is also in all that passes by like the wind and that no one can hold in his closed hands', p. 146).

If the river was the metaphor of narration in *La Lézarde*, it is the wind which sweeps all before it that typifies the spiral of bits and pieces of the past we see in *Le quatrième siècle*.[43] The old man's look brings back to Mathieu the memory of almost drowning during childhood.

Et s'il fermait les yeux il retrouvait à la fois le regard du quimboiseur et la longue clarté bleutée qui l'avait avalé, doucement montée en lui et autour de lui quand il s'était enfoncé dans la mer. (p. 253)

(And if he were to close his eyes he would face both the healer's look as well as the clear, blue infinity which had swallowed him up, softly rising in him and around him when he had sunk in the sea.)

This image of the individual's powerlessness before the complexity, the suction or the turbulence of history is further reinforced by Mathieu's frailty and disequilibrium. It is as if Mathieu's constitution is a victim of the conflicting forces in his past, the dialectical force of Mathieu's mixed heritage. This results not only from the frailty of his early years but from 'une propension au dérèglement, à l'éclat incontrôlé. [Mycéa] connaissait à coup sûr les causes véritables de ce déséquilibre chez Mathieu, le bagage qui est au fond' ('a propensity for derangement, for uncontrolled outbursts. [Mycéa] certainly was aware of the real causes of this disequilibrium in Mathieu, the baggage carried in his depths', p. 272). Mycéa, his companion, is herself a fragmented personality, prone to vertigo, because of the contradictions and ruptures in her past.

Towards the end of *Le quatrième siècle* we learn of the circumstances and dates of Mathieu's journeys into the *morne* and the world of Papa Longoué. These visits stretch from 1935, and the celebration of the tricentenary of relations with France, to the death of Papa Longoué in 1945. Details of Martinique's experience of Vichy control, the Allied blockade and the rule of the infamous Admiral Robert, who represented the Pétain regime in the island, are quickly sketched in (p. 266). The novel, however, does not concentrate on these contemporary events but rather on the accumulation of time, 'centuries' stretching

back to 1788. The past as related by Papa Longoué is filled
with elements of the mysterious and the inexplicable. For
instance, the names of the African slaves who arrive on the
Rose-Marie and who are destined to become the primogeni-
tors of the Longoué and Béluse families, are unknown.
Equally mysterious is the quarrel that divides them, that has
grown in intensity despite the horrors of the Middle Passage
and explodes into a fight on arrival in the Caribbean. The
novel frequently refers to the unknown origins of this bitter
rivalry between the two men. When Mathieu is tempted to
see this rivalry as simply an imitation of the tensions that
divide the planters to whom they are sold, he is told 'C'est
venu avec eux sur la mer' ('It came with them over the sea',
p. 73).[44]

The novel, then, consists of Papa Longoué's tracing of the
destiny of the two descendants of these two slaves. In this way
Glissant immediately focuses on the fundamental oppositions
that have tended to dominate a Caribbean view of the past, the
confrontation between the maroon and the plantation slave,
negation and acquiescence. One slave is sold to a planter, La
Roche, who owns the wealthy plantation l'Acajou, but he
almost immediately escapes with the help of a female slave.
The other is bought by a rival and less wealthy planter,
Senglis, and the slave, reconciling himself to his fate, accom-
modates to life on the plantation. The slave who escapes into
the untamed wilderness of the *morne* is later called Longoué.
His very name suggests a long defiant cry of freedom. The one
who remains in bondage is Béluse, whose name bears the mark
of servitude and his experience as a stud to produce children
for the plantation.

Predictably, Glissant's tale is not about a glorification of
those who resisted over those who collaborated. Rather, Papa
Longoué's story is one of mutual interdependence and the
emergence of a composite, creole culture. From the story's
heterogenous beginnings, Papa Longoué evokes a process of
interaction between individuals, groups and spaces. The
maroon clan is not privileged, especially since the line comes
to an end with Papa Longoué. The Béluse clan, despite its
inauspicious origins, ultimately produces Mathieu who inherits

the past both in terms of blood and in terms of knowledge. He represents the bridge to future action. In this regard he functions as an inverted image of the original Longoué. The latter escaped to freedom in 1788 with the help of a Martiniquan-born slave, Louise, from La Roche's plantation. In 1945 Mathieu begins a relationship with Mycéa, whose origins are on the *morne*. She provides the support and companionship for Mathieu as a female from the plantation once did for the original maroon.

The individuals who emerge in this story are not rigidly defined in terms of their origins but represent an unpredictability and adaptability that inevitably produce a wandering across zones of influence and an intricate web of relationships. These relationships are not restricted to these two families in particular. The two planters, La Roche and Senglis, themselves offer a contrast. La Roche is a renegade, a white maroon himself, and Senglis his submissive, decadent, 'other'. They are also a part of the story of the Béluses and the Longoués: the neurotic attachment of Marie-Nathalie, Senglis's wife, to Béluse is as much evidence of an irresistible attraction as is La Roche's obvious admiration for the maroon. Relationships are made even more dense by what Bernadette Cailler terms 'the quadruple family architecture'.[45] Indeed, the novel also includes two other families, the Targins and the Célats, who interrelate over two centuries to create the impression of an entire community. The *roman du nous* (novel of us all) that Glissant advocates is the result of the evocation of this network of relationships.

One of the more striking features of this treatment of Caribbean history, particularly so because it was written in the 1960s, is the way in which Africa slips away and individuals with no hope of returning 'home' become rooted in the new land. July 1788 and the arrival of the slave ship represented a true beginning for the Longoué and Béluse families and a rupture with the past.

1788 pour lui pour moi c'est le premier jour le premier cri le soleil et la première lune et le premier siècle du pays. Puisqu'il n'y avait plus que la terre minuscule entourée de la mer sans fin et qu'il fallait bien y rester. (p. 74)

(1788 for him for me is the first day the first cry the sun and the first moon and the first century of the land. Since there was only the tiny piece of land surrounded by the boundless sea and no choice but to stay.)

Arrival in the New World is also associated with a symbolic baptism by the rain (p. 21), and the washing of the slaves (p. 22). Similarly, when Louise is freed by Longoué Lapointe, she is taken to La Pointe des Sables and undergoes a ritual immersion with all its association of initiation and rebirth (pp. 88–9).

Along with this ritual cleansing and regeneration comes an Adamic sense of discovery, a sensation of discovering the world for the first time. Both primogenitors, Longoué and Béluse, experience this feeling of a new beginning. The 'primordial maroon' after the violent uprooting of the Middle Passage quickly gets to know his new world and to claim it as his own:

Cet homme qui n'avait de souche . . . et qui n'était pas encore Longoué mais connaissait déjà les moindres feuilles et les moindres ressources du nouveau pays, et qui savait déjà qu'il continuerait d'affirmer autour de la forêt . . . son incompréhensible et indéracinable présence. (p. 83)

(This uprooted man . . . who was not yet Longoué but already knew the most insignificant leaves and resources of the new land, and who already knew that he would continue to assert around the forest . . . his incomprehensible and rooted presence.)

This sense of belonging is no less true of Béluse who is equally drawn to the new world in which he has found himself. After the death of Marie-Nathalie, he frees himself from his house-bound state and begins to know the land: 'il decouvrait la terre nouvelle, triomphale' ('he discovered the land, new and triumphant', p. 117).

This process of belonging does not produce a lonely Promethean figure but leads to patterns of kinship and a set of intense, ambiguous relationships. What is evident in Papa Longoué's account of the past is both the process of creolisation as well as the gaps and uncertainties that emerge in family relationships. For instance, both Longoué and La Roche are aware that with the passage of time inexorable change will be created in their descendants. The Longoués will come down from the hillsides and become more accommodating and their line will survive in unpredictable descendants.

Taris, les Longoué reposaient en tous. Dans un Béluse, dont le vertige et l'impatience portaient la connaissance jusqu'au bord du chemin où elle était partagée entre tous. Dans un Targin, corps impavide, créé pour l'acte. (p. 287)

(Dried up, the Longoués came to rest in everyone. In a Béluse, whose dizziness and impatience took knowing to the edge of the path where it was shared between everyone. In a Targin, fearless body, made for action.)

The Longoué strain also turns up in the Célat family who are called 'les Longoué d'en bas'. La Roche too will descend through time to end up 'noyé au crâne stupéfait d'un crétin' ('drowned in the puzzled skull of a cretin', p. 110).

The changes over time can also be plotted in terms of the names of the various characters. First, Glissant seems to insist on an incomplete genealogy. For instance, we never know the name of the slave with whom Béluse has children on the Senglis plantation. Similarly, in subsequent generations, Anne, St. Yves, Zépherin have anonymous companions. Also names are repeated to create a greater sense of uncertainty. Mathieu's father is also called Mathieu. Longoué is the name of the first and last in that particular line of descent. Clearly names are significant in Glissant, even the irony of some names such as Marie-Rose whose name is the reverse of that of the slave ship. This issue of the instability of names has already been raised in *La Lézarde*. In *Le discours antillais* Glissant explains the function of names in the context of the process of creolisation.

Le Nom pour nous est d'abord collectif, n'est pas le signe d'un Je mais un Nous. Il peut être indifférencié (X) sa force vient d'être choisi et non pas imposé. Ce n'est pas le nom parental, c'est le nom conquis. Peu importe que je m'appelle X ou Glissant: l'important est que je ne subisse pas mon nom, que je l'assume avec et dans ma communauté.[46]

(The Name is for us first collective, is not the sign of an I but a We. It can be anonymous (X), its force comes from being chosen and not

imposed. It is not the given name, it is the chosen name. It does not
matter whether I call myself X or Glissant: the important thing is
that I am not subjected to my name, that I assume it with and in my
community.)

The process of naming is significant in *Le quatrième siècle*
because the maroon chooses his own name (p. 167) whereas
the plantation slave is named by his master. In the case of the
latter the name represents a humiliating state, 'bel usage'
(p. 116), inflicted on him by his mistress, Marie-Nathalie. The
mark of the plantation continues in the second generation of
Béluses with the son called Anne, whose name defines his
alienation. He is described as 'nervous and violent'. Not sur-
prisingly, he is drawn to his Longoué contemporary Liberté
who is not tied symbolically to servitude. The arbitrary and
absurd origins of the names given to freed slaves is evoked in
Chapter 10 of the section entitled 'Roche Carrée'. The names
are chosen from antiquity, nature, places in France and local
plantations. The height of the amusement of the clerks per-
forming this function was to reverse the names 'De Senglis en
résulta par exemple Glissant et de Courbaril, Barricou. De la
Roche: Roché, Rachu, Réchon, Ruchot' ('Senglis was for
instance turned into Glissant and Courbaril became Barricou.
La Roche became Roché, Rachu, Réchon, Ruchot', p. 178).

Ironically, these names represent not freedom but continued
servitude. For Glissant, however, it does not ultimately matter
whether names have ignominious beginnings, are self-imposed
or carry the weight of family and national history – as in the
case of the La Roche children who all have combinations of
Marie-France in their names. For example, the community
names the first Longoué La Pointe. This becomes his *nom
collectif*:

Il n'était pas Longoué. Les voisins, à cause de ses promenades au long
de la mer, disaient tout bonnement Monsieur-la-Pointe. (p. 96)

(He was not Longoué. The neighbours, because of his walks along the
sea, simply called him Monsieur-la-Pointe.)

It is not the origin or the ancestor that matters but the extent to
which relations with the surrounding community, the 'We',

are established. The last descendant of the maroon is called 'Papa' in recognition of his healing powers and his age. The names of La Pointe and Papa Longoué are destined to disappear because the bonding with the community is so fragile. The inability of a collective 'We' to be created from the past means that, in the end, it is only Mycéa who carries the mark of an emergent community. She was called 'mi Célat' ('there is Célat') which then became Mycéa (p. 267).

Ultimately the names from the past, the symbols of the community and the landscape itself become ambiguous. The process of creolisation means an erosion of original meanings and the creation of new ways of 'reading' or decoding one's world. The most obvious example of this process is the barrel that is given to the first maroon by La Roche and then handed down from generation to generation. The snake in this barrel is Longoué's sign of revolt and defiance as he forms it from the earth when he escapes.[47] This symbol is also used by the maroon as a magical device against his rival Béluse. The multiple meanings of this symbol demonstrate the kind of cultural crossing and metamorphosis that takes place in a New World context. Yet in the present, the memory of this symbol remains a vague source of fear in the Martiniquan unconscious. Not surprisingly, when the barrel finally comes down to Mathieu, it is nothing but a 'déballage de vieux débris' ('a scattering of old fragments', p. 274). The complex and ambivalent meanings of this symbol are lost in the present.

The history of the French dependencies is one of a progressive degrading of meanings. As the past dies with Papa Longoué and Mathieu becomes its only relay in the present, the land continues to hold secrets for those who are attentive. For Glissant, it is not the explosive force of the volcano which is the privileged sign ('Il n'était plus besoin d'un volcan', p. 287). The volcano is not a kind of gravitational centre for Glissant, imposing a symbolic order on surrounding space. Meanings tend to be latent, elusive and subject to indefinite detour and delay. Only a patient, imaginative decoding allows for a full grasp of complex historico-social realities. The land itself has an exemplary function in this regard. At the outset, it is a *tabula rasa*, with no predetermined meaning, on which various orders will be imposed.

[Longoué] voyait l'ancienne verdure, la folie originelle encore vierge des atteintes de l'homme, le chaos d'acacias roulant sa houle jusqu'aux hautes herbes . . . Toute l'histoire s'éclaire dans la terre que voici . . . Mathieu devrait . . . apprendre tout seul à sentir le frémissement de l'ancienne folie. (pp. 46–7)

([Longoué] could see the green world of the past, the original madness yet untouched by man, the chaotic acacias flooding down to the high grass . . . All of history lay in the land before him . . . Mathieu had . . . to learn all along how to feel the excitement of the madness of the past.)

Reading the signs in the landscape is, however, no easy matter. As relationships change, structures are dismantled and new institutions emerge, the land becomes a complex text. The community's historical *alexia* makes an understanding of the past impossible. Meaning will not spring full blown from nature or from an ideological concept. We leave *Le quatrième siècle* with an impression of the land with no plot, no beginning, no end but a Baroque luxuriance.

Et les terres rouges s'étaient mélangées aux terres noires, la roche et la lave aux sables, l'argile au silex flamboyant, le marigot à la mer et la mer au ciel: pour enfanter dans la calebasse cabossé sur les eaux un nouveau cri d'homme, et un echo neuf. (p. 285)

(And the red land had mixed with the black earth, rock and lava with sand, clay with dazzling flint, pools with the open sea, and the sea with the heavens: so as to produce in this battered calabash a new human cry and a new echo.)

CHAPTER 4

Writing the 'real country'

L'INTENTION POETIQUE, MALEMORT, BOISES, MONSIEUR
TOUSSAINT

> Ceux dont la survie chemine en la germination de
> l'herbe!
>
> Aimé Césaire

Glissant returned to Martinique in 1965 to take up a post as
professor of philosophy at the Lycée des Jeunes Filles, and
spent the next fifteen years in the Caribbean. Perhaps the most
dominant concern for Glissant during these years was the shift
in emphasis from the individual imagination to group
consciousness, from *intention*, to use Glissant's terms, to *relation*.
At this time, he was acutely aware of the difficulties faced by
the writer returning to the Caribbean, due to the differences
between his experience in France and the problems posed by
the home community. The situation in Martinique had been
aggravated by nineteen years of chronic dependence because
of departmentalisation. For Glissant, Martinique in 1965 was
a cultural desert and his challenge was to devise collective
solutions or at least a group response to the dilemma facing the
French Caribbean Department.

The total integration of Martinique within a French sphere
of influence meant a number of things: the destruction of local,
self-supporting productivity, the loss of control over internal
affairs, the erosion of a local creole culture and the relentless
europeanisation of all areas of life. Even Césaire himself, under
whom these changes were ironically taking place, would soon
recognise that departmentalisation carried with it the risk of

metropolitan tyranny and was relentlessly leading to what he called 'progressive underdevelopment'.[1] With the 'pays légal' officially in the hands of the French, and the 'pays rêvé' of Africa lost forever, Glissant looked to the 'pays réel' as the space that needed to be investigated and from which solutions had to be derived.

However, Martinique in the late 1960s was dominated by Céaire's ideology of negritude which was being compromised or at least neutralised within the process of departmentalisation. The cult of personality in local politics was, for Glissant, simply a fearful extension of the island's larger dependency complex.

L'obscur désir de s'identifier au faux père (qui prit la place de la mère terrassée) trouve en chaque élu son équivalent: dans le clair désir d'être le père immémorial. Le Césarisme est la tentation des déracinés.[2]

(The secret wish to identify with the false father (who replaced the vanquished mother) finds its equivalent in each susceptible person: in the open wish to be the primordial father. Césarism is the temptation of the uprooted.)

The suggestion of 'Césairisme' in 'Césarisme' is not accidental and the uncreative, dried-up state of the 'pays réel' could be traced, for Glissant, back to the failure of Césaire's politics, and the stranglehold of French cultural assimilation.

The extreme nature of economic and spiritual dispossession in Martinique marks Glissant's writing in these years. His so far unpublished and unperformed farce, *Parabole d'un moulin de la Martinique* ('Parable of a Martiniquan Windmill'), which relates the dramatic transformation of the plantation's windmill to a factory and then to a chainstore, satirizes the dismaying changes taking place in departmentalised Martinique. No image of Glissant's bleak view of the transformed Martinique is, however, more telling than that of the drying up of the Lézarde river. Losing a collective sense of purpose is likened to the vanished watercourse of the river that represented the freed spirit of the people in his first novel. As Ormerod points out, 'Glissant persistently forces the reader to confront the dismal

spectacle of the plundered river' which has become an insigni-
ficant trickle because of neglect and industrialisation.[3] Glissant
laments in *L'intention poétique*:

La rivière était naguère comme un delta d'infimes irrigations, pul-
peuses de sangsues, où les tournoiements de moustiques prenaient
l'ampleur de cataclysmes très naturels. J'y dérivais (avant même que
le souvenir m'en imposât l'image idéalisée) le rêve d'enfance, le désir
d'être. Mais c'est aujourd'hui un caniveau, son delta comblé.
(p. 220)

(The river was formerly like a delta fed by tiny canals, thick with
leeches, where the swirl of mosquitoes took on the proportions of
quite natural disasters. I derived from it (even before memory shaped
for me an idealized image of it) the dream of childhood, the desire to
be. But today it is a drain, its delta choked up.)

In the face of the personal loss of this youthful idyll, which
parallels the exuberance and promise of the end of the Second
World War in Martinique, Glissant established in 1967 his
Institut Martiniquais d'Etudes in order to oppose the drift
towards cultural oblivion. In the energetic pursuit of some kind
of generalised political and cultural awareness, Glissant hoped,
through this Institute, to make Martiniquans aware of the loss
of the countryside to industrialisation or *bétonisation* and the
potential for the *pays natal* to become little more than an
amusement park for metropolitan visitors. The aim of IME
would be seen as an attempt to revive collective, human
endeavour.

The Institute was run as an independent school and research
centre. Glissant invited a number of artists to Martinique,
notably the Chilean Roberto Matta, the Cuban Augustin
Cardenas and the Argentinian Antonio Ségui. Anglophone
Caribbean intellectuals and performing groups were also
among those invited and IME sponsored an annual cultural
festival from 1967 to 1972. The research interests of Glissant
and his collaborators were published in the journal *Acoma*
which appeared four times between 1970 and 1973. Beatrice
Clark, a member of a group of black American scholars who
attended summer courses at IME, gives a useful account of the
main thrust of Glissant's ideas at this time. In particular, she

stresses Glissant's thoughts on the threat to cultural diversity
because of the lure of universal civilisation promised by French
culture. Negritude, as Glissant provocatively urged in the
lectures mentioned by Clark, did not provide an antidote to
this possibility of cultural annihilation.[4]

Glissant's first published work after his return to Martinique
was the book of essays *L'intention poétique* (1969). This work is
important for two reasons. It marks the emergence of Glissant
as a major literary and cultural theorist. It also demonstrates
the value of using a form that consciously transgressed the
boundaries between creative and critical discourse. It could be
argued that there are two parts to *L'intention poétique*. On one
level, traces of Glissant as an attentive, passionate reader are
evident. On another level, most of the major ideas that would
dominate his later work appear in this book of essays. Terms
such as *opacité*, *relation*, *durée*, *errance* and *chaos* emerge with their
special range of meaning, in opposition to the negative values
of *transparence*, *fulgurance* and *l'universel*. Ultimately, these essays
are a thoroughgoing attempt to reconceptualise the problems
of Martinique and the Caribbean in the wake of the failure of
negritude and Marxism to provide satisfactory answers to the
problems posed by assimilationist policies.[5]

Glissant's overriding concerns in these essays are clear in
some of the headings of various sections of this work. 'De l'un à
l'univers' ('From Self to Universe'), 'Du divers au commun'
('From the Diverse to the Shared'), 'Dépassements de l'inten-
tion' ('Transcending Individual Intention') and 'Intention et
relation' ('Intention and Relating') all point to the writer's
concern with going beyond individual will to collective enter-
prise. This preoccupation with a demystification of the indi-
vidual self or creative genius and the attendant need to empha-
sise group consciousness is as much a reaction against Césaire's
politics of personality as an attempt to theorise an ideal
relationship between artist and community. In this regard,
Glissant's definition of the three elements of a poetics is telling.

Trois fois l'oeuvre concerne. En ce qu'elle est pulsion d'un groupe
d'hommes: communauté; en ce qu'elle se noue au voeu d'un homme:
intention; en ce qu'elle est ouvrage et drame d'humanité qui continue

ici: relation. La terre du groupe, le langage de cet homme, la durée
pour l'humain: tels, les éléments de la poétique, de l'un à l'autre,
joués. (p. 24)

(The work is important in three senses. In so far as it is the thrust of a
group of men: community; in so far as it is tied to what one man
wishes: intention; in so far as it is the working out of human drama
which extends to this space: relation. The group space, one man's
expression, the duration of human elements: such are the elements of
a poetics, played out from one to the other.)

L'intention poétique can be read as an unrelenting deconstruc-
tive critique of western notions of the self or rather the self-
certain subject. The compulsive pursuit of individualism, of the
sovereign ego, is proposed by Glissant as one of the major
thrusts of western thought.

L'occident se constitue dans la règle d'une spiritualité dont l'inten-
tion la plus systématique fut d'isoler l'homme, de la ramener sans
cesse à son rôle d'individu, de le confiner à lui-même. (p. 59)

(The west constitutes itself by the rule of a spirituality whose most
systematic intention was to isolate man, to restrict him to his role as
an individual, to confine him to himself.)

The effects of this obsession with the self and the mastery of the
other, are traced by Glissant in all areas of activity, political as
well as cultural. The important lesson for the Caribbean is to
combat this illusion of the sovereign subject. This is par-
ticularly true of literature where the artist must free himself or
herself of the didactic mode, the temptation of an avant-garde
asceticism, and re-establish links with the environment or the
collective consciousness. In those very essays which seem rather
to be poetic meditations, Glissant is self-conscious about not
succumbing to the posturing or rhetoric of an intellectual in
the French tradition. The authoritarian or magisterial self is
abandoned for a collective identity: 'je me groupe au je qui est
le nous d'un peuple' ('I huddle with the I who is the we of a
people', p. 38).

The writers whose work is discussed in this book of essays
represent attempts to break from the western notions of soli-
tude, inspiration and genius. Glissant is not as insistent as

Césaire is on the achievement of the surrealists.[6] The names of Lautréamont or Breton are not mentioned. Instead, the heroics of radical surrealist thought are replaced by a consideration of those writers who first questioned the ideal of the self-certain subject in anticipation of those who would seek self-definition through a relationship with the other as dialectical partner. In the first phase, described as 'le voeu du total' ('the wish for the whole'), the names of Rimbaud, Mallarmé and Valéry are mentioned among others. In the second phase, which describes a movement, both imaginative and physical, out of Europe and is called 'De l'un à l'univers' ('From Self to Universe'), Segalen, Perse, Leiris, Claudel, Césaire and Carpentier are analysed. Pride of place is reserved for three New World artists, Matta, Cardenas and Faulkner, whose work represents for Glissant the successful passage from *intention* to *relation*. His comments on the techniques of Matta's painting point to an exemplary poetics of chaos, which responds to the complex, heterogenous totality of the Americas.

Eclairs, entassement, matériau, prodigalité des matières, profusion interdisent le système, la pause, le médité ou l'expliqué. (p. 168)

(Flashes, accumulation, material, extravagant themes, profusion make systems, pauses, reflection or explanation impossible.)

In the non-literary expression of a non-French artist Glissant finds ways of escaping the entrapments of the western literary tradition and the pressures on the Caribbean writer to treat the metropolitan language in a fetishistic manner.

This emphasis placed on new forms of consciousness, a collective identity and aesthetics of chaos, and the demythification of the authority of the writer cannot be divorced from the actual situation of Martinique in the late sixties. Departmentalised Martinique had found itself in a static and paralysing relationship with France which could be likened to the nightmare, in Glissant's early *Soleil de la conscience*, of the woman who suckles a snake. Martinique was now living such a terrible vigil, which was a distortion of the important relationship which exists between self and other. Interrelating with other cultures is an important idea for Glissant. However,

Martinique ran the risk of being overwhelmed in this assimila-
tionist relationship with the metropole. Neither solitude nor
surrender were solutions to Martinique's crisis.[7] Glissant in the
late sixties created a model in which cultural diversity could be
preserved along with the cross-cultural relationship.

It is within such a context that Glissant uses the term *opacité*
to indicate cultural specificity. This is a crucial notion
because it is precisely this element that is denied in any
concept of universal culture. It is also this aspect of cultural
resistance that is distorted in the ideology of negritude or any
politics of cultural difference. Consequently, Glissant
advanced the theory of composite, hybrid cultures, the
process of *métissage* as a notion which would replace the ideal
of cultural authenticity or the obsession with origins or pure
beginnings. *Métissage* is, for Glissant, different from Senghor's
view of cosmic order and cultural synthesis. It means some-
thing more dynamic and even chaotic, neither a denial of self
nor a denial of the 'other' but a transcending which never
settles into a fixed state.[8]

La Relation porte l'univers au fécond métissage. Ceux qui vivent cet
état ne sont plus (en conscience) des victimes pathétiques: ils sont
lourds d'exemplarité. Au-delà du souffert, la communauté que
groups le métissage ne peut nier l'autre, ni l'histoire, ni la nation, ni la
poétique de l'un. Elle ne peut que les dépasser. (p. 219)

(Cross-cultural Relating sweeps the world towards an enriched creo-
lisation. Those who live this condition are no longer (in their
consciousness) pathetic victims: they are laden with an exempla-
riness. Beyond its experience of suffering, the community held
together by creolising forces cannot deny the other, or history, or
nation, or the poetics of self. It cannot but transcend them.)

The problem faced by Glissant was how to spread this
complex vision of composite cultures at a time when Martini-
que was ideologically polarised between those who sought
integration with the metropole and those who wished to wall
themselves up within a neo-African monolith. While the
Caribbean people as a whole lived this collective adventure,
intellectually and imaginatively they sought to deny it. The
writer's role for Glissant lay in an imaginative response to this

drama. The artistic imagination becomes a site where the process of interrelating is enacted.

Le poète ne cesse d'obéir à ce commandement . . . Il quitte 'l'éclair, le révélé', cette ponctuation de riens . . . pour se donner à une durée où se multiplie le rythme. Le poète choisit, élit dans la masse du monde ce qu'il lui faut préserver, à quoi s'accorde son chant. (p. 222)

(The poet never disobeys this command . . . He abandons 'the flash, the revelation', this punctuation of nothings . . . to give himself over to the ideal of duration where rhythms are multiplied. The poet chooses, selects out of the world's abundance what he must preserve, what is in tune with his song.)

Glissant in asserting this new literary vision joins the many artists in the Caribbean and the Americas who invoke the liberating properties of the creative imagination in a situation that seems bleak and hopeless. The essays of *L'intention poétique* give the impression of being both embattled yet excited in prescribing a strategy for weathering the degrading effects of departmentalisation. The energetic pursuit of innovative ideas seems even more startling in the face of a lack of local response to Glissant's concepts. As he admits at the end of his novel *Malemort* 'Les lecteurs *d'ici* sont futurs' ('Readers *from here* are still to come').[9] At this time, he has the self-confidence to believe that some time in the future what he is writing will be understood and have an impact locally.

Given the deconstructive critique of literary tradition in *L'intention poétique*, the obliviousness of a local reading public, and the need to inscribe literary activity within a collective endeavour, Glissant focuses on folklore as an important area for locating the literary enterprise:

Pour ceux qui n'ont disposé d'aucun des moyens par quoi la conti-nuité s'exerce (ni langue ni art ni communauté), le folklore constitue le seul champ où s'inscrire la visée commune. (p. 194)

(For those who have not had access to any of the means through which literary continuity functions (neither language nor technique nor public) folklore constitutes the only field in which is inscribed a common purpose.)

Folklore was both a vital means of identifying the cultural *opacité* of the Martiniquan people, in all its potential and its inadequacy, as well as an area of cultural life to be preserved from erosion through assimilation. There was already a tendency to turn folk culture into exotic entertainment for visitors and to empty all rituals, such as the carnival, of any real meaning. Glissant's ideas on folk culture, the collective unconscious and the importance of drama which were developed within IME and published in *Acoma* are crucial to understanding the kind of cultural resistance he proposed at this time.

Glissant's interest in popular culture is evident in his emphasis on the figure of the storyteller in his early fiction. Already the art of storytelling implied spectacle and even a form of ritual theatre. This interest intensified in the 1970s as Glissant works closely with members of IME on using folk culture as a route to popular theatre. As he explained in his 1978 foreword to the second edition of his play *Monsieur Toussaint*, before the 1960s nothing that could be called theatre and certainly no popular, experimental theatre existed in the French Caribbean.[10] In the sixties two forms of theatrical expression emerged – Aimé Césaire's tragic vision of solitary, Promethean heroes of the Third World and Daniel Boukman's fiercely anti-colonial street theatre. Neither the apotheosis of the tragic leader in the case of the former nor the mobilisation of the masses as conceived by Boukman seemed satisfactory to Glissant. The problem posed by the lack of theatrical expression pointed to difficulties that existed with the collective unconscious of the community.

Glissant's thoughts on drama are contained in the article 'Théâtre, conscience du peuple', published in 1971 in *Acoma*. In it he argued that theatre was the genre that was fed by a community's sense of itself, by a national consciousness. The lack of any such awareness in the French Caribbean made theatre impossible. However, the formation of a theatre was vital since it was through drama that a community could reflect on issues and transcend crises. Glissant's two propositions are:

Le théâtre est l'acte par lequel la conscience collective se voit, et par conséquent se dépasse. Il n'y a pas de nation sans théâtre.
Le théâtre suppose le dépassement du vécu . . . ce dépassement ne peut être pratiqué que par la conscience collective. Il n'y a pas de théâtre sans nation.[11]

(Theatre is the act which allows a collective consciousness to see itself, and consequently to move forward. There is no nation without theatre.
Theatre presupposes the transcending of the lived . . . This transcending can be managed only by a collective consciousness. There is no theatre without nation.)

The key ingredients for drama to flourish are collectivity and consciousness. The relationship between folklore and theatre is defined by the passage from lived experience to the level of conscious reflection.

The collective unconscious exists, for Glissant, in a latent, inert state within a people's folklore. Theatre is the means by which this unconscious is externalised and thought through.

L'expression théâtrale se fixe à partir de l'expression d'un fond folklorique commun, qui cesse alors d'être vécu pour être représenté, c'est-à-dire pensé . . . Cette expression théâtrale devient celle de la communauté (totale) car elle dépasse le fond folklorique en l'assumant.[12]

(Theatrical expression is fixed in accordance with the expression of a common folkloric base, which then ceases to be lived in order to be represented, that is thought . . . This theatrical expression becomes that of the (total) community for it transcends the folkloric base while incorporating it in the process.)

In Glissant's model, folklore = collective unconscious, while theatre = collective consciousness. The two forms of expression are two modes of the psychology of the group. In Martinique, however, the folkloric base is being eroded because of departmentalisation. The conditions for the evolution through drama to conscious reflection are absent, as are the groups within a society that facilitate this passage – 'l'émancipation par l'élite est radicalement impossible' ('emancipation through the elite is totally impossible'). Martinique, with its alienated elite, consequently never gets beyond the phase of the folkloric unconscious.

In the final section of this essay, Glissant offers a prescription for a popular, experimental Martiniquan theatre. It can be seen to some extent as a critical response to Fanon's recommendation of an agit-prop national drama in his influential work *Les damnés de la terre* (1961). Glissant suggests that theatre should be 'popular' in the most profound and sophisticated way. Theatrical spectacle should be located away from the official theatrical spaces in the towns. However, although this theatre is meant for the people, it need not necessarily be simpler and more accessible. He worries that this temptation, which manifests itself in a condescending 'doudouisme de gauche' ('folklorisation from the Left'), is just another form of intellectual alienation. It is important to believe in the sophistication of a popular audience: 'il n'est rien (en expression, forme, intrication) que le peuple ne puisse maîtriser' ('there is nothing (in expression, form, intricacy) that the people cannot understand'). Finally, the question of the use of Creole is raised. Here again, Glissant warns about the use of Creole in a superficial way to mask the lack of serious analysis:

on peut être amené a surdéterminer le créole (ou à en revendiquer ici et maintenant l'usage exclusif) simplement pour masquer une réelle insuffisance dans l'analyse des réalites.[13]

(one can be tempted to overdetermine Creole (or to demand its exclusive use here and now) simply in order to conceal a real inadequacy in the analysis of reality.)

These ideas are consistent with Glissant's general theorising about the relation between individual and collective at this time. His one published play, however, does not fit neatly into what is here prescribed.

Monsieur Toussaint was first published as early as 1961 but was later republished by *Acoma* in 1978. This republication is justified by the fact that the original version was not designed with theatrical production in mind. The second version is meant for acting. The stage version of this play does not quite overcome the problems posed by the structure of the original text. Static in drama movement, dense with speech and turgid with characters, Glissant's play remains interesting as text. It is conceived as a somewhat surreal journey into the mind of Toussaint Louverture and, in formal terms, can best be seen as a stylised oratorio. As Glissant points out in the 1961 foreword to this play, the return of the dead to speak with Toussaint is inspired by the Caribbean sense of the importance of the dead and their ability to communicate with the living. To this extent, the play can be likened to a funeral wake which allows for a patient reflection on events in the past.[14]

Whether conceived as wake or oratorio, the play is concerned with ambiguity and ambivalence. It goes back to Glissant's concern with the recuperation of the past that dominated his work in the early sixties. He makes this clear in his 1961 introduction, where he uses his much-cited expression 'a prophetic vision of the past' to describe the need for the Caribbean people to understand the present and future in terms of the past. The presence of the unpropitiated dead, the forgotten ghosts of the past, is an enduring preoccupation for Glissant. As he says in *L'intention poétique*:

Ici les rochers semblent de terre; amalgamés d'un sang de craie ils s'épongent et s'enracinent dans le tuf rouge. Leur antre est encombré des cadavres perdus, des corps fantômes. (p. 38)

(Here the rocks appear to be made of earth; held together by a chalk-like blood, sponged off, they take root in the red sub-soil. Their cavern is crowded with lost corpses, phantom bodies.)

Toussaint's mind is like this Caribbean landscape, bristling with the cries, accusations and screams of the dead. In his icy prison in the Jura mountains, an external representation of his mental space, Toussaint is visited by a series of historical figures who represent issues and positions in the Haitian War of Independence.

The title of the play points to the author's interest in Toussaint the man, not the hero or the historical figure. The contradictions and the ambivalence of the man are examined as he is increasingly overwhelmed by the events that he helped set in motion. As has been earlier noted, it is hard not to see the parallel with Césaire who can be seen as playing an ambiguous role in a chain of events that he set in motion when he returned to Martinique in the 1940s. In contrast to Glissant's depiction of Toussaint in terms of human frailty, a contemporary depiction of Toussaint by René Depestre in his *Un arc-ciel pour l'Occident chrétien* ('A Rainbow for the Christian West') in 1967 simply extols the virtues of the general's rebellious spirit and blurs the distinction between him and Makandal as well as Dessalines.

In facing the prospect of a slow death in Fort Joux, Toussaint is as enigmatic and ambiguous a symbol as any in Glissant's early poetry. The imprisoned father of Haitian independence is anything but the romanticized liberator. Rather, he is a man caught between icy prison and island space, the hills of the maroons and the sea that took him away, the flames of Makandal's pyre and the terrible cold of the Jura mountains. The play is constructed, not in terms of linear chronology, but according to a complex intertwining of present tragedy, historical reality and imaginary dialogue between Toussaint and those who are dead or merely absent. We consequently have a juxtaposition of historical fate, historical process and the unknown. There is a sense in which no one in this play is right or wrong but each character takes positions within the movement of history.

The swirl of events, values and ideologies is centred on Toussaint. The more he gets involved in public action, the greater his inner conflicts become. Each character who enters his imaginary world offers an insight into his troubled conscience. For instance, he must justify to his wife why he did not continue to live contentedly on the Breda plantation. His patriarchal former overseer, Bayon-Libertat, accuses him of ingratitude. In his values, he comes into conflict with Maman Dio, the Voodoo priestess, who represents the call of Mother Africa, while he is instinctively drawn to liberal notions of western humanism. Similarly, Makandal and the rebel leader, Macaia, urge him to distrust the whites and their ideas. The values of the forest are offered as an alternative to Toussaint's highminded ideals. As Juris Silenieks lucidly observes in his

introduction to the English translation, 'Every issue seems to be
entangled in an ambiguous morality where the values and the
nothingness of human effort are equally uncertain. Toussaint,
a man of high ideals of freedom and dignity, is forced to take
measures that tend to recreate the same order he is trying to
avoid.'[15]

Indeed, the central argument of the play turns on ideo-
logical choice. The debate between Makandal and Toussaint
pits the inward-turning maroon fighter against a man turned
towards the outside world, modernity, and the mainstream of
world history. It is this desire not to form a maroon enclave but
to participate in a world culture of modern technology and
democratic freedom that drives Toussaint. He makes this
explicit in declaring:

Construisons un pays, non pas un domaine partout fermé . . . La
terre pousse, fertile, jusqu'à la mer! La mer est ouverte sur le monde
entier. Toi, Maman Dio, les ancêtres, la croyance! J'ai connu la
croyance universelle, est-ce ma faute? (p. 65)

(Let us construct a country, not a domain sealed up everywhere . . .
The land grows, fertile, all the way to the sea! The sea is open to the
entire world. You, Maman Dio, the ancestors, the faith! I have
known the unversal faith, is that my fault?)

His advice to Dessalines is no different: 'Oublie la forêt, la
haine! Elles portent l'anarchie et la stérilité' ('Forget the forest,
hatred! They bring with them anarchy and sterility', p. 93).
Glissant is sympathetic to Toussaint's anxiety. But it is pre-
cisely this refusal to be confined within a narrow *marronnage*
that brings about Toussaint's downfall.

In the play Dessalines appears as an alternative to the in-
soluble conflict between maroon isolationism and Toussaint's
idealistic internationalism. He constantly warns Toussaint to
be on his guard against the fine words of the French and not to
be taken in by their schemes. Toussaint does not approve of
Dessalines whom he sees as too 'fond of wars'. For Toussaint,
building, 'the hoe', is as important as waging war, 'the rifle'.
But the times need a man who, as Dessalines asserts, can hate as
well as act. Dessalines, who describes Toussaint as a spent force

and actually allowed his arrest to take place, nevertheless sees him as a vital stage in the process of achieving Haitian independence.

Je suis né quand Toussaint l'a voulu, quand il a dit 'Voici!' . . . Pourtant un jour je vois qu'il faut le trahir et le laisser arrêter, oui, et le laisser emporter sur l'Océan pour le dernier voyage . . . Du moins, je ne trahirai pas Toussaint une seconde fois, en laissant pourrir son travail! (pp. 224–5)

(I came to life when Toussaint wanted it, when he said 'Look!' . . . Yet one day I see that I had to betray him and allow him to be arrested and, yes, be carried off across the sea on his last voyage . . . At least, I will not betray Toussaint a second time, by allowing his work to go to waste!)

In this strange sequence of historical events, it is the removal of Toussaint which allows the spirit of Makandal to be rekindled in Dessalines. Only in this way could the people's cause triumph. The play comes to an end with Makandal leading Toussaint beyond this earthly life and inviting the forces of the world beyond to embrace this man whose 'name will rise to the stars'.

In this play, all of Glissant's major preoccupations are evoked – the lure of the universal, the individual and collective destiny, the tug of the mainstream against an instinctive isolation and, as is the case in *Le quatrième siècle*, the complex relationships that make up the history of the Americas. To some extent, the story of the Longoué and Béluse families and the intricate web of relations that holds them together are reflected in this treatment of the Haitian War of Independence. The ironic yet real relationships between negation and acquiescence, revolt and acceptance, become in *Monsieur Toussaint* a shaping force in Haitian history.

Despite the shortcomings of *Monsieur Toussaint* as a script, its conception does present an original view of the hero of Haitian independence and of Haiti in general. Toussaint and the Haitian War of Independence are constantly mythologised inside and outside of the Caribbean. Toussaint is as much the romantic hero of Lamartine and Wordsworth as he is the legendary symbol of upright negritude of Aimé Césaire, C. L. R. James and René Depestre, to name a few from Caribbean literature. Glissant's special insight into Toussaint's predicament comes not only from his insistence on the Haitian leader's inner conflicts but also from his broader view of the historical process. Again with his creative juxtaposition of critical reflection on and poetic reconstruction of the past, Glissant sees in Haiti at the end of the eighteenth century the major issues that would haunt Caribbean thought from then onwards. As he makes clear in his introduction, the play's thrust is a poetic attempt to link past and present, since 'dévoiler le passé . . . permet parfois de mieux toucher l'actuel' ('unveiling the past . . . allows us sometimes to have a better grasp of the present', p. 8). If there was no turning back to a lost past, if the ideal of *marronnage* and isolation led to a dead end, what then would be an appropriate response to the crisis in the present? To this extent, Toussaint is not unlike all of Glissant's major protagonists who attempt to live through the dilemma posed by hill and plain, negation and acceptance. Thael, Mathieu, Mycéa are characters who are similarly poised. Indeed, given the political situation of Martinique and the neutralisation of negritude, the questions that needed to be asked have to be complex ones, since neither retreat nor total surrender could provide an answer to the pressures of assimilation.

It is perhaps significant that Glissant chose to write a play about Toussaint and not someone like General Louis Delgrès who, with his soldiers, committed mass suicide in Fort Matouba rather than surrender to General Richepanse, who had been sent to restore slavery in Guadeloupe. This romantic act of self-immolation is less interesting to Glissant than Toussaint's attempt to live through the tragic consequences of his ideological choices. In this regard, we must also pay attention to another figure who has fascinated Glissant, Behanzin, the last king of Dahomey who was exiled to Martinique in the nineteenth century. He incarnates, in an extreme way, the fate of the Caribbean people and can be seen as the tropical equivalent to the imprisoned Toussaint. The latter was exiled

from an island space to an icy continent by the colonial
authorities. Behanzin was moved in the opposite direction from
the continent of Africa to an island exile, also by the French.
Like Toussaint he remains within the Caribbean unconscious
as an unappeased and misunderstood figure. As Glissant writes
in *Boises*:

> Dans nos têtes ferrées le roi
> recommencé rit nos démences, crie
> notre nuit, meurt nos dénis.[16]
>
> (In our fettered heads the king
> Lives again mocking our delirium, he cries
> in our night, dies with our disavowals.)

Boises, the only book of poems published by Glissant during
his stay in Martinique, directly reflects the crepuscular atmo-
sphere of contemporary Martinique. It carries an illustration
by the Cuban sculptor Cardenas showing a wooden collar
(which is the meaning of 'boise') locked round a twisted
network of human bones. This image connotes all that is
suggested in the poetic text: spiritual impoverishment, dismem-
bered limbs and the stranglehold of the past. Glissant's epi-
graph to these poems makes these associations explicit: 'à tout
pays qui se détourne et s'exaspère de tarir' ('to any country
which turns away from itself and dries up in exasperation').
The graphic economy of the poems that follow seems to be a
visceral response to the spasms and contorted expression of a
threatened community.

The poems can then be seen as verbal extensions of Carde-
nas's graphic illustration. This desire to produce dense word
pictures again suggests Glissant's intense interest in the visual
component in literary expression as well as his open admiration
for the painter's or sculptor's ability to render the real. In *Boises*
poetic rhetoric is suppressed and there is little evidence of a
Baroque or lyrical excess of language. Rather one senses an
attempt to dip directly into reality in a series of short, startling
poems. The poem entitled 'Poétique' is typical of this book,
whose structure seems to be shaped by the word *tarir* and the
nightmare of the drying up of a community.

Comprendre temps chaleur
roche chaleur
douleur mariée
cri vaporant son mot
voyelle à voyelle
concrétées. (p. 175)

(To understand time heat
rock heat
grief conjoined
cry word of vapour
vowel to vowel
made concrete.)

In the explicit desire both to understand a landscape and to render this knowledge in a lapidary, almost material form, 'Poétique' makes us aware of Glissant's intention in *Boises*.

These poems take us from past to present, from the first section entitled 'l'Antan' ('Yesteryear') to the final poem 'Demains' ('Tomorrows'). All poems in the collection lead inexorably to the here and now and the 'pays réel'. Unlike the panoramic vistas of *Le sel noir*, *Boises* emphasises intense concentration. *Boises*, to this extent, can be regarded as Glissant's first poetic attempt to 'write the real country' after his return to Martinique. In doing so, Glissant seems to tackle the problem of the alienation of the Martiniquan from his landscape. In this poetic work it is not a matter of writing *about* an experience of contemporary Martinique but rather dissolving the thinking or writing subject and the conceptual framework within which the object would be conventionally placed. The 'pays réel' then becomes not so much an external world but an extension of inner feeling. In this consciously naive subversion of both the notion of independent reality and traditional thought processes, the 'pays réel' emerges in its full multiplicity of detail, disordered fragments and exposure of those contradictions that are normally denied or suppressed because they are intolerable.

Not surprisingly, the form of the poems bears the mark of this undermining of the conceptual process. Verbal collage, rapid enumeration, verbs left in the infinitive, and incomplete

lines that seem adrift on the page are the technical character-
istics of *Boises*. 'Demains', for example, is typical of these
poems, both stylistically and in terms of the contemporary
picture of Martinique – likened here to a mineral concreteness,
dried into a fixed form but still, perhaps, capable of being
reshaped and of yielding to vegetable growth.

Il n'est pas d'arrière-pays. Tu ne saurais te retirer derrière ta face
c'est pourqoui dérouler ce tarir et descendre dans tant d'absences,
pour sinuer jusqu'à renaître, noir dans le roc. (p. 186)

(There is no inner world. You cannot withdraw behind your surface,
that is why to live through this drying and to descend so many
absences, so as to work your way toward being reborn, black in the
rockface.)

The image of the rock, worked on from the inside and the
outside, seems central to these poems. The first poem "Brûlis'
('Burnt Out') laments the fact that the scars of the past are
forgotten in the present. The marks of 'la barre/la boise/les
ceps/le carcan' (the bar/the collar/fetters/shackles), instru-
ments of torture and subjugation, remain internal scars. Exter-
nally, wounds and a persistent process of erosion seem to
threaten, 'Dans la plaie au profond des verts sombres . . . Dans
l'affre au coeur des roches ton plein coeur' ('In the wound deep
in a green night . . . In the terror at the heart of the rocks your
full heart', p. 165). This two-fold cutting away at the rock
produces a condition of the living dead or *malemort*. The poem
with that title evokes both the state of lifelessness and the hope
for some liberation from such a condition.

> Rayon vert
> Sables rongés de blême
> Nous guettons le sursaut d'étincellement
> Nous coucher enfin dans l'usure, pâlir
> Nous enguêpons le temps. (p. 174)

> (Green ray
> Sands eaten by whiteness
> We look out for a sudden spark
> To end up sleeping worn out, growing pale
> We sting time with our curses.)

Other poems are miniature, enigmatic recordings of impressions of Martiniquan space. This poetic survey includes poems evoking the island's various moods, the force of the sea, the sun and the *morne*. There seems, in all this, a particular fascination with what Martinique has abandoned or cast away in its path to progress and modernisation. For instance, 'Monogamie' evokes bristling cactus forgotten on the hillside. Another, 'Usine encore', focuses on a sugar factory which has fallen into disuse and is related to Glissant's farce, written at about the same time, concerning the fate of a Martiniquan windmill, which eventually becomes a store in the Monoprix chain.

> Tortue
> rongée d'arbre sanguinolent
> elle meurt en bord de route sa transparence
> là se lisent
> déjà les fantômes, monoprisés. (p. 157)

> (Tortoise
> eaten away by a bloodied tree
> it dies at the roadside its transparency
> in it can be read
> already chainstore ghosts.)

The race towards modernisation and an identification with France means the abandonment of the world of the plantation; the factory is destined to become a centre not for production but for the passive consumption of foreign goods.

The section entitled 'Bois des Hauts' is of special significance in *Boises* because it was intended to accompany the appearance of the novel *Malemort*.[17] First published in *Acoma* in 1972 these poems were to be entitled *Poèmes de malemort*. They stand out in *Boises* because they form a kind of short narrative sequence within the larger collection of impressionistic poetic miniatures. By the time *Boises* appeared, 'Bois des Hauts' had been broken up into shorter fragments and entitled 'Dlan' and 'Le négateur'. This narrative sequence is reminiscent of the opening of *La Lézarde*. It returns to the world of the *morne*, its mute and unintelligible presences and the seductive tug of the sea.

In this sequence, a character is introduced by the name of
Dlan – an abbreviated form of 'De l'an', – suggesting a
relationship with time. Dlan is the fugitive who once fled into
the 'Bois des Hauts' for sanctuary and must now come down
from his hilly refuge. He feels with the passage of time an
increasing sense of belonging as his world becomes more open
and accessible.

> Tu cries tu erres ton poids ton flanc te
> nouent à ce que tu défends de terre. (p. 162)

> (You scream you wander your weight your side bind
>   you
> to the land you defend as your own.)

As was the case with Thael, the lure of the sea is a controlling
force and has the final say:

> La terre se vêt, commence à brûler.
> Mais la mer qui étreint, sèche par roches
> dans feuilles cannées.
> Mais la mer. (p. 103)

> (The land dressed up begins to burn.
> But the enfolding sea, dry with rocks
> in leaves of cane.
> But the sea.)

The journey settles into no final meaning. It takes us from the
morne to the inscrutable sea as an inevitable process which is
central to the movements of the novel *Malemort*.

The economic and political reality of departmentalised
Martinique hovers ominously over the events in Glissant's
third novel *Malemort*. The symbolic drying up of the Lézarde
river, the aggressive intrusion of assimilationist policies and the
destruction of local economic initiatives which are present in
this novel are evidence of Glissant's socio-economic concerns.
The destruction of a local utopian project of a farming
commune by the metropolitan company 'Somivag' is clear
evidence of Glissant's anti-assimilationist politics in the novel.
The character Medellus witnesses:

chaque jour, par-delà les derniers acacias, un tracteur jaune et rouge
. . . qui allant venant dans un boucan de tonnerre et ravageant tout
ce rêve de réforme agraire, entreprenait (bête aveugle) de déraciner
trois grands ébeniers.[18]

(each day, beyond the last acacias, a red and yellow tractor . . .
which moving to and fro with a devil of a noise, and ravaging this
whole dream of agrarian reform, was attempting (blind beast) to
uproot three ebony trees.)

Because of this aspect of *Malemort*, some critics have been
impatient with the complexity of the work as a whole. Many
would have been happier with a more directly political novel.
For instance, Frederick Ivor Case rejects the novel in the name
of 'social realism' and contends that the language of the novel
removes it 'entirely from lived reality and oversimplifies socio-
logical relationships through linguistic camouflage'.[19] Simi-
larly, the hostility of the *Présence Africaine* reviewer centres on
the 'quasi-incompréhensibilité' of the narrative. He is pro-
voked into declaring that *Malemort* is in no way Caribbean,
either in ideology, form or essence.[20] Such critical hostility has
today given way to unreserved praise for this novel in par-
ticular. The authors of *Eloge de la Créolité* describe *Malemort* as
the first literary work that revealed 'le réel antillais'.[21] The
literary history *Lettres créoles* ends in 1975, the year in which
Malemort was published, and sees the novel as a major aesthetic
breakthrough. Patrick Chamoiseau has openly declared that
Malemort was for him a novelist's novel and the single greatest
influence on his own writing.[22]

The literary fortunes of *Malemort* have changed dramatically
since its first appearance. Despite the early hostile critical
response to this work, it was anything but self-indulgent her-
meticism. This does not, of course, mean that *Malemort* is
accessible in a conventional sense, nor was the work intended
to be clear and straightforward. *Malemort* represents a break
from Glissant's earlier novels and is a product of this inten-
sively experimental phase in Glissant's writing.[23] Indeed,
Malemort manifests an acute awareness of the problem of
writing. In 1972, Glissant referred to what he called 'la crise de
l'écrit' ('the crisis of the written') and the fact that 'les littér-

atures des nations neuves semblent souffrir, sinon d'une impuissance, du moins d'une réticence à la production écrite' ('the literature of new nations seem to suffer, if not from impotence, at least from a reticence in their literary output').[24] *Malemort*, consequently, is Glissant's response to the crisis faced by French Caribbean literature in the 1970s. It is equally the product of an intense interest at this time in the traumatised consciousness of departmentalised Martinique and the pathological nature of self-expression.

In a speech given in May 1972 at the first international conference of AUPELF held in Quebec, Glissant raises the issue of language within a modern multilingual context. Some of this is aimed at the expansionist policies inherent in the notion of *francophonie*. However, Glissant's main contention is that what is important to a community is not so much the language it speaks but the idiom through which it understands the world. This opposition between *langue* and *langage*, already raised in a preliminary way in *L'intention poétique*, becomes increasingly important to Glissant's ideas in the seventies. He argues that it is within a multilingual situation that the *langage* or 'idiom' of the community evolves. In so doing, he brings a new perspective to the traditional debate over the merits of Creole or the spoken, against those of French, or the written. The *langage* of the community is seen as a manifestation of cultural interrelating and consequently feeds on both Creole and French, spoken and written.

l'opposition entre langage parlé et langue écrite n'a pas ici – et pour moi – plus de sens, car le parler créole qui m'est naturel vient à tout moment irriguer ma langue écrite, et mon langage provient de cette symbiose.[25]

(the opposition between spoken language and written language no longer has, for me, any meaning, for Creole speech which is natural to me feeds at every turn my written language, and my idiom results from this symbiosis.)

In his insistence on the particularising force of *langage*, Glissant criticizes both the universalist pretensions of the French language as well as the ideals implicit in the policy of assimilation. His call to the members of AUPELF, to 'relativiser la langue française' ('make the French language relative'), is as much a provoking declaration before professionals concerned with the dissemination of the French language as evidence of Glissant's major preoccupation at this time. For him, the problem in Martinique is that this Overseas Department does not live lucidly and freely within a multilingual situation. Martinique runs the risk of being overwhelmed by French language and culture and of never evolving its own *langage*. As Glissant warns:

Pour qu'un multilinguisme ne soit pas dévastateur, il faut qu'il soit consenti et vécu librement, par delà son institutionnalité, par la conscience libre de la communauté.[26]

(For a multilingual encounter not to be devastating, it must be agreed to and lived freely, beyond its official status, within the free consciousness of the community.)

Because this is not the case in Martinique, the writer's special role is to demonstrate the possibility of the emergence of this special idiom or at least reflect the anguished nature of the confrontation, the 'tormented' interfacing, of *langue* and *langage*. What Glissant would later call a 'forced poetics' will result from 'cette opposition entre une langue dont on se sert et un langage dont on a besoin' ('this opposition between a language one uses and an idiom one needs').[27] In opposing the centripetal, conservative values of *langue* to the centrifugal, creolising force of *langage*, Glissant is again invoking his preoccupation with the non-systematic, the chaotic in the Caribbean sensibility. He also seems to be aware of the capacity of narrative or fiction to voice the special diversity of *langage*. This capacity of the novel to represent linguistic plurality is remarkably close to Bakhtin's view of the dialogic principle in the novel.[28]

The concept of *langage* is extended by Glissant beyond specifically linguistic concerns to refer to a repertoire of responses created within a given society, and within a given language situation, in response to its experience of the world. *Langage* becomes then in his words a structured and conscious series of attitudes, and refers to that zone in which the peculiarities of a community's world view or sensibility are formed. What the multilingual encounter has not produced in Martinique is a *langage*. Rather, French has progressively caused Creole to become impoverished while itself reflecting the tortured impulses of a dependant mentality. As consumers and not producers of culture, Martiniquans project their inner contradictions into the language they speak or write, whether Creole or French. The linguistic peculiarities of the Martiniquan situation and the psychological distortions that underpin them are extensively explored in the essay 'Sur le délire verbal' ('On Verbal Delirium') which appeared in the last issue of *Acoma* in 1973.

Glissant's theoretical approach to the psychological problems of Martiniquan society is made clear in *Acoma* in 'Action culturelle et pratique politique'. He contends that while poverty has receded, because of the material advantages of departmentalisation, there has been an 'aggravation du désarroi moral'. He sees this as the inevitable product of a non-productive community:

la dépropriation, l'irresponsabilité technique, la non-maîtrise du quotidien et des circuits économiques privent la collectivité martiniquaise de ses chances d'évolution, en l'amputant d'une conscience et d'une personnalité propres.[29]

(dispossession, lack of technological responsibility, absence of control over the every day and the circuits of the economy deprive the Martiniquan community of its opportunity to evolve, of its own consciousness and personality.)

In his study of what he calls the 'délire verbal coutumier' of Martinique, his hypothesis is that ordinary discourse in Martinique bears the marks of the mental disequilibrium of the group. Martinique is experiencing an extreme form of alienation because it may well be the only case of successful colonisation in the modern world. It is, indeed, a collectivity on the verge of disappearing.

The use of language as an index of mental trauma had been raised previously in a more limited way by Frantz Fanon.[30]

Glissant concentrates exclusively on discourse as distorted by internal conflicts that cannot be resolved. Powerlessness has created deviation in behaviour, such as an impulse to violence, depression and forms of hysteria. In a more everyday and 'normal' way, language is subjected to the turbulence within the Martiniquan unconscious. In this essay, Glissant meticulously lists the manifestations of this delirium and the conditions under which it erupts: an unnecessary accumulation of words, a fetishistic attitude to French, overcompensation and a predilection for the theatrical. Language then is not a process of communication but becomes a form of aggression or evasion. Finally, he focuses on the chronic need for verbal eloquence among Martiniquans. As he says, '"Parler français" est plus important que dire quelque chose' ('"To speak French" is more important than to say something').[31] Language becomes, for the entire community, a pathetic attempt to create the illusion of power.

The central focus of *Malemort* is a particular aspect of 'le réel martiniquais' – the verbal coding through which a collective neurosis manifests itself. To impose a clear, orderly rhetoric on the Martiniquan situation would be to falsify the alienated reality of that culture or worse, further to reinforce the linguistic aberration. From its epigraph, *Malemort* openly declares its concern with linguistic deviation: 'Hormis du bien, lu [sic] nègre peut tout faire' ('Besides good, the black man is capable of anything'). In this mocking representation of the speech of members of the Martiniquan middle class, Glissant clearly demonstrates his concern with cultural and economic alienation and the distortions it produces in every day speech. These symptoms of inner disequilibrium are characteristic of the society as a whole as represented in *Malemort*. The excessive ornamentation of the language of the bourgeoisie as well as the deviations of popular speech reflect economic impotence, 'une réponse pathétique et incontrôlable à une éradication économique. Le délire verbal coutumier est substitutif du pouvoir économique néantisé'('a pathetic and uncontrollable response to economic dispossession. Everyday verbal delirium is a substitute for neutralised economic power').[32] Language turns into parody; vision becomes hallucination; political action is either impulsive or absent; and characters lack a psychic wholeness.

Malemort is a difficult work because it is meant to shock and disorient. Glissant's earlier novels seem almost straightforward and conventional by comparison, although the intense scepticism in *Malemort* is present in the previous novels in an embryonic form. The poetic embrace of the world and the explosion of metaphor in the first two novels have yielded in the 1970s to self-doubt and pessimism in the face of the socioeconomic transformation of Martinique as well as an intensifying sense of the limitations of traditional literary expression. This sense of the need to go beyond the literary, to doubt the illusions created by the word, is clearly stated in these terms: 'sortir aussi du papier. Déborder au loin de la page. La terre n'est pas dans la page' ('also leave paper behind. Overflow far from the page. The land is not in the page', p. 200). The point is reaffirmed later when Glissant expresses doubt about the whole literary enterprise in the face of terminal cultural assimilation, 'dans l'horrible sans horreurs d'une colonisation réussie. Qu'y peut l'écriture? Elle ne rattrape jamais' ('in the horrorless horror of successful colonisation. What can writing accomplish? It can never retrieve anything').[33]

The world of *Malemort*, the Martinique of 1974, is dominated by a pervasive and aimless drifting. We are presented with a community of *drivés* – the Creole word which echoes the French *dérive* and the further resonances of delirium and deviation. Bonds with the land are forgotten, the past buried and no kind of collective self-consciousness seems possible. In contrast to the ecstatic discovery of the world in previous works, Martiniquans are now deprived of any sense of a heartland.

il leur était refusé cet unique plaisir, qui est pour l'homme de se dilater sur sa terre comme un fanal de lumière, jusqu'à ce lieu caché où sa terre et lui se confondent, dans les ténèbres profitables de ce qu'on appelle un arrière-pays. (p. 201)

(they were denied this singular pleasure, which is for the individual to spread out over his land like light from a lantern, up to that hidden space where his land and his self become one, in the resources of the dark that we call one's heartland.)

Because this essential process cannot take place, the scattered cries of Martinique cannot coalesce into a *langage*; violent impulses do not produce consciousness; fragmented selves cannot constitute a collective *Nous* and the individual *traces* or journeys do not yield to a common path or *chemin*. It is the *autoroute* or highway, an emblem of modernisation and *bétonisation*, because of departmentalisation, that predominates.

Martinique, consequently, becomes the land of the happy zombi. Neither alive nor dead, these *malemorts* wander like uninvited guests, exiles in their own land. With no sense of an ancestral space, no real access to a legal space, they are 'êtres de passage'. Glissant's novel focuses on the most extreme examples of this aimless drifting, the Martiniquan working class who, uprooted from the land, incapable of creating productive enterprises, live off welfare handouts and eventually migrate to the metropole, courtesy of the government agency BUMIDOM. These are the *djobeurs* of contemporary Martinique who are driven to the towns and eke out an unsettled, somewhat mysterious life there. Characters who once were, if not flesh and blood, at least representative and coherent points of view, now yield to fragmented creatures who are neither whole nor can produce a collective wholeness. In *Malemort*, the barely alive *djobeurs* are Dlan, Medellus, Silacier, all of whom form a composite multiple character. They represent different aspects of the collective neurosis: religious mysticism, utopian fantasy and blind violence.

Glissant's characters are obsessed by treasure hunts, delusions of grandeur and the senseless impulse to violence: 'ils s'accrochent à n'importe quoi qui taille tranche couteau rasoir coutelas n'importe quoi qui coupe' ('they grab hold of anything that slashes slices knife razor cutlass anything that cuts', p. 203). The only example of stability is a marginal character Lomé, who first appeared in *La Lézarde*. He has not lost 'la trace depuis les hauts jusqu'au sable . . . il était planté dans la terre' ('the path from the heights to the sand . . . he was planted in the land', p. 204). The maroon or 'négateur' is almost a figment of the imagination and has become a figure of derision and fear. If those in contemporary Martinique are barely alive, the legendary maroon is undead and haunts the imagination of those who wish to deny the past, who in 1974 pose the questions: 'le passé, Négateur quel négateur' (p. 189). The 'négateur', in the conformist docile present, has become 'une vague douleur' (p. 129), 'un vague noeud au ventre, un cri sans feuille ni racine' ('a slight knot in the belly, a cry without leaf or root', p. 61). He reappears in the figure of the fugitive Beautemps and paradoxically in the policeman Tigamba and the paymaster Odibert who serve metropolitan interests. They are reminiscent of the turncoat Garin in *La Lézarde* who works against his own community. These figures echo the greater treachery in the New World of the black executioner, Verdugo, who tortured and killed Tupac Amaru (p. 178) and the maroons of Jamaica: 'les descendants des Enfuis devinrent les spécialistes policiers; la mémoire du Négateur diminuée en Beautemps et abolie en Tigamba' ('the descendants of Escapees became specialists in policing; the memory of the one who said no diminished in Beautemps and abolished in Tigamba', p. 183).

This pervasive picture of submissiveness and impotence prevails, oddly enough, at a time when there are violent incidents in Martinique. The events of the novel take place between 1788 and 1974. Both dates represent a violent reaction against the *status quo*. In 1788 there was a slave revolt and in 1974 there was a strike, brutally put down, of workers on a banana plantation in the north of Martinique. Within this period there were also riots and strikes in Martinique and Guadeloupe, in 1959, and 1967 and 1971, for example. However, Glissant wishes to demonstrate that these events are impulsive and spasmodic. They do not lead to a collective 'prise de conscience'. The collective consciousness is clogged like the Lézarde river with debris and refuse from the past which form no coherent pattern. In order to make this view of the chaotic passage of time more emphatic, Glissant does not provide a picture of an accumulation of events or even temporal duration. The *datation* or dating of each chapter follows no sequence. These dates are divided by slashes, linked by hyphens and listed by commas. Indeed, we have an impression here of time lived in an incoherent way as opposed to the empty, official record of contemporary Martiniquan 'history'. *Malemort* reconstitutes the 'pays réel' at this level – the banal, sometimes funny and arbitrary truth of a community which lacks internal coherence.

In this regard, it is hardly surprising that the introduction to the text is entitled 'péripéties' ('ups and downs'). Made up of multiple plots, drifting characters and a cacophony of styles, *Malemort*, despite the fact that Glissant declares that there is no local public for this text, can only be fully decoded by readers with an intimate knowledge of events, expressions and a sense of the magical, peculiar to Martinique in the mid-seventies. The 'péripéties' of this world describe events as everyday as a domino game and a country funeral; riots where the past and present collide in a stream of unbroken and unpunctuated narrative (1788–1974); the stream of consciousness episode when Silacier steals a car for seven and a half minutes; the corrupt electoral practices (1945–6) of Lesprit which almost reads like a satirical sketch. One has a constant sense of movement, of a swirl of events which include chases, boat races and a general fascination with speed to give a temporary and artificial illusion of power. Not surprisingly, the first words of the novel are 'Il danse' in reference to a dancing coffin carried in a funeral procession. The *danse macabre* of this opening can be extended to refer to all the events in the novel. The characters 'réunis pour le repos de l'âme' ('gathered together for the repose of the soul', p. 21) are pulled together by the frenzied movement of a community whose soul is moribund, whose history is a procession of the unpropitiated dead, 'ce défilé de mort qu'on pourrait appeler leur histoire' ('this procession of death that we could call their history', p. 132).

If Glissant's characters are not 'planted in the land' but condemned to physical and emotional instability, their language is also deeply affected by their inner trauma. The verbal delirium that surfaces in much of the text of *Malemort* is a symptom of the fragmented psyche. Unresolved internal conflicts surface in the language of the group. It is not directness and clarity that characterise the speech of Martiniquans in

Malemort. Language becomes coded, allusive and circuitous. It is sometimes hard to tell if some of the passionate tirades in this novel are meant to communicate or to conceal. *Malemort* is as much as anything a record of twisted speech patterns, linguistic excess, juxtaposed with inexplicable silences:

Nous les aimons, eux qui tant parlaient et tant se taisaient; comme s'ils avaient cherché, de cet excès de style à ces extrêmes de silence, la tresse de quelque chose que nous eussions pu nommer: mais nous ne pouvons rien nommer, nous avons été sans en apercevoir usés en nous-mêmes, réduits non pas tant à un silence qu'à cette absence défilée qui est la nôtre et où les caricatures de parler aussi bien que les mutités elles-mêmes ne signifient plus rien. (p. 150)

(We love them, they who spoke so much and concealed so much; as if they had sought, from this stylistic excess to extremes of silence, to weave something that we could have named: but we can name nothing, without realizing it we have been eroded within, reduced not so much to a silence as to this emptiness which is ours and in which caricatured speech as much as our very silence no longer have any meaning.)

Singled out for satirical attention in this regard are the franco-phile school teachers 'intoxiqués du savoir universel', who attempt to convey in an ornate language the ideals of universal humanism. But there is a constant slippage in language that is more generalised, as is seen in the stickers on cars that clog the streets of the town. The permutations of the sign 'Ne roulez pas trop près' are fully recorded (p. 154) in Creole and pseudo-Creole versions, suggesting even in the banal phenomenon a natural impulse to linguistic improvisation, but one that is directionless and betrays an inner emptiness.

This question of physical and psychological *errance* or within the island space *drivage* is crucial to the community's inability to create a collective *Nous*. Instead there is the artificial, folkloric *Nous* created by the metropolitan administration, an aberrant *Nous* created by the elected representatives of the people, and the *Nous* who figure in development projects. The episode entitled 'Télés' (p. 194) gives a sense of the cacophony of official slogans that have little to do with the 'pays réel' – 'l'identité culturelle', 'un Francais est un Francais', 'cette histoire commune'. In a desperate attempt to forge a community, Medellus establishes his commune. His utopian 'Assemblée générale des Nations' is ultimately bulldozed by one of the construction companies that multiply in the island Department and he goes mad.

Technically, the difficulty in creating a collectivity in *Malemort* is seen in the proliferation of narrative voices in the text. Polyphony in *Malemort* is a product of the pathological nature of the collective consciousness of the group. The changing perspectives in the novel correspond to shifts in style, rhythm, pace and speech pattern. This aspect of the novel has been carefully plotted by Elinor Miller who notes each interruption of or deviance from the *Nous* viewpoint.[34] The ultimate effect of this confusion of juxtaposed, sometimes random, voices is to create 'Le spectre des choses et des gens sans ordre ni mémoire' ('The spectre of things and people with neither order nor memory'), as one chapter is entitled. Like the 'tombés-levés' who resist only to be shot down and to rise again and inevitably be once more suppressed, events take place in this novel which escape being narrated either by the community or by a detached omniscient third party. Collectivity emerges in an ephemeral way from time to time only to dissolve into fragmented individual selves. Even when the collective voice is used, the tone of this voice shifts from the humorous, to the critical or the nostalgic.[35] This inability to understand lived experience seems to be most touchingly caught in the uncomprehending dying gaze of a child who witnesses the shootings of 1959. This represents the aborted consciousness and conscience of the group as a whole.

Il y avait avec eux un enfant aux yeux élargis, comme si l'ancienne forêt disparue avait continué de supporter dans l'air ces yeux qui l'avaient emplie, l'enfant tombant les regardait. (p. 133)

(There was with them a child with wide-open eyes as if the absent forest of the past had continued to maintain in the air these eyes that had filled it, the child falling looked at them.)

In this picture of contemporary Martinique, traditional *marronnage* is not possible: 'nulle part derrière cette terre à travailler, ni pardessous ni au loin ni à l'infini audessus . . . ne se trouvait d'espace où se retirer pour comprendre, où dormir et prendre joie' ('nowhere behind this land of work, nor below in the distance nor in the infinite above . . . could one find space to retire in order to understand, or sleep or feel happy', p. 200). The town, the welfare state and spreading construction have created a false order and transparency. The compulsive mobility of Dlan, Selacier, Medellus and their role as *driveurs* represent some kind of fitful resistance, *opacité* to a petrifying stasis. The picture of Martinique in *Malemort* is that of a world filled with 'nègres habitants' since 'la terre entière est une Habitation' ('the entire land is a plantation'). This is not the plantation of the past which was based on local productivity. The vestiges of that world lie, strewn like phantoms all over the landscape. All traces of the past slowly vanish:

tapie en un détour de poussières et de branchages, fantôme de zincs, d'étains rongés, des brèches figées dans leur rouille . . . la rhumerie abandonnée dormait son rêve tropical: lézardée de bêtes insoupçonnables, son toit de tôles ouvrant de grandes gueules bées dans les après-midi. (p. 66)

(crouching at a turning of sand and branches, zinc phantom, corroded tin, holes fixed in rust . . . the abandoned distillery slept its tropical dream: gnawed at by unthinkable creatures, its zinc roof gaping wide open in the afternoons.)

Hotels, shopping centres, high rise buildings now replace the world of the plantation as Martinique slips irretrievably into a dependant, consumer society.

The image that recurs in *Malemort* to describe the relationship between France and its Department is the nightmarish scene of the woman who is forced to suckle a snake. No one in the dried-up, slowly disintegrating world of *Malemort* thinks of 'la femme outragée abandonée'. The image is as much one of the exploited female in Martinique society as of the island itself 'qui jamais n'abdique sa force et jamais ne crie sa fatigue' ('which never surrenders its strength and never screams out its exhaustion', p. 56). The source of the woman and the country's agony is the snake or, as Glissant calls it, 'la bête longue'. It is such a creature that at the end of the novel swallows in a hallucinatory scene Silacier's body:

La bête longue l'enroula de vents brûlés. Elle l'étouffa. Elle le noya, le souleva sur l'air. Elle s'arracha de lui en emportant la moitié de lui qui restait encore. Elle le laissa retomber sans corps. (p. 227)

(The long beast twisted around him with a burning wind. It strangled him. It drowned him, raised him in the air. It tore itself from him taking away the half that was still left of him. It dropped him back without a body.)

This final episode of the novel reads like a parody of the denouement of Césaire's *Cahier d'un retour au pays natal*. Not only is the snake turned into a sinister image in Glissant's text but Silacier sees yawning before him a 'trou blanc', a symbol of French-induced oblivion.

Already in *Malemort* Glissant was beginning to elaborate his notion of *Antillanité*. Martinique is oblivious to the nature of the region that surrounds it. There is no longer salvation in the *morne* but it might just lie in the interrelationships with the world on the outside. The idea of a Caribbean identity for Martinique is sketched out as Dlan, Medellus and Silacier gaze out to sea. St. Lucian workers who were brought in to break a strike and sided with the Martiniquan workers; the self-sustaining productivity of Dominica; Haiti with its legendary past and frightening present; the exploits of the Cuban general Maceo – all these are juxtaposed with a Martinique more and more alienated from itself and prone to self-destruction: 'le grattement de tant de terres alentour dont nous ne savons pas que le cri nous hèle' ('the scratching of so many lands around who we do not know are calling out to us', p. 183). The chapter ends with the frenzied ravings of a madman who lists all that the metropole has provided and wildly strips off his underwear in a desperately comical effort to jettison the trappings of metropolitan largesse.

Despite its depressing atmosphere of helpless rage and sullen resignation, *Malemort* was written with a corrective purpose in mind. As Glissant would later reveal, the novel was meant to 'Surprendre quelques aspects de notre usure collective et peut-être par là de contribuer à ralentir cette usure' ('Eavesdrop on some aspects of the erosion of our community and perhaps, in doing so, contribute to the slowing down of such erosion').[36]

Glissant, consequently, managed to focus not only on the main features of contemporary Martiniquan reality but also on the figure of the *djobeur* who has become the central focus of much of today's writing in Martinique. In a world of tragic absurdity, the *djobeur* represents a kind of wilful and embattled sanity. In acknowledgement of their unheroic resistance, Patrick Chamoiseau later declared they were the 'nègres marrons de l'en-ville' ('runaways in town').[37] *Malemort* has recently been hailed as the work that revealed 'le singulier dévoilement du réel antillais ... l'outil premier de cette démarche de se connaître: la vision intérieure' ('the unique insight into French Caribbean reality ... the first instrument in the process of knowing ourselves: the inner vision').[38] Fifteen years after *Malemort*'s appearance, the 'lecteurs d'ici' began to decode its complex meaning.

CHAPTER 5

Towards a theory of 'Antillanité'

> Les hommes sont si nécessairement fous, que ce serait être
> fou . . . de n'être pas fou.
>
> Pascal, *Pensées*

Approximately two decades after the deaths of Frantz Fanon
and Jacques Stephen Alexis, and at a time when the fathers of
negritude had begun to succumb to creative exhaustion,
Glissant published two major works. In 1981 *La case du com-
mandeur* ('The Overseer's Cabin')[1] and *Le discours antillais*
('Caribbean Discourse')[2] appeared simultaneously. The
former, a novel that picks up where *La Lézarde* left off, has been
praised as 'the most beautiful story in a Caribbean language'.[3]
The latter, a massive book of theoretical essays, was greeted by
the reviewer in *Le Monde* as 'a great book, only three or four of
which appear in a decade'.[4]

Both works, which are necessarily related to each other, are
marked by the research into and diagnosis of Martiniquan
reality that were done at IME before Glissant left for Paris as
editor of the UNESCO *Courrier* in 1980. Indeed, as the author
states at the end of the notes in *Le discours antillais*, the themes
and ideas of this work were drawn from a series of public
lectures sponsored by IME between 1978 and 1979. In par-
ticular, the sections on 'Le vécu antillais' ('The lived Experi-
ence of the French West Indies'), 'Sur délire verbal' ('Verbal
Delirium') and 'Théâtre, conscience du peuple' ('Theatre, the
People's Consciousness') had already appeared as essays in the
review *Acoma*.

In these two works Glissant returns to the idea of the generalised morbidity of Martiniquan society and the theme of mental disequilibrium. The approach to mental illness in 1981 seems, however, different from the view of madness evoked in the earlier novel *Malemort*. Insanity in *Malemort* is associated with impotence, mysticism and violence. From the empty rhetoric of politicians and schoolteachers to the senseless ragings of the dispossessed poor, the world of *Malemort* conveys a sense of verbal delirium as a symptom of economic destitution. In 1981 madness and eccentricity, or various forms of behaviour, are interpreted as positively deviant, a kind of escape into the irrational.

The subversive potential of the *driveur* or *djobeur* in *Malemort* is given fuller expression in *La case du commandeur*. In 1981, Glissant looks at the shadowy, mysterious underside of the zombified, consumerist society of Martinique with a more constructive eye. If the heartland has died on the outside, then it may continue to exist in the fevered brain of those who once came from such a world. In fact, in Pascal's words, Martiniquans who wish to resist the homogenising socio-cultural forces of departmentalisation, may be 'nécessairement fous', almost ironically as a form of self-protective therapy. Where order leads inexorably towards political absurdity and cultural extinction, insanity becomes a kind of restorative counter-order.

The end of *La case du commandeur* makes this point very forcefully. Marie Celat's father, Pythagore, sits mindlessly before a colour television set, bought on credit, from the beginning of transmission at four o'clock to the end at ten o'clock (p. 238). Both Marie Celat's sons are dead. The older one, Patrice, driven by a demonic addiction to speed, has been killed in a motorcycle accident at the age of nineteen. At the same age, his younger brother, Odono, has died by drowning, lost to the underwater dream world that obsessed him. Like the primogenitor who bore the same name, he was lost in that in-between world, neither part of the past left behind nor rooted in the new land. In all this, Marie Celat predictably suffers a nervous breakdown and is placed in a mental hospital.

The French-made institution, with its metropolitan doctors and gendarmes, is supposed to restore the mentally ill to sanity. But sanity as defined in contemporary Martinique is a kind of madness. Marie Celat must perform an act of *marronnage* in order to save herself. She escapes with the madman Chérubin, who inhabits an abandoned sugar factory, and finds peace contemplating the counter-order of the dark in a chapter revealingly entitled 'Roche de l'opacité' ('Rock of Opacity').

Papa Longoué had predicted earlier in the novel that 'la fille perdue allait se trouver dans sa nuit' ('the lost girl would find herself in her night', pp. 191–2). The healer's clairvoyant prediction refers to the night of Marie Celat's escape from the asylum and her vigil in the overseer's cabin. Ultimately, Glissant's novel is about the capacity of the restless, disturbed Marie Celat or Mycéa, as she is called, to find herself. However, as the newspaper items that open and close the narrative reveal, this is not by any means the official version of Mycéa's story. The first excerpt from the newspaper *Quotidien des Antilles* includes an eye-witness account of a deranged woman's behaviour and the passing comment that she spread ideas that most people did not like (p. 12). The event is quickly passed over as the newspaper report moves on, no doubt to more pleasant matters. The novel closes with a report of an inquiry into the status of psychiatric care in the Department. The final words of this report are loaded with irony as the inquiry has found that psychiatric care in Martinique is the envy of neighbouring independent islands which send psychotic patients to the French Department for therapy.

What makes *La case du commandeur* different from Glissant's earlier work is the figure of Mycéa, who is very different from any of the major protagonists encountered before in his works. Hers is a split personality. Caught between *ceci* and *cela*, day and night, the *autocensure* of the present and the irresistible power of the past, she incarnates a creatively fissured mind not unlike the creative fissure of the Lézarde river in the Martiniquan landscape. She is different from characters such as Thael and Mathieu who have been used previously as perspectives on Martiniquan reality. She is an exemplary 'tête en feu' ('head on fire') who transcends both the silent man of the mountains, Thael, and the incarnation of the limitations of intellect, Mathieu. The bipolar world of Thael and Mathieu dissolves in Mycéa. One can even conceive of her in terms of a mental landscape, a psychic territory extended through space towards the hole of time in the past.

La case du commandeur begins with Mycéa's birth in 1928 and ends with her release from the asylum in 1978. Both Mathieu and Thael are marginal and ultimately absent. Mycéa is left on the island as the sole representative of the four major families whose experiences are traced throughout Glissant's 'oeuvre'. The Longoué, Béluse, Targin and Celat families all inhabit the fevered unconscious of Mycéa. Unlike those around her, she cannot shut out the past. The difficulties between Mathieu and Mycéa as well as their mutual interdependence stem from the inevitable conflicts that exist between raw experience and the rational mind. Indeed, in focusing on this issue Glissant seems to be confessing to his own problems as a topographer of mental landscapes:

Mathieu produisait en idées ou en mots ce que Mycéa gardait au plus intouchable d'elle-même et défoulait par bouffées en grands balans de vie exagérée . . . mais à mesure qu'ils avançaient ils s'écartaient l'un de l'autre. D'où leur passion. Car ce qu'on devine en idées ou qu'on expose en mots devient tellement étranger à ce qu'on accumule en soi comme roches. (pp. 88–9)

(Mathieu would translate into ideas words that Mycéa kept in the most untouchable part of herself and gave vent to in gusts like great swirls of exaggerated animation . . . But as they went forward they grew away from each other. Whence their passion. For what you learn through ideas or reveal in words becomes so alien to what you accumulate inside yourself like rocks.)

What is interesting about this inner landscape is that it retains traces of the past, latent meanings that have been obliterated in the outside world due to 'progress' and modernisation. It is no coincidence that Chérubin inhabits the last vestige of the past, an abandoned sugar factory, and that Mycéa should find herself in the abandoned hut of an ancestor.

Mycéa's problematic relationship to the society and her past seems to be related to her mother's legacy.[5] In some ways, Mycéa's own relationship with Mathieu echoes the difficult union between her mother and father, Cinna Chimène and Pythagore Celat. Mycéa is impatient with Mathieu's theories, in fact with any attempt whatsoever to intellectualise experience. Experiences are to her 'like rocks' and she expresses a fear of theories or any attempt to explain or to manipulate them.

Vos discours sont comme la farine qu'on distribuait à l'hôpital, il fallait trier les mites avant de mettre à cuire. (p. 189)

(Your discourses are like the flour that was shared out at the hospital, you had to sift out the mites before cooking it.)

Cinna Chimène equally embodies mystery and the unconscious. She is a foundling whose age, origins and relatives are unknown. Allied with this mystery is her visionary talent, that she has gained from contact with Papa Longoué. She has also 'la tête en feu' and is described in almost the same words as Mycéa. She becomes in Papa Longoué's hut 'un pan de roche' ('a rock face'). She too, as her daughter later does, plunges 'au ventre inviolé de la forêt' ('into the unviolated womb of the forest', p. 72), much to the consternation and bafflement of her husband.

Pythagore carries 'la même brûlure . . . le même trou dans la tête' ('the same burning . . . the same hole in his head', p. 44). However, he responds by creating a fictional Africa and is fascinated by Mycéa's schoolbooks as a means to understanding the past, not realizing, as his daughter already has, that 'les livres n'ont cessé de mentir pour le meilleur profit de ceux qui les produisirent' ('books never stopped lying to the greater advantage of those who produced them', p. 34). Pythagore never understands, like his wife and daughter do, that the answer to the mysteries of his past lies within himself. Consequently, on accidentally learning of Behanzin, the Dahomean king exiled to Martinique, he feels that this exiled monarch is the key to his search for the 'pays d'avant'. He assumes, using the popular method of dating events by natural disasters, that Behanzin arrived with the explosion of Mt Pélée in 1902. He then continues his search through official records in government offices, only to encounter humiliating contempt from officials who see him merely as a cane cutter with pretensions at doing historical research (p. 41). Just as in the relationship between Mathieu and Mycéa, now Pythagore in contrast to Cinna is lost in futile archival research in a vain attempt to master a private trauma.

Mycéa in the novel is not only intimately connected with the past and internal space, she is also the one who senses the protective presence of 'toutes les îles que vous ne voyez pas plantées dans la mer alentour' ('all the islands you do not see planted in the surrounding sea', p. 235). Just as the dark heartland has a restorative and healing function for Mycéa, so does wandering along the sea shore and the infinite space beyond. Within this space, she descends to join the bodies of African slaves weighted down at the bottom of the sea (p. 195). What distances Mycéa from her contemporaries is her sensitivity to the islands that surround the French Department.

Marie Celat courait aux endroits des bords de mer d'où par temps découvert on reconnaissait la Dominique au nord, avec l'accompagnement rugueux des côtes en escarpe et des vagues déchirées, ou Sainte-Lucie au sud, qui semblait se découper sur les sables tranquilles et l'eau verte étalée; elle apostrophait les îles. (p. 215)

(Marie Celat ran to places on the seashore where on a clear day you could make out Dominica to the north, with its rugged accompaniment of steep slope and shattered breakers, or Saint Lucia to the south, which seemed to rise above serene sands and smooth green water; she called out to the islands.)

Having inherited, because of her ancestry, the legacy of Cinna Chimène and Liberté Longoué, the two previous generations of maroon women, Mycéa is difficult and sceptical. She is far less credulous than Mathieu concerning Papa Longoué's stories. Ultimately, she represents a kind of endurance and defiance that makes relationships with others impossible. This is evident from the outset in her relationship with her father Pythagore. Her character is summed up in this description where she is likened to hot pepper:

Sèche comme un pied de piment, ses yeux fixes vous repoussaient jusqu'au point où vous ne vouliez pas reculer et où vous vous retrouviez soudain, criant qu'une enfant n'avait pas le droit de déporter ainsi les gens. (p. 45)

(Dry like a pepper stalk, her staring eyes kept you at a distance, so much so that you did not want to withdraw and you suddenly found yourself screaming that no child had the right to put off people like that.)

The author insists on this aspect of Mycéa as he later points to her dislike for 'le goût sucré de [ces] légumes' ('the sugary taste of certain vegetables', p. 45). Her grandmother Ephraîse displays a similar distaste for sweet or sugary food, suggesting an aversion to the world of the cane field as well as an inner stoicism and toughness. 'Elle n'offrait jamais de sucreries ni aucune sorte de douceurs, et nul n'en attendait d'elle' ('She never offered sweets nor any kind of confectionery, and no one expected any from her', p. 71). Mycéa, consequently, can be seen as descending from a line of women who appear to embody the complexities, the anguish and a kind of spiritual resistance which are necessary to combat the assimilationist reality of the present. Perhaps, also, they are associated with the primal image of the *femme outragée* which appeared in Glissant's earliest essays and which bears mute witness to the terror of being suckled all night long by a snake.

Despite the emphasis on the heroic suffering of Mycéa and this line of 'femmes marronnes', *La case du commandeur* is neither a feminist work nor is it a celebration of resistance. The title of the novel is drawn from none of these fierce figures of female resistance. Rather, the gravitational centre of the work is the realm of moral ambiguity, the inadmissible horror that the community wishes to shut out. In no other work by Glissant has the question of moral paradox been so clearly the centre of focus. The overseer's cabin to which Mycéa makes her pilgrimage houses the ambivalence of her ancestor's actions. This cabin is both the symbolic opposite of the mental asylum from which she escapes and different from other *cases* or cabins that have turned up in previous works. In Glissant's first two novels, the main characters went to Papa Longoué's cabin where the past and the future were revealed to them. Even in *La case du commandeur* Cinna Chimène goes into the forest to her own seances of initiation in the cabin of the defiant maroon, Papa Longoué (p. 78). However, for Mycéa and by extension for post-abolition Martinique, the overseer's cabin is a zone of inauspicious beginnings.

The abandoned cabin is that of a distant ancestor, Euloge Alfonsine, whose daughter, Adoline, was Mycéa's great grandmother. Euloge, the first slave to be made an overseer, turned against his own people. He was a severe *commandeur* who identified with the values of his white master (p. 86). He ran a shop in his cabin on the plantation. When abolition was decreed in 1848, he retreated into the world he had previously ignored, the forest. The decree was symbolically pinned to this cabin after Euloge, a fugitive from freedom, ironically took refuge in the world of the maroon. For him the whole song and dance over abolition was nothing but 'simagrées' ('pretence'). He turns out to have been right as abolition is later described as a 'cérémonie vide' (p. 144). Euloge is a figure of disturbing ambivalence in his shrewd, self-seeking nature. He incarnates a defiant individualism that has nothing to do with collective values. In giving his actions prominence in the novel, Glissant is suggesting that, more than the maroons Odono or Longoué, he is the shaping force of modern Martinique. Euloge's fierce individualism and defiant self-advancement point to Glissant's hypothesis that Martinique's history is one of missed opportunities. The choice of French citizenship and of Departmental status in 1946 are seen by Glissant as inevitable given the fiercely self-improving nature of individuals like Euloge.

The short-circuiting of the collective whole or the *Nous* symbolised by Euloge's actions is central to *La case du commandeur*, as it is to Glissant's writing as a whole at this time. *La case du commandeur* can then be read as an illustration of the difficulties that exist in writing the 'roman du nous', defined in *Le discours antillais* as 'le roman de l'implication du Je au Nous, du Je a l'Autre, du Nous au Nous' (p. 153) ('the novel of the involvement of the I and the We, the I and the Other, the We and the We').[6] Predictably, the novel begins and ends with the relentless striving to create a 'We' from the disjointed 'I's. The second sentence of the novel deals with collective destiny and is picked up in the closing lines:

Nous, qui avec tant d'impatience rassemblons ces moi disjoints; dans les retournements turbulents où cahoter à grands bras, piochant aussi le temps qui tombe et monte sans répit; acharnés à contenir la part inquiète de chaque corps dans cette obscurité difficile du nous. (p. 239)

(We, who so impatiently put together these disjointed I's; in troubled writhings we jerk along, arms flailing, in the process excavating time which falls and rises relentlessly; eager to contain the restless part of each body in this difficult obscurity of the we.)

Consequently, *La case du commandeur* can be seen as a case history of 'cette obscurité difficile du nous'. The entire novel, conceivably, takes place in the overseer's cabin during Mycéa's vigil after her escape from the psychiatric hospital. The narrative has been described as a 'géohistoire'[7] and it is true that language and landscape are once more interrelated in Glissant's text. Chérubin makes this link for Mycéa during her night in the cabin when he says that the word is planted in the earth which is turned over (p. 235). One of the epigraphs for the novel also emphasizes this relationship between word and land as the word is compared to a yam whose nourishing roots extend deep into the land. The narrative structure is likened by Beverley Ormerod to a pyramid rising through four generations in pursuit of the meaning of 'Odono', the primordial ancestor: 'At the top of the pyramid, the identity and fate of Odono are at last revealed. But the narrative, after this privileged pause continues down the reverse slope.'[8] The slope deals with Mycéa's tribulations after 1946. This is a useful model for explaining the story of *La case du commandeur*. The book is arranged in three sections. These sections also seem to correspond to Martiniquan topography as 'La tête en feu' can refer to the hilly north and Mt Pélée, 'Mitan du temps' ('Centre of Time') to the central plains, and 'Le premier des animaux' ('The First of the Animals') to the sands of the south. The overall structure of the novel is based on the 'espace-temps' of the island of Martinique which ironically is not understood by those who inhabit it.

The novel takes us backwards from the birth of Mycéa in 1928. The first chapter deals with Mycéa's parents Pythagore Celat and Cinna Chimène. The second narrates the childhood of Mycéa's foundling mother and her grandparents Ephraîse and Ozonzo. The third recounts the meeting of Mycéa's great-grandparents, Adoline Alfonsine and Augustus Celat, and the period of abolition. The fourth and last chapter takes us back to Liberté Longoué and Anatolie Celat. Anatolie is the first person to bear the name Celat and, most importantly, is a storyteller, 'semeur d'histoires' or 'historieur'. This prodigious patriarch, who fathered thirty-five children, is the gateway to the past and the obscure beginnings of this family. Through Liberté Longoué, Anatolie learns of the first maroon or *négateur*. But here the story becomes blurred and confusing. There turn out to be two blood brothers called Odono. To complicate the picture further Odono and Longoué both seem to have identical experiences of betrayal, escape and survival, so much so that when the name Odono was called no one knew which of the two was being addressed (p. 125). There can be no further clarification as Anatolie does not know, and even Liberté admits that the beginnings of the story 'tombait dans un trou sans fond, où plus personne n'était visible' ('fell into a bottomless pit where no one was visible', p. 123).

No one can unravel the mystery of these stories. The wife of Anatolie's white master dies 'sur un tas de vieux papier de toutes les couleurs qu'elle s'était effrenée à découper ('on a pile of colourful old papers that she was desperately trying to cut up', p. 129) in a vain attempt to piece together these stories. This puzzle continues from generation to generation as an insoluble mystery. The 'trou du temps passé' ('pit of time past') haunts each succeeding generation. The legacy of contemporary Martinique is this void in the past and the myths, illusions or 'rocks' that have been used to fill it. Liberté's advice is the only proper response to this 'pit of time past': 'il valait mieux contempler ainsi le passé dans un fond de nuit, sans préciser les noms ni les moments' ('it was better to contemplate the past

like this, in the depths of night, without being precise about
names or incidents', p. 125). Nevertheless, the *Nous* of the
present continues to be haunted by

Ce trou débondé que déferla sur nous la foule des mémoires et des
oublis tressés, sous quoi nous peinons à recomposer nous ne savons
quelle histoire débitée en morceaux. (p. 126)

(This exploding pit which the flood of interwoven memories and
forgetting unleashed on us, under which we strive to put together we
do not know what story cut up into pieces.)

As Ormerod again points out, this mystery is the shared
puzzlement of the 'nous' of the story. The identity of the 'nous'
shifts from one chapter to another (now Pythagore's drinking
companions, now Ozonzo's children and their playmates, now
the group of slaves gathered before the driver's hut to gaze at
the official announcement of abolition).[9] But as we have seen
before, the past for Glissant cannot be easily unravelled. In
discussing the relationship between literature and history in *Le
discours antillais*, he refers to the longing in the Caribbean for an
ideal past which history cannot provide. Consequently, Mycéa
cannot derive her true nature from this dark pit of the past nor
can the 'we' of the story piece together a tale of heroic exploits.

The ideal notion of historical time first appeared in
Glissant's work in the symbol of the surging Lézarde river.
Now that the river is dried up, time is represented in terms of
rocks or boulders that contain the past but in a disjointed way.
The ambiguous nature of 'la roche du temps' is the key to
Glissant's reference to history in *La case du commandeur*. The
section entitled 'Mitan du temps' is filled with references in
italics to leaping from one rock to another and to pulverising
rocks: '*Nous sautons de roche en roche dans ce temps*' (p. 138), '*nous
ravageons la roche, nous sommes les casseurs de roches du temps*'
(p. 143). The image of the rock appears as an external manifes-
tation of this mythical view of the past. In *Le discours antillais*,
Glissant describes the mythical view of the past as the raw
material for the literary work. Myth disguises just as it signifies,
it obscures while rendering intense and fascinating that which
is established in a time and place between men and their

surroundings. The rock has certain characteristics of myth. Opacity, the primordial quality of the rock, is seen as the first obstacle that the fugitive maroon opposes to the transparency of the coloniser. The rock then is the maroon's strategy of negation.

The rock which was once opposed to the *trace* or track as a way of protecting the refuge of the maroon has now become a puzzling legacy for the latter's descendants. Cailler rightly refers to the 'polyvalence symbolique' of the image of rock in *La case du commandeur*.[10] Rocks take us through the past but do not clarify. Each memory that surges up from the unconscious in 'Mitan du temps' is rock, and the same image is repeated towards the end as Mycéa, symbolic of the tortured collective consciousness, refers to 'ce qu'on accumule en soi comme roches' ('what we accumulate in ourselves like rocks', p. 189). The past, then, is not penetrated by following the track. The only route is marked by rocks. The question then is how to deal with these obscure blocks of historical time.[11] The temptation is to become 'casseurs de roches' ('stonebreakers'). Glissant sees this role as the temptation offered to the Caribbean writer faced with the opacity of the past. The impulse is to shatter these rocks but that does not mean that the fragments left behind lead to greater clarity. After all, the second chapter of this middle section of the novel begins 'La poussière de roche dans quoi nous dérivons' ('The rock dust in which we drift along', p. 145). If history has become a congealed mineralised calendar, then an inventory of rocks, a regrouping of these frozen units of meaning, may be all that the writer can manage. The use of words like *Inventaire*, *Bestiaire* and *Registre* suggests such a concern.

What may be more interesting is Glissant's speculation concerning the use of opacity and the symbolic deployment of subterranean rocks as a counter-poetics. In *Le discours antillais*, in a discussion of what he calls the poetics of the unconscious, Glissant sees the practice of opacity in language, whether the 'détours' of Creole or the Baroque excesses of French, as an instinctive counter-poetics. It marks 'le déni instinctif, qui ne s'est pas encore organisé en refus collectif conscient' ('the instinctive rejection which is not yet organised into a conscious collective negation', p. 279). The creative deformation of the car sticker 'Ne roulez pas trop près' is used as a mundane illustration of the instinct towards a counter-order (p. 280). This general area of investigation is advanced by Glissant at this time as an unorganized but positive strategy on the part of Martiniquans. As he affirms, again in *Le discours antillais*, French West Indians are not condemned to 'la déculturation sans retour' ('inexorable deculturation', p. 16).

The question of a counter-order is raised in *La case du commandeur* as Glissant speculates about the possibility of a rhetoric of inner speech, the rudiments of an internal *langage* or idiom which he had despaired of finding in *Malemort*. Interestingly, this issue emerges in the context of psychoanalysis. The official therapy for the mentally disturbed in the psychiatric hospital is revelation, confession and catharsis. The impulse to self-enclosure, to a fierce reticence, is a form of resistance on Mycéa's part. The outer speech of externalized discourse is the approved idiom of the asylum and by extension of official Martinique. It is the voice that appears at the end of the novel on the colour television as yet another technocrat, politician or visiting French official goes on about development plans for the Department. In contrast to this form of discourse, shared by some males in the novel who put inordinate faith in the intellect,[12] Mycéa opts for a defiant retentiveness, and accumulation of rocks of feeling. In the novel, the forest encroaches on the brightly-lit world of the mental hospital. Mycéa, 'opaque par nature' (p. 173), quietly affirms her loyalty to the dark at the end of the novel: 'je retiens tout' ('I retain everything', p. 238).[13]

The extent to which this instinctive practice on Mycéa's part is followed by the community is an intriguing dimension of the novel and of Glissant's own poetics of narration. Glissant does not go so far as to suggest a syntax of the collective unconscious of Martiniquans. The artist for Glissant is not a psychoanalyst. He does not focus on externalisation and elucidation. He does not bring to light and, consequently, betray the intensive private discourse of *opacité*. The important thing is not to cure but to register this vital pathological zone of resistance. Mycéa's intense inner discourse is responsible for her disequilibrium. The community as a whole seems to participate in a form of instinctive counter-poetics. The twisting or the explosion of meanings may be a kind of system or codification of inner speech. The first practitioner of this method is Anatolie Celat, the ancestral 'nègre errant', who is a legendary storyteller. He tells each of his many female conquests a piece of his family story. Neither his master nor his white mistress can make anything of 'ces histoires cassées' ('these broken stories', p. 115). This 'discours éclaté', as it is called in *Le discours antillais*, is described during Mycéa's vigil as a form of 'déparler' ('anti-speech'). This strategy is reflected in the need to take hold of one's name as in the case of the maroon who calls himself Aa-a in a mocking representation of the French language. He is significantly punished for this violence inflicted on French by having a burning torch stuffed down his throat (p. 167).

The *Nous* of the novel also have this tendency to twist meanings and deform words so that they now have a local internal resonance. The very word 'Odono', which haunts the consciousness, never quite disappears but keeps recurring in various forms, such as Ozonzo or the transformation of Mycéa's son's name Odono into 'Donou' by his friends. Similarly, the fate of the area where the *case du commandeur* was sited also reveals a process of verbal inventiveness which both reclaims and obscures. Here we see how the oral tradition of the community works. Grand Congo and la Petite Guinée became the site for a bar where locals returning from France recount their adventures. One of them renamed the place:

un ancien Parisien s'avisa que c'était là Barbès. Barbès remplaca la Petite Guinée. (p. 210)

(a former Parisian got it into his head that it was called Barbès. Barbès replaced la Petite Guinée.)

Barbès-Rochechouart then became Barbès-Roches-tombées because two drinkers threw rocks at each other. Finally, because it was so small, one self-important patron of the bar felt that it should be called Barbès le Mouchoir. This name stuck and remained part of the local collective consciousness. 'Ces variations n'avaient pas tant d'importance; nous étions seuls à en rire, les réservant pour notre usage' ('These variations were not so important; we were the only ones to laugh at them, keeping them for our use', p. 210).

Glissant develops the idea of a community taking the shape of Barbès. The 'soirées de Barbès' becomes a means of keeping in touch with distant members of the Celat family who come to visit. These evenings become the occasion as well for the telling of stories, of jokes that suggest the beginnings of a community. In the final analysis *La case du commandeur* ends on a hopeful note, as Glissant suggests in the world of Barbès the possibility of an independent and homogenous culture, whose conscience is embodied in Mycéa.[14] The latter teaches the people of the area not to forget the past, in the face of the non-productive and impotent present.

si Marie Celat nous avait quittés ou si du moins nous en prenions peu à peu une si douloureuse conscience, c'est parce que nous levions les yeux sur ce qui de l'alentour nous échappait tellement. Nous ne savions à la fin comment faire marcher notre usine ni par quoi remplacer sa vacance terrible. On nous divertissait d'activités de remplacement, qui nous saturaient d'une jouissance au bout du compte insupportable. (p. 212)

(if Marie Celat had left us or if at least we slowly became more painfully aware of the fact, it is because we lifted our eyes to see what around us was really disappearing. We no longer knew how to run our factory, nor how to fill in the terrible emptiness left behind. We were entertained with substitute activities, which saturated us with a pleasure that was ultimately unbearable.)

This embryonic sense of collective unease may well be what is responsible at the end of the novel for the fact that people began to 'parler vraiment des partisans d'indépendance' ('really speak of those advocating independence', p. 239).

There is a feeling at the end of *La case du commandeur* that the story is not yet complete, that the potential exists for some kind of collective self-affirmation. In a way, *Le discours antillais* develops this aspect of the novel. This book of essays is an attempt to articulate a theory of *Antillanité* or Caribbeanness while recognising the inadequacy of all systematic theorizing. Indeed, one can say that in *Le discours antillais* Glissant tries to turn the rocks or frozen units of feeling in the Martiniquan unconscious into words and theories. Nevertheless, there is the recognition that not everything can be brought to consciousness and voiced, as the epigraph from Jean-Jacques Rousseau states: 'Mais le langage le plus énergique est celui où le signe a tout dit avant qu'on parle' ('But the most powerful language is the one in which all is said without a word being uttered').

In these essays, Glissant spells out in great detail the predicament of Martinique. The reality of its condition of dependency and stagnation is elaborated in terms of statistics, official data, as well as small telling details of Martiniquan life. For instance one is as likely to find extensive charts on economic dependency and the tertiarisation of the Martiniquan economy as comical details of daily life in Martinique. For instance, the use of the four seasons to advertise events in tropical Martinique, the story of the white tramp who visits a primary school and is taken for the school inspector, and that of the Martiniquan who, when asked to donate blood for his wife in labour, said that he thought blood was supplied by France (p. 175) – all point to the disturbing effects of departmentalisation in the seventies. Less comical are the psychological responses to this state of alienation and impotence. Glissant's analysis of verbal delirium, swear-words and psychic disequilibrium is used to illustrate the symptoms of self-repudiation and chronic reliance on French paternalism that have eroded the natural tendency to self-affirmation in a people.

This has not, in Glissant's view, always been the case. Martiniquan history is interpreted by him as a series of *occasions ratées* ('missed opportunities'). From 1848, date of abolition of slavery, to 1946, that of departmentalisation, Martinique intensified its alienating relationship with the metropole to the extent that passive consumerism alone is all that is needed in the present to keep this relationship intact. The last period of self-sufficiency for Martiniquans, Glissant points out, was during World War II. Blockaded by the Allied fleet, Martinique was isolated from the metropole. During this time, 1939–45, Martinique was ironically 'freer' than after 1946. As he concludes in the essay 'Faire et créer', Martinique became for a few years resourceful and creative:

nous n'avons jamais été aussi libres que sous l'Occupation . . . les Martiniquais apprirent, en même temps que les pratiques du marché noir, les ressources de l'auto production. (p. 40)

(we have never been as free as under the Occupation . . . Martiniquans learnt, along with the operation of the black market, the skills of producing for themselves.)

He produces an impressive list of items that were made in Martinique during the six years of the Occupation: salt, leather, glasses, baskets and various food products. The spirit of the *djobeurs* of *Malemort* is behind this collective inventiveness provoked by economic necessity.

However, such a period of creativity is shortlived. 'Le réel Martiniquais' is characterised by loss – a loss of language, memory, political will and local culture. Nevertheless, it would be misleading to treat *Le discours antillais* as simply a litany of the pernicious effects of prolonged dependency. The real importance of this book of essays is that it goes beyond the bleak diagnosis to suggest the possibility of resistance that still exists. Glissant's intelligence is too restless and creative to accept this apparent deculturation as absolute and immutable. Consequently, *Le discours antillais* has a certain upbeat tone to it from the very outset. On the second page of the book, and repeated several times in the text, Glissant declares 'je crois à l'avenir des petits pays' ('I have faith in the future of small countries'). The last section of the work, entitled significantly 'L'avenir antillais', concludes with this optimistic observation:

La colonisation n'a donc pas été aussi réussie qu'il y paraît à première vue. L'irrésistible pulsion mimétique se heurte à des foyers de résistance dont l'inconvénient est que rien, dans une situation littéralement éclatée, ne les relie entre eux. (p. 465)

(Colonisation has therefore not been as successful as it appears at first sight. The irresistible mimetic impulse comes up against areas of resistance for which the difficulty is that nothing in a literally fragmented situation can link them together.)

In the face of this declared dearth of organized and sustained resistance, Glissant, as is apparent in *La case du commandeur*, takes an interest in those practices that suggest some kind of self-affirmation among French West Indians. On the first page of these essays, Glissant indicates where his interest lies. He announces 'Nous réclamons le droit à l'opacité' ('We demand the right to opacity'). This notion of *opacité* is central to Glissant's broad philosophical preoccupations in the text. 'Opacity' or the recognised impenetrability of a culture (*opacité consentie*) is a complex idea and one which, as Glissant is well aware, can lead to a kind of dangerous cultural reductionism.

Nevertheless, the notion of *opacité* as developed in *Le discours antillais* is a dynamic and subtle one. On one hand it is contrasted with the dangerous lure of universal culture. On the other, it attempts to distance itself from the false opacity of ideological folklorism or the romanticising of cultural essence and authenticity. The question, Glissant asks, is to what extent have Martiniquans constructed a particular thought-world, to what extent has a counter-poetics developed in the face of the threat of 'colonisation réussie'. Glissant seeks answers to these questions in the folktale, orality, and some of the most banal episodes of Martiniquan life. The ingredient of *opacité* creates the cultural diversity without which the ideal of *relation* (cultural interrelating) is impossible.

In the folklore, for instance, Glissant isolates the practice of a counter-poetics. The tale points to the realities of Martiniquan life, such as space which is not possessed. Also, in the area of language, even as there is an erosion of Creole, there is an irrepressible impulse towards a Creolisation of French, as Glissant demonstrates with the instinctive deformation of windshield stickers. These ideas are most coherently developed in the essay 'Poétique naturelle poétique forcée' ('Natural Poetics, Forced Poetics'). Martinique does not have a 'natural poetics', that is, a condition in which there is no incompatibility between expression and pressures within the community. Rather Martinique struggles with a 'forced poetics' because of the confrontation between feeling and expression, internal discourse and the problems, both linguistic and political, in externalizing this discourse. It is within this 'forced poetics' that zones of *opacité* can be identified.

For instance, Glissant points to the coding of Creole which does not have the 'structuration naturelle' of traditional languages but rather, a negative or reactive linguistic structuration. In the scrambled sounds ('non-sens accéleré) of Creole, the pitch, the deliberate cacophony at times, the patterns of detours and delays (p. 32), Glissant identifies a strategy of counter-poetics. The verbal delirium that results Glissant characterises as habitual ('coutumier') and not 'pathologique'. The point here is that Martinique is caught between an inability to liberate itself completely and an insistence on trying to do so (pp. 241–2). As he concludes in this essay, the ideal would be for Martinique to enter a relationship with the region and the rest of the world with an acknowledged *opacité*, because:

consentir à l'opacité, c'est-à-dire à la densité irréductible de l'autre c'est accomplir véritablement, à travers le divers, l'humain. L'humain n'est peut-être pas l' 'image de l'homme' mais aujourd'hui la trame sans cesse recommencée de ces opacités consenties. (p. 245)

(to accept opacity, that is the irreducible density of the other is truly to accomplish, through diversity, a human ideal. The human is not perhaps defined today as the 'image of man' but the ever growing network of recognised opacities.)

The question of *opacité* as it is raised in *Le discours antillais* is inextricably linked to Glissant's ideas on creolisation and *Antillanité*. Both these notions locate what Glissant sees as the network of recognised opacities within the specific reality of the Caribbean and the Americas. Indeed, the notion of *opacité* for Glissant has as much an internal momentum as an external field of reference. In his introduction, he makes a clear statement on the passage from negritude to a more Caribbean identity that is taking place.

Aujourd'hui l'Antillais ne renie plus la part Africaine de son être; il n'a plus, par réaction, à la prôner comme exclusive. Il faut qu'il la *reconnaisse*. Il compréhend que de toute cette histoire (même si nous l'avons vécue comme une non-histoire) est résultée *une autre réalité*. Il n'est plus contraint de rejeter par tactique les composantes occidentales, aujourd'hui encore aliénantes, dont il sait qu'il peut choisir entre elles . . . Il conçoit que la synthèse n'est pas l'opération d'abâtardissement qu'on lui disait, mais pratique féconde par quoi les composantes s'enrichissent. Il est devenu antillais. (pp. 17–18).

(Today the French West Indian no longer denies the African part of his being; he no longer has, through reaction, to flaunt it as exclusive. He must *recognise* it. He understands that from all this history (even if we have lived it as a non-history) has emerged *another reality*. He is no longer forced to reject tactically the western components, still an alienating force today, between which he knows he can choose . . . He knows that the synthesis is not the process of bastardisation as he has been told, but a fertile experience through which the constituent parts enrich each other. He has become Caribbean.)

These ideas raised earlier in his theorising about *métissage* in *L'intention poétique* are now given a more thoroughgoing treatment.

In this regard, *Le discours antillais* is not an inward-looking or nationalistic view of Martiniquan identity. *Opacité* as an idea is tied to the specificity of the Martiniquan experience. However, Glissant sees in creolisation and the concept of *Antillanité*, a possible external orientation for the French Departments that would take them beyond *francophonie* or negritude.[15] As he puts it, there is another *Nous* within which Martinique must take its place. It is only by so doing that Martinique can fully understand itself.

La question à poser à un Martiniquais ne sera par exemple pas: 'Qui suis-je?' question inopératoire au premier abord, mais bien 'qui sommes-nous?' (p. 153)

(The question to be asked of a Martiniquan will not be for instance: 'Who am I?' from the outset a question that goes nowhere, but rather 'Who are we?')

The answer to the latter question is given in a later essay. In 'Poétique de la relation' Glissant points out that the space that Martiniquans need to claim in order to escape the threat of cultural anonymity implied in the idea of universal civilisation is that of the region as a whole.

Contre l'universel généralisant le premier recours est la volonté rêche de *rester au lieu*. Mais le lieu en ce qui nous concerne n'est pas seulement la terre où notre peuple fut déporté, c'est aussi l'histoire

qu'il a partagée (la vivant comme non-histoire) avec d'autres com-
munautés, dont la convergence apparaît aujourd'hui. Notre lieu,
c'est les Antilles. (p. 249)

(Against a generalising universality, the first resort is the fierce
insistence on *fixing oneself in one's space*. But the space for us is not only
the land where our people were deported to, it is the history they
have shared (living it like a non-history) with other communities,
whose relationship with us is apparent today. Our space is the
Caribbean.)

In claiming the right to a Caribbean creole identity for the
French West Indian Departments, Glissant carefully avoids
elaborating a rigid and narrow model of cultural identity. The
two outstanding features of his view of Caribbean creole identi-
ties are firstly, the creatively unstable nature of the identity
proposed and, secondly, the refusal to exclude other cultures
and nations from this interculturative process. Glissant's defi-
nition of the Caribbean is a revealing one.

Qu'est-ce que les Antilles en effet? Une multi-relation. Nous le
ressentons tous, nous l'exprimons sous toutes sortes de formes
occultées ou caricaturales, ou nous le nions farouchement. Mais nous
éprouvons bien que cette mer est là en nous avec sa charge d'îles enfin
découvertes. (p. 249)

(What is the Caribbean in fact? An example of multi-relationships.
We all feel it, we express it in all kinds of hidden or exaggerated ways,
or we fiercely deny it. But we sense that this sea exists within us with
its weight of now revealed islands.)

Within such a system of multiple interrelated cultures, the
Caribbean represents not a closed space but one that is open
both internally, within the archipelago, and externally,
exposed to the continental mass of the Americas and the
Atlantic Ocean. In this context, as Glissant concludes, insula-
rity takes on a new meaning. It is no longer an agoraphobic
condition ('une névrose') for in the Caribbean 'chaque île est
une ouverture' ('each island is an opening').

The panoramic picture of the Caribbean is almost one in
which a shared part and a common landscape remain a sub-
marine and unconscious reality, and the 'field of islands' repre-

sents zones of consciousness where *Antillanité* is manifested in a given linguistic, national and political configuration. As Glissant writes, *Antillanité* is lived 'de manière souterraine' ('in a subterranean manner') by the people of the Caribbean. Here, the vision of *Antillanité* is of hidden, unifying forces that have been lived for centuries but are only now surfacing:

> nos histoires diversifiées dans la Caraîbe produisent aujourd'hui un autre dévoilement: celui de leur convergence souterraine . . . le poète et historien Brathwaite, dressant dans la revue *Savacou* un récapitulatif des travaux effectués sur notre histoire . . . résume la troisième et dernière partie de son étude en une seule phrase: 'The unity is submarine'. (p. 134)

> (our diverse histories in the Caribbean produce today another revelation: that of their subterranean convergence . . . the poet and historian Brathwaite, in his recapitulation in the magazine *Savacou* of the work done in the Caribbean on our history . . . summarises the third and last part of his study with the single phrase: 'The unity is submarine'.)

This image releases a whole new cluster of ideas which mark a significant shift from the traditional ideals of filiation, *enracinement* and belonging.[16] Glissant proposes 'racines sousmarines: c'est-à-dire dérivées, non implantées d'un seul mat dans un seul limon' ('submarine roots: that is floating free, not one shaft fixed in a unique spot', p. 134).

In this definition of the Caribbean in terms of openness, of *errance* and of an intricate, unceasing branching of cultures, Glissant is careful not to claim an exclusive right to this experience by Caribbean peoples. In deconstructing the notions of pure and impure, he sees the world in terms of ceaseless cultural transformation and subverts the old temptation to essentialist and exclusivist strategies.

> Si nous parlons des cultures métissées (comme l'antillaise par exemple), ce n'est pas pour définir une catégorie en-soi qui s'opposerait par là à d'autres catégories (de cultures 'pures') mais pour affirmer qu'aujourd'hui s'ouvre pour la mentalité humaine une approche infinie de la relation . . . Le métissage comme proposition souligne qu'il est désormais inopérant de glorifier une origine 'unique' dont la race serait gardienne et continuatrice . . . Affirmer

que les peuples sont métissés, que le métissage est valeur, c'est déconstruire ainsi une catégorie 'métis' qui serait intermédiaire en tant que telle entre deux extrêmes 'purs'. (p. 250)

(If we speak of creolised cultures (like that of the Caribbean for example), it is not to define a self-contained category which by its very nature would be opposed to other categories ('pure' cultures), but to assert that today the infinite vistas of interrelating are open to the human mind . . . Creolisation as a hypothesis emphasises that it is henceforth pointless to glorify 'unique' origins which the race would protect and propagate . . . To assert that peoples are creolised, that *métissage* has a value, is to deconstruct the category of 'creolised' that would be seen as halfway between two 'pure' extremes.)

In developing this vision of global creolisation, Glissant sees the Caribbean as an intense and sustained version of a larger phenomenon. Unlike other Caribbean theorists of creolisation, he begins to conceive of the Caribbean not as a New World Mediterranean but rather as a sea exploding outwards, not concentrating inwards.[17]

With these ideas on creolisation and *Antillanité* Glissant fully enters the arena of post-colonial theory. In *Le discours antillais*, the epistemological break with negritude is complete, even if the word *Antillanité* does suggest through its ending an ideological *prise de position* as opposed to a process. Glissant's vision is different from earlier nationalisms and counter-discursive ideologies because it not only demystifies the imperialistic myth of universal civilization but also rejects the values of hegemonic systems. In breaking free from the ideas of cultural purity, racial authenticity and ancestral origination, Glissant provides a way out of the temptation to relapse into identitarian thought. His vision of inexhaustible hybridity is an ideological breakthrough. However, it must be noted that Glissant is careful not to make *Le discours antillais* into a manifesto for a new post-negritude ideology. In the glossary to these essays, he defines *Antillanité* as more than a theory, a vision ('plus qu'une théorie, une vision', p. 495).[18] In *Le discours antillais* there are only three short sections entitled 'l'Antillanité'. In the first, he maintains that Martinique can survive without France 'dans son contexte antillais' (p. 178). In the second, he develops this idea by saying that the love–hate relationship between Martinique and the metropole could be transcended if there existed 'la multi-relation de la diversité antillaise' (p. 281). *Antillanité* is ultimately, in the third section, a dream but a fragile one (p. 422).

Le discours antillais does not stop at the notion of Caribbeanness and creolisation. Glissant speculates about the larger New World or American identity of Martinique and the Caribbean. In the shift away from what Glissant sees as an earlier generation's concern with exile to his present concern with 'insertion' (p. 265), that is establishing the Caribbean's context, Glissant sees the Caribbean as 'l'autre Amérique'. In considering what the archipelago of tiny islands could mean to the continental mass of North and South America, Glissant calls the Caribbean sea the estuary of the Americas (p. 249), a zone where the richest possibilities of the New World are deposited; their exposed nature and the intensity of the process of hybridization make the Caribbean, in Glissant's view, 'l'avancée de l'Amérique. Ce qui échappa à la masse du continent et pourtant participe de son poids' ('the vanguard of America. That which escapes the mass of the continent and yet forms part of its weight', p. 230).

Consequently, an important dimension of these essays is the projection of Martinique and the Caribbean into a New World poetics. Glissant identifies three Americas: 'Toute cette Amérique . . . vit trois héritages: l'indien, l'africain et l'occidental' ('All this America lives three legacies: the Indian, the African and the Western', p. 229). He agrees with the systems of clarification advanced by theorists such as Darcy Ribeiro and Rex Nettleford, who identify three American spaces: Euro-America, Meso-America, and Plantation America. It is within Plantation America that the Caribbean figures prominently with its history of repopulated space, the shaping force of the plantation and the resulting experience of *marronnage*, multilingualism and creolisation. The world view or poetics of this American space is investigated by Glissant in terms of the imaginative activity that is evident. This activity goes beyond literature to include dance, music and the visual arts.

His poetics of the 'other' America focuses on three areas: space, history and language. The question of Caribbean and now American space has been a constant preoccupation of Glissant's from his earliest essays. The need to liberate the Caribbean as a docile referent, to give full expression to the 'primordial chaos' of Caribbean landscape, is articulated in *Soleil de la conscience*. These ideas are extended in *Le discours antillais* to the larger context of the 'other' America. Again painting and sculpture provide insights into the special imaginative idiom of this world. 'La lecture du paysage' ('a reading of space') is a central consideration in Glissant's comments on the visual arts. Two exemplary painters are, not surprisingly, cited here as illustrating the poetics of American space: Wifredo Lam and Roberto Matta.

Chez Wifredo Lam, la poétique du paysage américain (accumulation, dilatation, charge du passé, relais africain, présence des totems) est *dessinée* . . . Matta figure les conflicts ardents où la psyché des hommes se forge aujourd'hui. Peinture de la multiplicité; j'ose dire: du multilinguisme. (p. 230)

(In Wifredo Lam, the poetics of American landscape (accumulation, expansion, force of the past, the African connection, presence of totems) is *part of the design* . . . Matta represents the intense conflicts that shape men's minds today. Paintings of multiplicity; I even dare to say: of multilingualism.)

Glissant's approach to Haitian art is no less novel. In 'Sur la peinture haïtienne' he again displays his gifts as an art critic in arguing that the painted sign can be seen as the true realm of Haitian oral expression (p. 269). He goes so far as to say that where literature and the French language have failed to translate a sense of 'le merveilleux' Haitian art has succeeded.

The collective imagination of the 'other' America comes up against certain difficulties in the use of the written word, the contaminated world of the book. The latter, because it is indirect and inevitably freezes the dynamic nature of lived reality, becomes an unnatural idiom, a forced poetics, for the freed slave whose natural reflex is physical excess. For Glissant, it is the written word, more specifically the book, that paralyses the body. Music and painting which allow for a more direct, corporeal expression permit truer representations of imaginative activity in Plantation America. Naturally, because of Martinique's status as a Department, neither music nor painting have the same vigour and creativity that are visible where the poetics of the 'other' America is more freely expressed. Again the lack of productivity is directly related in Martinique to a dearth of creativity in these forms of artistic expression.

However, Glissant does not leave out of account the literary expression of an American poetics. The most important essay on this is 'Le roman des Amériques'. This study is the continuation of ideas raised previously as a new orientation for Caribbean literature. Here Glissant raises the question of the importance of history, landscape and language to the novel of the Americas. His hypothesis is that landscape in a New World poetics is not a form of *décor consentant* (sentimentalised background), but inscribed in the text as in painting or music. More powerful than the characters in a novel, landscape becomes an externalization of the profusion and chaos of an American aesthetic. In this regard, it can be distinguished from a European poetics:

la poétique du continent américain, que je caractérise comme étant d'une quête de la durée s'oppose en particulier aux poétiques européennes qui se caractériseraient par l'inspiration et l'éclatement de l'instant. (p. 254)

(the poetics of the American continent, which I characterise as being a search for temporal duration, is opposed in particular to European poetics, which would be characterised by the inspiration or the sudden burst of a single moment.)

In order to demonstrate his point, Glissant cites the works of Jacques Roumain, Alejo Carpentier, Gabriel García Márquez, William Faulkner, among others. In these writers he identifies the forest as the 'parole du paysage' and not the economy of the meadow or the serenity of the spring (p. 255), that forms Europe's pastoral tradition.

Time and space are, as always, inextricably intertwined in Glissant's thinking. *Le discours antillais* also offers a sustained meditation of the quarrel with history in the New World. Glissant quotes with approval the St. Lucian poet Derek Walcott's affirmation, 'sea is history'. He develops Walcott's idea that a linear, progressive view of history is a dangerous longing in the New World. Both those who venerate the past and those who violently reject it inevitably perpetuate it.[19] Glissant too eschews this view of history, which he characterises as History with a capital 'H' for a multiplicity of histories. As he says, 'Les histoires lézardent l'Histoire' ('histories [stories] fissure History', p. 433). The totalizing, triumphant view of history as a single process is rejected for a vision of intricate branching and unceasing accumulation in which adaptation and creolisation are the prevailing forces. Traditional 'History' is not only, as Orwell wrote, 'written by winners' but is part of a larger impulse to shape and control human experience. As Claude Lévi-Strauss explained, 'the historian and the agent of history choose, sever and carve . . . for a truly total history would confront them with chaos'.[20] History as universal design is then doomed to selection omission and distortion. It is in opposition to this paradigm that Glissant advances the *opacité* of histories, which subverts the coherent, transcendental pattern.

Le discours antillais can be read, then, as an elaboration of a discourse, poetics of a rhetoric of the Caribbean. In this regard, Glissant is not overly prescriptive and he refrains from turning the text into a manifesto. The American artist is described in terms that immediately recall the imagery of *La case du commandeur*:

Nous sommes les casseurs de pierre du temps. Nous ne le voyons pas s'étirer dans notre passé (nous porter tranquilles vers l'avenir) mais faire irruption en nous par blocs, charroyés dans des zones d'absence où nous devons difficilement, douloureusement, tout recomposer si nous voulons nous rejoindre et nous exprimer. (p. 225)

(We are time's stonebreakers. We do not see it stretch into our past (calmly carry us into the future) but thrust up in us like rocks, transported in fields of oblivion where we must, with difficulty and pain, put it all back together if we wish to make contact with ourselves and achieve self-expression.)

The role of 'stonebreaker' is related to another reference to the writer as a 'forceur de langage', someone who creatively forces the idiom of the community to the surface.

In this concern with language, Glissant projects into writing values and energies associated elsewhere with the graphic and oral sign. This means that the ideal language of literary expression will not be a Mallarméan 'purification' or asceticism, a cleaning up of a clogged, contaminated language. Nor will there be the emphasis on the hallowing, ordaining power of the word (*verbe*) that one finds in Claudel or Perse. Glissant argues for a discourse that is more intuitive, looser, more Baroque (p. 463). His poetics of the 'other' America dictates that the artist must:

'provoquer' un langage-choc, un langage antidote, non neutre, à travers quoi pourraient être réexprimés les problèmes de la communauté (p. 347)

('provoke' a shock language, an antidote language, a non-neutral one, through which could be expressed the problems of the community.)

The ultimate ambition of producing a 'poétique liberée' for the Caribbean, whose form remains unknown, means the modest acceptance of literature of the present as a preface to a future literature.

Glissant, in recommending a sustained and radical demystification of languages, both French and Creole, accepts that the writer runs the risk of at least temporary isolation.

La fonction de l'écrivain dans un tel contexte, fonction de chercheur et d'explorant, l'isole souvent du langage 'actuel' et par conséquent d'un lecteur 'quotidien'. (p. 347)

(The function of the writer in such a context, function of researcher and explorer, often isolates him from the language 'in present use' and consequently from the 'everyday' reader.)

Until a liberated poetics emerges, the writer must practise a forced poetics, for the book is 'l'outil de la poétique forcée' (p. 451) ('the tool of a forced poetics').

Le discours antillais comes to a close with the feeling that literature is inadequate where other imaginative strategies are more successful. In the final part of the work, Glissant examines the sculpture of the Cuban Augustin Cardenas, whose work is featured on the cover of this book of essays. In the work of this artist of the 'other' America, Glissant identifies the poetics of orality, duration and cultural relating. Cardenas's art is not 'un cri'; it is 'un discours'. It becomes not simply a masterpiece but the exemplary expression of a communal Caribbean discourse, described in the following terms:

La poétique de Cardenas . . . rejoint la tradition de fêtes orales, le rythme du corps, le continu des fresques, le don de la mélopée. D'une oeuvre à l'autre, c'est le même texte qui se dit . . . Il assemble ainsi une rhétorique de la durée. (p. 448)

(Cardenas's poetics . . . connects with the tradition of oral celebration, the rhythm of the body, the continuity of frescoes, the gift of melody. From one work to another, the same text is articulated . . . In this way he puts together a poetics of duration.)

In Cardenas's creation of what Glissant calls the sculpted word, an American discourse manifests itself.

In contrast to the writer's struggle with a forced poetics, frozen rocks of time and an inchoate collectivity, the sculptor works more freely within the *langage* of the group. Cardenas's sculpture straddles the traditional and the modern. His work draws as much on Arp and Brancusi as it is shaped by orality and a carnival of forms. In his effusive praise for the work of the Cuban sculptor, Glissant suggests an ideal poetics of *Antillanité*. A Caribbean discourse is epitomised in Cardenas's sculptured forms in a way that cannot be fully conveyed through theoretical exposition.

CHAPTER 6

A poetics of chaos

The art of our time is noisy with appeals for silence.

Susan Sontag

Glissant's work in the eighties is marked by an increasing distrust of the written word and a marked unease with the literary text. This trend is already apparent in 1981. In *La case du commandeur*, Mycéa rejects Mathieu's continuous theorizing and defiantly accumulates feelings as mineralised units or 'rocks' within herself. In *Le discours antillais*, the exemplary artist of the Americas is not a writer but the Cuban sculptor Cardenas, who does not suffer from the constrictions of the 'forced poetics' of writing. This scepticism is intensified in the 1980s as later works question radically, even self-consciously at times, the role of the writer and the act of writing.

The grandiose concept of the writer as visionary, of writing as an ordering process and of the *discours généralisant* of intellectuals is the cause of great anxiety for Glissant in this decade.[1] This disaffection was first glimpsed in his early anti-Mallarméan impulses. Glissant now fiercely rejects any belief that the world was meant to be raw material for a book or could be fully explained by any theory. The notion of *Antillanité* is never developed into a full-blown theory. On the contrary, Glissant seems to move towards a more thoroughgoing exploration of models of disorder or chaos.

The implications of his new emphasis on unpredictability are significant. It means that his notion of *opacité* is given further prominence as he explores more singlemindedly the realm of the intuitive and the indeterminate as a corrective response to the systematizing pressures of assimilation and deculturation.[2] This form of resistance is not the heroic act of negation of the maroon. Rather, Glissant now concentrates on a more anonymous and pedestrian form of resistance. This he identifies in the patient, reticent presence of women who become increasingly important in his later work. As he argued in 1983, the Caribbean female 'porte en elle *une connaissance du réel camouflé* dont l'homme antillais ne maîtrise pas la pleine dimension' ('carries within herself *a knowledge of camouflaged reality* that Caribbean man cannot fully master').[3]

The epitome of this subversive *opacité* is the character Mycéa who dominates his later work. In *Pays rêvé, pays réel* ('Dream Country, Real Country') he describes her as:

Celle dont le poète est enchanté, qu'il nomme à chaque ventée. Mais dont les mots ne rendent compte.[4]

(The one with whom the poet is enchanted, that he names with each breath. But for whom words are inadequate.)

She represents the view that language and ideas need to be reinserted in the everyday and shaped by the corporeal, concrete particularity of given situations. Global theory and literary stylization run the risk of being inauthentic and irrelevant. In this regard, she appears as the author's *porte parole* in *Mahagony*.

Je vais barrer ma tête pour m'empêcher de retomber dans la cadence, dans les phrases jolies. Je vais m'entêter pour mettre un mot bosco . . . sur toutes les choses sans grandeur ni vanité. Un mot une [sic] herbage. Un herbage une parole.[5]

(I will tie my head to prevent myself from lapsing into rhythm, into fine phrases. I will force myself to put a crude word . . . on all things without grandeur or vanity. One word for one field of grass. One field of grass for one utterance.)

Glissant seems to be appealing for a kind of silence around words, for an eschewing of stylization and pedantry. There has always been in Glissant's work an acute awareness of the capacity of abstract thought to falsify experience, of the risk of gratuitous stylization that exists in the literary text. Now there seems to be greater urgency in his desire to close the gap between art and experience in order to create a more immediate, oral, corporeal language. As he writes towards the end of *Mahagony*:

A la croisée des vents, le bruit des voix accompagne les signes écrits; disposés en procession pathétique sur la cosse ou le parchemin; le dessin gagne encore. Mais qui parle, c'est l'écho infinissable de ces voix. (p. 230)

(At the crossroads of winds, the sound of voices accompanies the written signs; arranged in a pathetic procession on the pod or parchment; the design still takes shape. But who is speaking, it is the unending echo of these voices.)

This chapter, not surprisingly, ends with a glossary, an inventory of words, which are allowed to have a fuller resonance outside of writing and narrative: 'la chose écrite a besoin de glossaire, pour ce qu'elle manque en écho ou en vent' ('the written thing needs a glossary, to make up for what it lacks in resonance or air', p. 230).

It is, perhaps, significant that after his monumental book of essays *Le discours antillais* Glissant should turn to poetry. *Pays rêvé, pays réel* deals with one of the thematic commonplaces in the region's literature, Africa and the Caribbean, the dream country and the real one. Glissant, however, deals with this important issue in an unusual way. A key to Glissant's approach to this theme can be found in a short essay on Wifredo Lam published in 1983 and entitled 'Lam, l'envol et la réunion'. Again it is a non-literary work that provides Glissant with an insight into how a subject would be treated. He observes that in Lam's paintings you have a rehabilitation of African forms not in a clichéd way but 'dans leur mouvement essentiel'. This essential movement is identified in forms and signs which 's'élancent dans *toutes les directions* et s'achèvent, c'est-à-dire se réalisent, dans l'inattendu de l'énorme relation mondiale' ('shoot off in *all directions* and achieve a final form, that is their fullest manifestation, in the unexpected expanse of global relating').[6]

What Glissant is insisting on in his treatment of Lam's use of African symbols in their transmutation and recuperation. The multiplying of forms, the profusion of vegetation, the proliferation of signs are central to Lam's aesthetic. It is, as Glissant defines it, 'une poétique non pas de l'arbre mais de la végétation' ('a poetics not of the tree but of vegetation').[7] This shift in emphasis to *végétation* or *herbage* we have already seen is part of Glissant's present insistence on the value of the multiple over the unique, the pedestrian over the heroic. Africa is not now evoked in terms of defiant maroons or exiled kings. Instead Glissant argues that Africa has always been a living entity in the collective unconscious of the Caribbean people.

Au fond, la trace est vraiment trace, c'est-à-dire que c'est une donnée de l'inconscient collectif . . . Mais ce qui me paraît fondamental, s'agissant de cette question, c'est le tourment du Martiniquais qui, même quand il se clame citoyen francais . . . le clame avec une telle agressivité qu'on sent bien qu'il y a là quelque chose d'autre.[8]

(Deep down, the trace is really a trace, that is a component of the collective unconscious . . . But what seems essential to me, on this same question, is the torment of the Martiniquan who, even when he declares himself a French citizen . . . does it so aggressively that one feels that there is something else involved.)

Consequently, *Pays rêvé, pays réel*, unlike *Boises*, is not the tortured evocation of a dried up culture but a more passionate affirmation of Martiniquan *opacité*. It is an investigation of how the past remains a fundamental trait in the unconscious, in the form of 'une sorte de douloureux regret' ('a kind of painful remorse'). He adds, 'c'est pour moi, en littérature, ce qui est le plus passionant à pister' ('it is for me, in literature, what is the most exciting to track down').[9] Caribbean literature must, for Glissant, transcend the mere celebration of Africa for an exploration of the dynamic, hidden reality of Africa within the context of the Caribbean and the Americas. The poem's epigraph points to this new emphasis in referring to unspoken marvels and to liberty flowering on stumps of trees.

The dramatic poem begins and ends with sections entitled

'Pays'. They act as an overture and a finale to the main themes of the work. The musical parallel is further reinforced by the use of the word *chant* to describe the intervention of various voices in the text. This also suggests the poet's interest in the oral as against the written. This opposition is visible from the outset as a collective visceral scream is opposed to the coloniser's abstract notations:

> Nous râlions à vos soutes le vent peuplait
> Vos hautes lisses à compter
> Nous épelions du vent la harde de nos cris
> Vous qui savez lire l'entour des mots où nous errons
> Déassemblés de nous qui vous crions nos sangs. (p. 11)

> (We groaned below deck the wind filled
> Your heights smooth for counting
> We spelt the shreds of our screams in the wind
> You who can read the expanse of words in which we wander
> We broken up screaming our blood to you.)

'Pays' is a zone of calculated ambiguity. It is as much the dream land of Africa, as it is the dream land of the island and even the dreamscape of the text. Perhaps, even more significantly, it is the equivalent of a kind of speech that makes expression possible.

The identification of 'pays' and 'parler' comes early in *Pays rêvé, pays réel*:

> Ce pays qui s'efforce par semence et salaison
> Ce doux parler déraisonnable, d'étoiles rousses
> Entre roche d'eau et vert des profonds. (p. 13)

> (This country which tries seed and salt
> This soft unreasonable speech, of reddish stars
> Between sea rocks and the green depths.)

This country is carried in the wind as a scent, a cry and the past can be read in the waves of the sea. It is continuously shaped and fed by the 'sang de mer mêlé aux rouilles des boulets' ('the blood of the sea mixed with the rust of the weights'). The past is not lost but permanently wedded to the present.

> Nous fêlons le pays d'avant dans l'entrave du pays-ci
> Nous l'amarrons à cette mangle qui feint mémoire. (p. 17)

(We shatter the former country in the fetters of this one
We tie it to this mangrove which feigns memory.)

The poem then traces the 'pays d'avant' and its creatures of legend who 'communiquent par des sens dont nous avons perdu l'usage' ('communicate with senses which we can no longer use', p. 29). These spirits have names – Ata-Eli, Laoka, Ichneumon, Milos – which are apparently invented by the poet. They live on in the tale. The peculiarities of the Caribbean folktale are suggested here, as it contains neither founding myths nor stories of filiation.

> Il n'est filiation ô conteur
> Ni du nom à la terre ni du vent
> A la cendre. Les fonds levèrent
> Il lève ces fonds marins dans nos antans et nos faims.
> (p. 33)

(There is no filiation O storyteller
Neither from the name to the earth nor from the wind
To the ashes. The depths arose
It raises the depths of the sea in our yesterdays and our
    hunger.)

A section of the poem is devoted to the storyteller Ichneumon's song. His advice is about finding one's sense of self in the world.

> Ne soyez pas les mendiants de l'Univers
> Quand les tambours établissent le dénouement. (p. 53)

(Do not be beggars of the Universe
When the drums herald the end.)

Among the creatures of legend, Glissant invents a spirit called Laoka who appears to be the spirit of the land, perhaps even the spirit of *opacité*. In this figure, Glissant locates the secret, repressed survival of the past, of the *pays d'antan*.

> Tu es l'autre raison, qui chemine au-dedans, où les boues
> Sont rouges de nos cris et la graisse sur les cheveux cille
> Tu es le goût caché que nous donnons à nos mots
> Dans la nuit quand la paille bouge le bambou craque. (p. 57)

(You are the other reason, which makes its way on the inside, where the mud
Is red with our screams and the grease on our hair seals
You are the hidden taste we give to our words
In the night when the straw moves the bamboo creaks.)

Laoka is also the spirit of the people that is retained despite the pressures of deculturation.

Tu es ce peuple, il le faut, qui gravit et son souffle
s'alourdit aux ravines où ne croît que notre trace. (p. 58)

(You are this people, of necessity, climbing upwards and whose breath
grows heavy in the gullies where only the trace of you grows.)

In Laoka's song, Milos the blacksmith and Ichneumon, the storyteller, live again to make the link between 'Le souffrir du pays d'antan/De la ravine délitée du pays-ci' ('The suffering of the former country/Of the exposed gully of this country', p. 63). In *Pays rêvé, pays réel*, the dense truncated fragments of earlier poems give way to a more relaxed, even celebratory mode. The warning is nevertheless apparent that if Milos, symbolizing productivity, and Ichneumon, the imagination which depends on productivity, are forgotten, the past dries up and the future remains unrealized.

Cantos 6 and 7 of the poem deal with the 'pays réel' through the fictional characters of Thael, Mathieu and Mycéa. Here images of privation and aridity are evident: 'Un homme très vieux ses jambes droites maigres' ('A very old man his legs straight thin'); 'Un enfant rond ses jambes rondes écartées' ('A round child its legs bowed splayed out'); 'Une mangouste fracassée' ('A mangoose shattered to pieces'); 'L'agouti s'entête/Sa patte droite est lacerée d'un épini' ('the bush rat persists/Its right paw ripped by a thorn'). Thael and Mathieu representing mountain and plain, past and present, dream and reality, symbolise a collectivity whose hidden *opacité* is likened to 'La roche accorée au coeur' ('The rock wedged in the heart'). This section ends with an evocation of the past as humbly, imperceptibly present in the spreading grass and the community's problematic relation to the country. Here 'dévirons', meaning turning away, suggests *dérivons*, drifting.

> Nos aieux tout du long couchés sur l'herbe à couresse,
>   soigneusement
> Nous dévirons au pays. (p. 77)

> (Our ancestors lying along the spreading grass carefully
> We turn away from the country.)

The penultimate section entitled 'Pour Mycéa' is about this increasingly important figure, the night that is within her and her intimate relationship to the land.[10] The land is first presented as the end of the journey, 'toute en jour où nous sommes venus . . . tes mots m'ont déhalé de ce long songe' ('the full light into which we came . . . your words woke me from this long dream'). This praise song to the land is extended to its incarnation, Mycéa.

Je t'ai nommée Terre blessée, dont la fêlure n'est gouvernable, et t'ai vêtue de mélopées dessouchées des recoins d'hier. (p. 83)

(I have named you wounded Earth, whose crack cannot be controlled, and I have dressed you with melodies unearthed from the crannies of yesterday.)

The poet's words are like water, flowing and drifting and incapable of taking hold of or penetrating the rocks of an opaque reality: 'l'eau de mes mots coule, tant que roche l'arrête, où je descends rivière' ('the water of my words flows, as long as rocks stop it, where like the river I come down'). Mycéa is the elusive opacity of this land, the fictional evocation of Laoka who forces the poet to confess his impotence.[11]

> Je hèle inattendue errance
> Tu sors de la parole, t'enfuis
> Tu es pays d'avant donné en récompense
> Invisibles nous conduisons la route
> La terre seule comprend. (p. 89)

> (I will call out to you unexpected drifting
> You come from the word, you fly away
> You are the former country given as recompense
> Invisible we wend our way
> Only the earth understands.)

In the final movement of the poem, Glissant affirms the existence of a stubborn capacity for resistance in the French Caribbean people. In 1984 Glissant expressed open amazement at the continued existence of 'la force de résistance' which is celebrated in the closing pages of *Pays rêvé, pays réel*.[12] In neither a preachy nor polemical way but in one of the more personal episodes of the poem, Glissant describes the exercise of the poetic imagination. He appears in his customary role as a poet on the beach facing the ocean's voices:

> La où pays et vents sont de même eau intarissable
> . . .
> J'ai tendu haut ce linge dénudé; la voix de sel
> Comme un limon sans fond ni diamant ni piège bleu
> A cet empan où toute lave s'émerveille de geler
> Devenant être, et elle prend parti d'un pur étant. (p. 94)
>
> (Where land and wind are all the same everlasting water
> . . .
> I have stretched high this bare cloth, the voice of salt
> Like timeless silt neither diamond nor blue illusion
> On this span where lava marvellously freezes
> Becoming form, and taking shape in a pure being.)

As was first suggested in *Soleil de la conscience*, it is the threshold of the sand facing the open sea that is the poet's exemplary space.

The poem does not linger on this personal note but presents the collective 'we' growing from 'le cri, éclaboussé/Le long cri des oiseaux précipités dans cette mer' ('the shriek, spattered/ The sustained shriek of birds plunging into this sea') to the sense of the sea as all-embracing, restless and ever-changing, from which a certain truth must be drawn as with a net.

> L'oeuvre que nous halons est un songe de mer
> Nous reconnûmes le sésame et la soierie émerveillée.
>   (p. 97)
>
> (The work that we haul in is a dream of the sea
> We recognised the sesame and the silken marvels.)

The poem ends with a vision of a sea-derived people, who find a new space, a new identity and ultimately the experience of healing old wounds. The 'pays rêvé' becomes real.

Voici ô dérivée nous nous levons de bonne houle
Tu es nouvelle dans l'humus qui t'a hélée
Une grotte a ouvert pour nous sa parenté
D'île en cratère c'est éclat de lames bleuité
Encore et brûlis de l'eau d'un mancenillier
Je prends ma terre pour laver les vieilles plaies. (p. 99)

(Here O drifting one we rise from the good surf
You are new in the humus that called out to you
A grotto has prepared for us its welcome opening
In this cratered island there is the explosion of waves,
Still blue and the burning sap of the machineal
I take my earth to wash away old wounds.)

Despite its title, what is most striking about the pattern of imagery in the poem is the predominance of aquatic symbols and nautical terms throughout the text. The work itself, defined as 'un songe de mer', points to this insistence on marine symbolism. The transforming, restorative power of water and the harsh, bitter truth of the sea is central to the inscrutable, ambiguous nature of the experience of the 'pays réel'. This system of imagery and the faith in a kind of modest but persistent resistance dominate Glissant's creative imagination in these later years. Images of closure and oppression are explored in terms of openness and creative possibility, whether the hold of the slave ship or the closed world of the *habitation*.

The novel *Mahagony*, which appeared in 1987, turns specifically to the process of 'hauling the work from the sea of the unknown'. This prose fiction, in exploring variations on the theme of *marronnage*, focuses on the always inadequate process of attempting to note down, chronicle or relate the experience of *opacité*. The three predominant themes of *Mahagony* can be said to be the view of the writer as incompetent 'stonebreaker', the need to relate heroic negation to more generalized, modest forms of resistance, and the fragmentation of fiction into a polyphonic quiltwork of stories. It is as if in this novel Glissant is enacting a complex and necessary dialogue between *marronnage* and *relation*, between life and literature, and even between characters and author. There is the overriding preoccupation with the need to create a literary language that would be palpable with convincing detail and would tingle with the specificity of lived experience. In all this, the aspect of Glissant's work that becomes increasingly evident is what one critic calls the tone of 'celebratory epiphany'.[13] *Mahagony*, while maintaining a sceptical attitude to the literary act, expresses an abiding faith in the tenacity of the collective subject.

This novel returns to characters and the relationships first raised in *La Lézarde*. Mathieu, Thael and Mycéa all recur in this text but in different roles. Mycéa and Mathieu dominate and Thael now has a minor part. Glissant focuses even more attention on the figure of the narrator who had originally appeared as the 'narrateur enfant' of *La Lézarde*. In *Mahagony* Mathieu refers dismissively to the author as 'ce chroniqueur' or 'mon portraitiste'. In fact, there is an important relationship between Mathieu and Mycéa that is repeated in Mathieu and 'ce chroniqueur'. In the same way that Mycéa distrusts Mathieu's theorizing, so Mathieu claims a kind of *opacité* for himself in *Mahagony* and criticizes the narrator for distorting and simplifying his experience.

je ne savais pas qu'un raconteur d'histoires ce chroniqueur m'allait prendre bientôt (l'image qu'il avait de moi) pour personnage de ses récits, me conférant une exemplarité dont j'étais loin d'approcher la mécanique simplicité. (p. 18)

(I did not know that a storyteller – this chronicler – would soon take me (the image he had of me) as a character, endowing me with an exemplariness whose mechanical simplicity I was not even close to approaching.)

This tension between art and experience, or experience and writing, is a sustained motif in the text and is reflected in other relationships such as that of Eudoxie and the literate slave Hégésippe.[14] As the former says:

Il gratte sur papier ça même que je bouleverse dans ma nuit. C'est un jeu entre nous, il a son mystère, j'ai le mystère de son mystère. (p. 60)

(He scratches on that paper the same thing I turn upside down in my night. It is a game between us, he has his mystery, I have the mystery of his mystery.)

If *Mahagony* can be called a narrative for mixed voices, some of those voices are subversive and dissident.

Another feature that is shared with *La Lézarde* is the importance of landscape. *Mahagony*'s title is drawn from nature as is that of the earlier novel. In the same way that the Lézarde river represented freed consciousness, the mahogany tree represents the force of resistance that can be identified in various ways in the different characters. In this novel, the major figures in the narrative all are intimately related to the tree. The names Gani, Maho and Mani are all derived from 'mahogani' thereby intensifying the relationship between the natural and the human. Indeed, the title of the novel which suggests 'my agony' is related to human suffering. However, the reality of the *mahogani* hovers behind this apparent anguish, 'brûlant d'une foule muette et têtue' ('burning with a silent and stubborn multitude').

The mahogany is not the symbolic equivalent of the Césairean volcano. It is not the tree's tenacious solitude that provides a stable gravitational centre for Glissant's vision of time and space. Rather it releases a set of tensions, continuities and mutations that are part of a future-directed, outward-growing process. As a result this tree does not embody authentic origin or identity but is part of a series of trajectories that ultimately undermine or at least modify its supremacy and pre-eminence. In landscape, the patriarchal subject yields to a signifying chain of relationships. The landscape reveals a poetics of the decentred subject. The solitary tree gives way to spreading vegetation, dominated by the smell of charcoal pits.

Les ébéniers . . . leurs branchages et leurs racines partout alentour en forêt inachevée mais inviolée . . . la savane qui s'étendait plus loin et qui ondulait entre de maigres touffes de vétiver changeait de couleur avec les sautes du vent; elle paraissait aussi vierge que la jungle enfantée par les ébéniers, en sorte qu'on s'étonnait de découvrir soudain quatre ou cinq cases en contrebas . . . Une ravine courait au fond, qui marquait par en bas la ligne d'un horizon incalculé. Derrière l'embroussaillage des ébéniers un four à charbon grossissait inépuisable.

(The ebony trees . . . their branches and roots all around like an inviolate but incomplete forest . . . the savannah spreading further on and rolling between thin clumps of vetiver changed colour with changes in the wind; it seemed as virgin as the forest born from the ebony trees, so much so that you were surprised to discover suddenly four or five houses lower down . . . A gully ran along in the distance, marking the lower edge of an unexpected horizon. Behind the tangle of the ebony trees a charcoal oven burnt, fertile and inexhaustible.)

Further to strengthen this process of decentring, the tree, at the end of the novel, becomes 'multiplié en tant d'arbres dans tant de pays du monde' (p. 252).

It is because of the vital truth embodied in this landscape which represents the collective psychic life of the community that Glissant contemplates with horror the possibility of Martinique becoming a sanitized, harmless distraction for foreign tourists. The latent possibilities of growth and change are suppressed as Martinique becomes a successful experiment in the ultimate colony.

On a installé une verrière sur tout le pays, pour le distinguer des autres. Les cargos aériens entrent par des fenêtres qu'on ouvre à des heures fixes. On filtre l'air du dehors, pour que les microbes n'envahissent pas. (p. 178)

(A glass partition has been installed all around the country, in order to keep it apart from the rest. Transport planes enter through windows opened at specific times. The outside air is filtered so that no microbes can enter.)

This is an extreme version of the psychiatric hospital in *La case du commandeur*. Social and ecological engineering has ensured that the place is safe and the native, benign. Mt Pélée has been neutralized and a mechanical contraption placed within and snow planted at the summit. As Glissant wryly observes, 'seuls les natifs y ont pris goût' ('only the natives took to it'). As is observed at the end of this nightmare vision of the future, Martinique will have entered a phase of happy oblivion: 'Les gens heureux n'ont pas d'histoire' ('Happy people have no history').

The chaotic, unstable human and natural reality of *Mahagony* is the exact opposite of the sanitised order of this vision of dystopia. Chaos, *opacité* and resistance are all intertwined in the story of *Mahagony* which is centred on three episodes of *marronnage*. Each episode has a title that suggests past, present and future. 'Trou-à-Roches' refers to the chasm of the past filled with petrified moments of history; 'Malendure' suggests 'malemort' but with the more positive potential for endurance, and 'Le tout-monde' pulls together the lives of Glissant's main characters and their survival into the future. The last words of the novel are 'je vivrai longtemps'.

Each of these episodes is centred on a specific act of *marronnage* or *négation* – that of a youth named Gani in 1831; that of Beautemps, renamed Maho, in 1943; and that of Mani, a young misfit, in 1978. As Mathieu suggests, they represent at different times and in different contexts, 'la même figure d'une même force dérivée de son allant normal' ('the same expression of the same force derived from its normal momentum', p. 22). These stories epitomise the necessary and inevitable transformations of primordial *marronnage*. Less heroic, less noble than that of the original maroon, the stories of these latter-day *négateurs* nevertheless represent the persistent capacity of a community to resist. More than the primordial act of defiance, the poetics of duration and interrelation is essential to a history of the collective subject.

In the first story, the child Gani is from birth closely related to the mahogany tree. Indeed, he is called 'l'enfant le plant' as, according to the literate slave Hégésippe 'le père planta le placenta lors même que le plant' ('the father planted the placenta at the same time as the seedling', p. 39). As, following an African custom, plant and placenta are planted together, they grow as human and vegetable extensions of the same spirit of the landscape. We learn from Hégésippe's wife Eudoxie, that Gani's mother Jésabel did not want the child and that the night before Gani's birth, Jésabel was suckled by a snake. Her silent endurance of this nightmare allowed the child within her to survive. This motif, repeated in various earlier works, reappears here as an event in the life of an important character. Gani's father killed the snake and buried the placenta along with the snake's skin in the same hole in which the tree is planted (p. 52). To the origins of the child Gani is added the magical and fearsome force of the snake.

Gani epitomises pure revolt. Just as the tree grows to reveal human configurations, the branches suggesting a human face whose look resembled that of the Christ of Corcovado (p. 77), so Gani is irresistibly drawn to the freedom latent in the vegetation. He lives a life of *vagabondage* in defiance of the plantations and is secretly fed by the womenfolk, in particular a woman called Tani. The tree at this time is an extension of Gani's fierce and solitary revolt against the plantation system: 'il figurait un volcan bouillant dans la nuit' ('it looked like a volcano bubbling in the night'). Despite Tani's pleadings he does not give up his way of life as a maroon. Ultimately he is killed by the armed overseers who have been tracking him down. He is buried at the root of the mahogany tree which symbolically carries on his spirit of resistance (p. 95). Equally significant in the Gani episode is the fact that the young maroon could never survive as long as he did without the help of the women, that of Tani in particular. As important as Gani's act of defiance is the chain of reactions and consequences that follows. The modest collective efforts of the community are at least as significant as the act of the maroon that provoked them in the first place.

In the second episode, Glissant revives the story of the overseer who first appeared in *Malemort*. He is a legendary character called Beautemps, and as we learn in *Mahagony*, also called Maho, whose wife is raped by a *béké* (white creole) in 1936. In attempting to avenge her, he fails to kill the *béké* and is destined to live as a fugitive from then on. Beautemps/Maho is also witness to a political assassination by a hired killer called Odibert. Through sheer luck Odibert and the police manage to kill Beautemps. The latter is not a heroic rebel against the plantation system. Rather he is driven through circumstance to become a fugitive. If he is the reincarnation of the spirit of the mahogany or Gani, it is in a more ambiguous and certainly less glorious way.

The story of Beautemps/Maho is told in Felix's barber shop. He is a fugitive for seven years during which time, we are told,

he does not stray far from the mahogany tree (p. 149). He too is
provided with food by the women. In his case, Adoline plays
the same role as Tani in the earlier story. Even after her death
other women continue to provide food for this legendary fugi-
tive. He is finally killed under the mahogany tree by the forces
of the law. The story ends with Odibert, the traitor and reincar-
nation of Garin of *La Lézarde*, for whom the community has no
name. He claims that it is his bullet that killed Maho, and
escapes to Dominica. His life is destined to be one of pointless
errance as he turns his back on *voisinage* with a stream of curses.

The third episode in *Mahagony* brings us into the present.
Here, the predominant motif is not the great trees of the past
but the tenacious, anonymous and disorderly grass that swarms
over everything. 'Cette herbe-là prend avantage sur les plants,
mal à l'aise dans ces temps-ci. L'herbe est en douce, elle couvre
sa misère' ('That grass overcomes plants, ill at ease in these
times. The grass spreads softly, it covers its mystery', p. 169).
Here, the story focuses on two episodes of *marronnage* – those of
Mani, friend of Mycéa's son Odono, and Marny, an outlaw
who benefited from the goodwill of the people of Saint-Thérèse
(pp. 198–9). Mani is the incarnation of disorder. The words
désordre and *driver* are associated with him as he is described as a
specialist in disappearances. He is part of a turbulent younger
generation. We have already had an insight into the self-
destructive force of these young people, this new 'herbage', into
the fascination that Odono had with speed in *La case du com-
mandeur*.

Mani's story is told by someone of his generation, Ida, the
daughter of Mycéa and Mathieu. Mani, who is unstable and
given to sudden disappearances, is not seen for seven days. No
one knows for sure what transpires during this short period of
marronnage. Ida collects what she can of the facts from 'L'enfant
des marins', a friend, a soldier, his girlfriend and a fisherman.
No one can furnish the full story. To complicate matters,
Marny escapes from prison at the same time and the latter's
escapades completely obscure what happens to Mani.

L'actualité de Marny refoulait au plus fond l'obscurité de Mani.
Celui-ci était allé au bout de sa solitude . . . Mani est entré seul dans

ce désert, simplement parce qu'il estimait qu'il devait essayer encore. C'est là qu'il a disparu pour toujours. (p. 205)

(The news of Marny pushed deep into the background Mani's obscurity. The latter had gone to the end of his solitude . . . Mani entered alone this desert, simply because he felt he should try again. That is where he disappeared for good.)

Both Marny and Mani, we are told, survive because of the daring and concern of various women. Ultimately their paths diverge. Mani's journey comes to an end when he encounters the mahogany tree. During the night of Mani's final disappearance, he and the tree become one.

Son corps . . . se fond dans la masse de feuillage qu'il a traînée jusqu'à cette cache. Le rêve le prend une fois encore. Il se réveille en sursaut. 'C'est le mahogani', pense-t-il. Alors, il se laisse aller au sanglotement de toutes ces ombres, de ces débris, devient roche qui dure, bois qui résiste. (p. 224)

(His body . . . melts into the mass of foliage which he has brought to his hideout. The dream takes hold of him once more. He wakes up with a start. 'It is the mahogany', he thinks. Then, he yields to the sobbing of all these shadows, this refuse becoming durable rock, resistant wood.)

Mani's final identification with the tree brings to a close the process started by Gani in 1815, when the tree was planted.

The story of parallel yet succeeding lives lies at the centre of *Mahagony*. However, this is not a simple story of heroism or celebration of the spirit of resistance. The point is made repeatedly that solitary resistance is not possible without the assistance of those who remain behind to endure hardship. This role is played by a series of women in this novel – Eudoxie, Tani, Jésabel, Adonie, Artémise, Adelaide, Ida and Mycéa. In the figure of Mycéa we have, perhaps, the ultimate act of *marronnage*, the subversion of the symbol of negation. It is Mycéa's hand that takes hold of a small plant and pulls it out of the ground. It comes up attached to a small rock by its roots. It is by defiantly facing the plant and its hidden mineralised treasure that she is free to turn away.

A la fin je vous déracine, dit-elle, mais je sais bien que vous allez repousser n'importe où, vous allez voir. Elle jeta loin la roche et la tige violacée, marcha au large du trou infinitésimal . . . Il y avait dans l'air une légèreté d'herbage. (p. 236)

(At the end I uproot you, she says, but I know full well that you will sprout again somewhere, you shall see. She threw the rock and the bluish stem far away, walking away from the tiny hole . . . In the air there was the lightness of grass.)

For the spirit of the mahogany to survive, there must be a new flexibility and capacity for adaptation. As in other works, Glissant is urging that the single act of defiance, of *fulgurance*, be seen in terms of a chain of relationships which involve more humble and less glorious forms of resistance. The quiet resolve of the women in these stories falls into this category of patient yet tenacious courage. As Mathieu says, he dreams of telling the stories of these women who 'avaient maintenu la force, permis la survie, qui avaient amassé suffisamment d'énergie pour préserver les plants et les herbages' ('had maintained the strength, allowed the survival, who had amassed enough energy to preserve plants and clumps of grass', p. 246). Mycéa's discourse on grass emphasizes the nameless, uncontrollable nature of this vegetation that survives even after huge trees have fallen. As she says, do not ask for the names. Grass is classified by categories: climbing grass, staining grass, medicinal grass, wild grass, rebellious grass, razor grass and so on.

Along with this procession of women that keep the idea of resistance alive, Glissant points to the equally important and equally modest *marronnage* of the storyteller. *Mahagony* is also about a succession of storytellers who keep the dream alive.

Gani confie son rêve à Tani qui le rapporte à Eudoxie qui le conte à la veillée. Le rêve est embelli de place en place, d'âge en âge . . . Le rêve est-il de Gani ou, tout autant, de la procession de conteurs assurés qui se relayèrent pour le sauver de l'oubli? (pp. 213–14)

(Gani entrusts his dream to Tani who reports it to Eudoxie who relates it at the wake. The dream is embellished from occasion to occasion, from time to time . . . Is it Gani's dream or, as much, that of the procession of confident storytellers who succeed each other in order to save it from oblivion?)

Mahagony is filled with these storytellers or chroniclers who relay and relate. They include those who gather data like Mathieu and Ida, those who use their literacy to subvert like Hégésippe and the 'chroniqueur', those who simply tell stories, like Longoué, Lanoué, Mycéa and Eudoxie. No one has a particular hold on truth. They all, to a greater or lesser extent, depend on legend. Mathieu's experience is characteristic of them all:

Relayant ce vieux houeur, comme l'amarreur pas à pas suit le coupeur, et il assemble et lie de feuilles sèches mêlées aux feuilles vertes les bouts que celui-ci a taillés, ainsi amassai-je bruits et rumeurs tombés à la fin de cette histoire, en quantité suffisante pour m'y perdre. (p. 76)

(Relaying this old hoer, like the tier following step for step the cutter, and he bundles and ties dry leaves along with green ones, the joints of cane the latter has cut, so I collected sounds and rumours fallen at the end of this story, in a sufficient quantity to lose myself.)

The image of the storyteller as necessary but inevitably inept 'stonebreaker' recurs again and again here. The apologetic, self-effacing narrator in *La Lézarde* was the first manifestation of this image of the person whose relating is vital to the process of interrelating. This view of the narrator is in keeping with the subversion of the heroic and the patriarchal in this novel.[15] He does not possess superior knowledge or understanding. In the same way as the maroon is demystified, so is the author. The unpretentious voice of the one 'whose name is the reverse of Senglis', appears directly in a short section towards the end of the novel. In confessing his inadequacies as 'l'homme d'écriture', his narrative breaks down to a glossary, an alphabetical list of words which are allowed to have their own freed resonance. As he admits, 'La raideur à élucider l'histoire cède au plaisir des histoires' ('The rigid elucidation of a single history yields to the pleasure of many stories'). This chronicler or portraitist suffers the, not unexpected, indignity of his protagonist Mathieu rebelling against him to become a *conteur* in his own right and suffer the same anxieties as his original creator.

Where words are unreliable and writing falsifies, sensation becomes the only reliable form of contact with reality. In the first chapter of the book, Mathieu admits to this need for bodily contact, a palpable relationship with reality. 'Le bord du monde est là, il n'est que de le toucher en avancant la main comme une feuille' ('The edge of the world is there, you can touch it by reaching your hand out like a leaf', pp. 34–5). The sensuous immersion of the self in the world, ever present in Glissant's work, is made even more emphatic in *Mahagony*. In this shift from the cerebral to the physical, Mycéa attains her true importance. In the chapter entitled 'Remontée' ('Climb Back'/'Recovery'), Mycéa's hand fumbles in the dark pushing past leaves into the hole of the unknown ('l'abîme') beyond vision. The hand like an autonomous, sensorial field tentatively probes the diverse, unsuspected, multiple life forms in the dark. It is a kind of corporeal therapy for Mycéa but does not bring immediate elucidation. The importance of this kind of contact is signalled by the hand on a tree trunk on the cover of the novel.

What the dark teaches, in terms of renewal and endurance, is a significant dimension to this novel. This is where the storyteller attempts tentatively to offer a meaning for the dark. Mathieu, in his new role of *conteur*, reflects on three phases of the unknown in the journey to the New World. Mathieu defines these three experiences of the unknown or the 'gouffre' as: the belly of the slave ship, the depths of the ocean and the unknown destination of the vessel. Interestingly, Glissant offers an alternative to the traditional commonplace of Mother Africa. He suggests the slave ship as a mother, a terrible womb that reshaped a people definitively:

C'est que cette barque est une matrice, le gouffre-matrice. Généra-trice de votre clameur. Productrice aussi de votre unanimité. Car si vous êtes seul dans l'épouvante, vous partagez déjà l'inconnu avec quelques-uns que vous ne connaissez pas encore. Cette barque ronde, si profonde, est votre mère, qui vous expulse. (pp. 215–16)

(The fact is this ship is a womb, the gulf-womb. The genetrix of your screams. Procreator also of your shared experience. For if you are alone in your fear, you already share the unknown with some you do not yet know. This round, so deep vessel is your mother, which pushes you out.)

Ultimately, *Mahagony* can be seen in terms of the agony of rebirth and survival. It is this theme and the very image of the 'gouffre-matrice' that is elaborated in Glissant's most recent book of essays *Poétique de la relation* ('Poetics of Relating') which appeared in 1990.[16]

A 'poetics' here implies not a political manifesto or a polemical text but an imaginative reflection on the notion of *relation* in the sense of cross-cultural relating, intra-cultural relating and relating through narrative or storytelling. *Poétique de la relation* is an exuberant tangle of puns, neologisms and *double-entendres* which inevitably reminds the reader of the earlier essays. Glissant is conscious of the fact that these recent essays are an elaboration of old ideas and not a brand new departure. He says, for instance, that the present work can be seen as 'l'écho recomposé ou la redite en spirale' ('the reconstituted echo or the spiral repetition') of the earlier works *L'intention poétique* and *Le discours antillais*. Towards the end, he responds to the observation that many of the present ideas were previously raised in *Soleil de la conscience*, thirty years earlier, by saying that:

Nous nous déplaçons à la surface, dans l'étendue, tramant notre imaginaire, et ne remplissant pas les vides d'un savoir. (p. 223)

(We move along the surface, across the expanse, weaving our imaginative pattern, and not filling holes with knowledge.)

The image of weaving, of a texture or a quiltwork of ideas, recurs constantly in *Poétique de la relation*. It is as if Glissant is deliberately avoiding the temptation of a conceptual linearity or progression for a process of amalgamation, accumulation and circularity.

In this regard, these essays also seem to pick up where *Mahagony* left off. The image of the 'gouffre-matrice' is repeated in *Poétique de la relation*. It is the controlling image of the first essay 'La barque ouverte' ('The Open Ship'), but, as

Glissant has observed, repeated in a spiral pattern. The idea of the productive experience of the unknown leads Glissant to speculate about the Caribbean experience in terms of the global fear of the unknown, 'une inquiétude généralisée' (p. 176). In a world where the ruins of ideology, the devastation of technology and the failure of old certitudes proliferate, the Caribbean is one of those exemplary spaces where the unknown is part of the shared experience. In these essays, the system of the plantation is also conceived as a 'gouffre-matrice': 'La Plantation est un des ventres du monde' ('The plantation is one of the wombs of the world', p. 89). From this early concept of the unknown, Glissant speculates that there is another contemporary 'gulf' – the chaos of today's world – that is the challenge of the future.

Some of these essays were first given as talks on a diverse range of occasions, from a meeting of Martiniquan science teachers to literary colloquia. Consequently, they retain elements of improvisation, digression and orality that point to their beginnings as public performances. However, despite this aspect of mental and professional *errance*, the essays are rooted in and shaped by what seems as much a mathematical as a poetic concept of chaos. Glissant's hypothesis is that the world today has become quite simply a zone of rapid, unceasing and often violent cultural encounters. In such a context of uncertainty and unpredictability, old symmetries are irrelevant and any attempt at systematic explanation is doomed to failure.

In his use of chaos theory, Glissant is suggesting that even the tiniest fluctuations in the most remote part of the world are interconnected with disproportionately larger, more important events elsewhere. Just as the flutter of a butterfly's wings in South America can produce a tornado in the Mid-West, so the systems of culture in the world are prone to massive convulsions from imperceptible causes. Modern physics is used by Glissant to elaborate a theory of creative disorder that transcends earlier notions of abject dependency and the deadly equilibrium that is the inevitable result of static ideas of centre and periphery. This dynamic, swirling vision of contemporary culture is central to Glissant's poetics of relating. It leads to new terms for describing this sense of global flux and fragmentation – 'le tout-monde', 'écho-monde', 'identité-relation' – and a revaluation of old terms such as *Baroque, opacité* and *nomadisme.*

It is within this context of indeterminacy and contingency that Glissant elaborates his poetics of relating which is the positive result of global chaos. Chaos for Glissant is a salutary state because it means the breakdown of systems of standardisation and uniformity, of 'l'universel généralisant' that is produced by imperialistic ideologies. If chaos means the alternative to this homogenizing force, it does not signify incomprehensible turbulence. 'Le chaos-monde n'est ni fusion ni confusion . . . Le chaos n'est pas "chaotique"' (p. 108). Here chaos theory and the poetic imagination have something in common.

la science du Chaos renonce à la puissante emprise du linéaire, conçoit l'indéterminé comme une donnée analysable, l'accident comme mesurable. La connaissance scientifique . . . développe ainsi une des façons du poétique, rejoignant l'ancienne ambition de la poésie de se constituer en connaissance. (p. 152)

(The science of Chaos rejects the powerful hold of the linear, conceives the indeterminate as analysable data, accident as measurable. Scientific knowledge . . . thereby develops a poetic mode, coinciding with the old ambition of poetry to constitute itself into a science.)

Science and poetry converge around the significance of the accidental and the unpredictable. Chaotic patterns, fractal swirls, entropic energy, all of interest to physicists and mathematicians, lead inexorably, for Glissant, towards the elaboration of a poetics that breaks with a mechanistic and systematizing view of the world.

The importance of the imagination as a form of knowledge recurs constantly in these essays. The book begins with the image of the gulf and ends with a final paragraph that is an actual prose poem, first published in 1989.[17] Poetry is seen here as an investigative tool, 'la pensée poétique'. As Glissant explains:

L'analyse nous aide à mieux imaginer; l'imaginaire, à mieux saisir les éléments (non premiers) de notre totalité. (p. 184)

(Analysis helps us to better imagine; the imaginative process, to better grasp the elements (not primary) of our totality.)

The value of poets and poetic systems in advancing thought is considered in 'Poétiques'. After a survey of the Baudelairean 'poétique des profondeurs' and the Mallarméan 'poétique du langage-en-soi', Glissant examines the 'poétique de la relation' that emerges in Rimbaud's sense of otherness within, as well as the attraction of otherness. The lure of diversity attracts Segalen, Malraux, Leiris and Claudel. Others like Saint-John Perse are drawn from the periphery to the centre. At present, centre and periphery become abolished as a 'nomadisme circulaire' becomes part of a modern poetics.

There is an interesting overlap between the kind of text described as 'neo-baroque', that transmits the experience of chaos, and the scientific reading of the world: 'Les conceptions actuelles des sciences recontrent et confirment cette extension du baroque' ('Present-day notions of the sciences coincide with and confirm this extension of the Baroque'). The Baroque with its emphasis on proliferation, excess, exuberance, becomes naturalized in a world of uncertainty and indeterminacy. The ideal text then becomes a kind of hyper-text which is not unidirectional or fixed but a web of segments that are interactive and polyvocal. These ideas raised in earlier essays now become part of a global phenomenon as rationalism becomes powerless in the face of the unknown (p. 91) and 'la parole baroque' becomes the only adequate representation of 'la relation vécue'.

It is this emphasis on textual *errance* and celebration of poetic error or accident that reveals Glissant's faith in the creative imagination and in the force of poetry. The 'chaos-monde' is capable of releasing a generalised poetic energy.

La force poétique (l'énergie) du monde, maintenue vive en nous, s'appose par frissons fragiles, fugitifs, à la prescience de poésie qui divague en nos profondeurs . . . la force jamais ne tarit, car elle est à elle-même turbulence. (p. 173)

(Poetic force (energy) in the world, kept alive within us, coexists in fragile elusive spasms with the visionary potential of poetry that rambles on deep within us . . . the force never dries up, because it is a self-activating turbulence.)

In confronting the question that poetry guarantees no concrete form of action, Glissant replies that it allows us better to understand 'notre action dans le monde' (p. 215). In a sense all theory is driven to poetic excess. A poetics then becomes the only possible theoretical response to the turbulence of the modern world.

The theory of *relation* is the main thrust of this book of essays. It takes notions of *errance*, *métissage* and creolisation to a new global level. Within this vision of widespread cultural encounter, whole cultures become fragmented into archipelagos of cultural units. In a world of several Africas, several Europes and so on, an extreme multilingualism is the inevitable destiny of all countries. Modern communication further exacerbates contact and diversity. What Glissant envisages is a new tower of Babel (p. 117). The major consequence of such dynamic linguistic diversity is the need to redefine old notions of identity. The old mechanisms of identity, the traditional process of recognition and delimitation, can no longer be maintained in a situation of cultural chaos. Identity is no longer stable and becomes threatened by otherness. Glissant uses the model 'identité-racine' ('root identity') yielding to 'identité-rhizome' ('rhizome identity') to describe a new concept of identity (p. 23). 'Root identity' is typified by a central, predatory downward-growing shaft. 'Rhizome identity' is characterised by horizontal encounter, not depth, and an infinite, multiple network of branching roots. This is the theoretical extension of the image of 'herbage' that replaces the giant mahogany in Glissant's *Mahagony*.

In this problematic area of self-definition, Glissant explores the twofold dynamic of *opacité* and *altérité*. The former is directed inward and the latter part of a necessary dialogue of mutual recognition. In a constant process of making and unmaking the subject, the 'other' is a necessary dialectical partner. Again, Glissant marks the break with traditional

identitarian thought: 'Aux idéologies d'indépendance nation-
ale, qui ont conduit les luttes de la décolonisation, se sont peu à
peu substitutués les pressentiments d'une interdépendance'
('The ideologies of national independence, which have led the
struggles for decolonisation, have been gradually replaced by
the intuition of interdependence', p. 157). This does not mean
a bland notion of universal culture. Glissant keeps alive the
notion of *opacité*, the irreducible singularity of a culture or a
language: 'La théorie de la différence est précieuse' ('The story
of difference is invaluable'). However, it must not exist in
either a hierarchical or a defensive way or lead to cultural
autism.

Glissant's vision of an ideal multilingual, multicultural
world is one in which one must generously accept 'le principe
d'altérité'. *Opacité/altérité* become the diastole and systole of
human relationships, the give and take of self-denial, self-
affirmation and recognition of the other.

Des opacités peuvent coexister, confluer, tramant des tissus dont la
véritable compréhension porterait sur la texture de cette trame et non
pas sur la nature des composantes . . . Il y aurait grandeur et
générosité à inaugurer un tel mouvement, dont le référent ne serait
pas l'Humanité mais la divergence exultante des humanités. (p. 204)

(Opacities can coexist, converge, weaving kinds of fabric whose true
meaning would be related to the interweaving of this weft and not to
the nature of its component threads . . . It would be a grand act of
generosity to launch such a movement, whose referent would not be
Humanity but the exuberant divergence of humanities.)

The texture of hybrid components is translated into a textual
strategy in the glossary of the text as Glissant presents a list
('litanie') of words that are held together by a comma, signify-
ing relationships; a hyphen, signifying opposition; a colon,
signifying a consecutive union.

This global vision is centred on the Caribbean. Here,
Glissant's often professed faith in small countries feeds the idea
of the 'chaos-monde': 'je cite la Caraïbe comme un des lieux
du monde où la relation le plus visiblement se donne, une des
zones d'éclat où elle paraît se renforcer' ('I cite the Caribbean

as one of the places in the world where interrelating most visibly operates, one of the flashpoints where it seems to be reinforced', p. 46). The Caribbean, unlike the Mediterranean, is not for Glissant the region of the transcendental self, of monotheism. As opposed to the Mediterranean, which concentrates, the Caribbean sea explodes outwards ('Une mer qui diffracte'). Here the experience of *relation* is expressed as *créolisation*, defined in terms of the accidental, the unpredictable, 'une dimension inédite qui permet à chacun d'être là et ailleurs, enraciné et ouvert' ('an unprecedented dimension which allows each one to be here and elsewhere, rooted and open', p. 46).

As formidably self-aware as he always is, Glissant relates this dazzling theoretical performance to a particular place where the work was put together – a beach at Diamant in Martinique.[18] Once again on this island–threshold, he can see St. Lucia in the south, while to the north are the looming heights of Martinique. The mechanism of *opacité/altérité* is suggested not only in this topography but in the sand itself. In the essay 'La plage noire', the beach at Diamant is described as covered with black sand, volcanic deposits brought down from Mt Pélée in the north 'Comme si la mer entretenait un commerce souterrain avec le feu caché du volcan' ('As if the sea maintained a subterranean relation with the secret fire of the volcano', p. 135). In the final essay in *Poétique de la relation*, 'La plage ardente', the volcanic lava is replaced on the beach by shining white sand. A different kind of order emerges within disorder and the beach becomes a haunt for tourists, at least for a while. In this cyclical process, this ordered disorder, Glissant senses the deeper truth about the region and the modern world.

The powerful subterranean force that regulates the surface manifestation of chaos appears as the force of poetic undertow in the creative imagination. This force is, for Glissant, almost impossible to control or suppress. In this final essay, an image of resistance, again drawn from landscape, sums up the irrepressible voice of the community:

On s'acharne à combler cette mangrove, pour y établir la patente de zones industrielles, de hauts lieux de consommation. Mais elle résiste encore. Mes amis m'ont mené là, dérivant à la découverte des points chauds, ces vases d'eau rouge qui glougloutent leurs brûlures, de place en place, dans les palétuviers. (p. 222)

(They struggle to cover this mangrove, to put in place the open space of industrial zones, of the commanding heights of consumerism. But it still resists. My friends took me there, wandering around to look for hot points, the pools of red water which gurgle their burning, from one place to another, in the mangrove.)

The opposition to *bétonisation*, the need to transcend a narrow *indépendantisme*, the defence of creole culture and the new regionalist resistance to assimilation are part of the legacy of Edouard Glissant's thought in the French Caribbean at the end of the twentieth century.[19]

As the 'lecteurs d'ici' become more numerous and a regional literary tradition becomes established, the importance of Glissant's oeuvre becomes increasingly apparent. This oeuvre is still very much a 'work in progress'.[20] This will always be the case because of its innate restlessness and circularity, as each theoretical construct is undone or extended by a deconstructing poetic energy. In a sense, there has always been a creative chaos to Glissant's thought because of the complexity that he brings to issues as well as the capacity of his imagination to renew itself. As *Poétique de la relation* ends Glissant withdraws from the beach at Diamant realizing that he cannot have the last word. Reality remains a sea of indeterminate flux, resisting total explanation. As in the final words of Walcott's *Omeros*, 'When he left the beach the sea was still going on.'[21]

Notes

1. CONTEXTS

1 *Le discours antillais*, Paris: Seuil, 1981, p. 258.

2 Glissant rewrites the Césairean lines by referring to 'ceux qui n'ont pas eu de voix et dont nous ne saurions être la voix: pour ce que nous ne sommes que partie de leurs voix' ('those who have no voice and whose voice we could never be: for the simple reason that we are but a part of their voices'). See *L'intention poétique*, Paris: Seuil, 1969, p. 197.

3 Richard Burton, 'Comment peut-on être Martiniquais? The recent work of Edouard Glissant', *The Modern Language Review*, Vol. 79, No. 2, April 1984, p. 302.

4 *The Middle Passage*, Harmondsworth: Penguin, 1969, p. 212.

5 *La Lézarde*, Paris: Seuil, 1958, p. 12.

6 *Soleil de la conscience*, Paris: Seuil, 1956, p. 43.

7 See Frantz Fanon, *Towards the African Revolution*, Harmondsworth: Penguin, 1970.

8 'Le romancier noir et son peuple', *Présence Africaine*, No. 16, October–November 1957, p. 29.

9 See Gaëton Picon, *Panorama de la nouvelle littérature française*, Paris: Gallimard, 1960, p. 243. Glissant refers to his admiration for Henri Pichette in a talk given at Temple University in 1988 entitled 'La Caraïbe, Les Ameriques et la poétique de la relation'. Also he speaks of Pichette and a number of other poets as his French contemporaries in *L'intention poétique*, pp. 241–2.

10 *Soleil de la conscience*, p. 19.

11 *Soleil de la conscience*, p. 61.

12 *Le discours antillais*, Paris: Seuil, 1981, p. 36.

13 A useful personal account of the activities of IME can be found in Beatrice Stith Clark's 'IME revisited' in *World Literature Today*, Vol. 63, No. 4, Autumn 1989, pp. 599–605.

14 The word *malemort* was used earlier by the Haitian novelist

Jacques Stephen Alexis in *Les arbres musiciens* (1958) in reference to the assault of American imperialism on the Haitian countryside: 'C'était la malemort, l'engloutissement d'un passé qui n'avait pas fini de durer' ('This was the undead, the swallowing up of a past which had not ceased lasting', p. 83).

15 *Monsieur Toussaint*, Paris: Seuil, 1961, p. 233.

16 *Acoma*, No. 2, July 1971, p. 42.

17 Amadou-Mahtar M'Bow, *Le temps des peuples*, Paris; Laffont, 1982.

18 *Magazine littéraire*, No. 221, July–August 1985, p. 52.

19 Priska Degras and Bernard Magnier, 'Edouard Glissant, préfacier d'une littérature future', *Notre librairie*, No. 74, 1984, p. 20.

20 *CARE*, No. 10, April 1983, p. 17.

21 In *Mahagony* the omniscient authority of the novelist is mocked as the main character Mathieu refuses to be manipulated by an inept *chroniqueur*. Glissant's self-consciousness in this regard seems very different from Césaire's grand declaration in 'Entretien', *Tropiques*, Vol. 1 (1941–5, reprint 1978) that he was personally responsible for an entire generation of Martiniquans: 'ils sont tous sortis de moi' (p. x).

22 Degras and Magnier, 'Edouard Glissant, préfacier d'une littérature future', p. 16.

23 *Le nouvel observateur* numero special 1991, p. 13.

24 Instead of seeing himself as the theoretician of a movement, Glissant simply refers to himself as 'préfacier'. In any case, the image of the *conteur*, recurrent in his work, recalls a time when tales were told and circulated without any concern about the author's identity or individuality.

25 Jean Bernabé, Patrick Chamoiseau and Raphael Confiant, *Eloge de la Créolité*, Paris: Gallimard, 1989, p. 26.

26 Maryse Condé, *La poésie antillaise*, Paris: Nathan, 1977, p. 71.

27 Patrick Chamoiseau, 'En témoignage d'une volupté', *Carbet*, No. 10, December 1990, p. 144. Raphael Confiant, a contemporary of Chamoiseau, has also acknowledged a debt to Glissant and dedicated his novel *Le nègre et l'amiral* (1988) to him.

28 Milan Kundera, 'The Umbrella, the Night World and the Lonely Moon', *The New York Review of Books*, Vol. 38, No. 21, 19 December 1991, p. 48.

29 Glissant's interest in dynamic and open-ended systems of thought has an interesting parallel in the movement called *Spiralisme*, begun by the mathematician and writer Franck Etienne in Haiti in the late sixties.

30 *Soleil de la conscience*, p. 69.

31 Chamoiseau, 'En temoignage d'une volupté', p. 143.

2. THE POETIC INTENTION

1 Léonard Sainville, *Anthologie de la littérature négro-africaine*, Paris: Présence Africaine, 1963, p. 93.

2 *L'intention poétique*, p. 35.

3 *L'intention poétique*, p. 36.

4 Barbara Johnson, *A World of Difference*, Baltimore: Johns Hopkins University Press, 1987, p. 60.

5 *L'intention poétique*, p. 64.

6 *Le discours antillais*, p. 258.

7 'Saint-John Perse et les Antillais', *La nouvelle revue Francaise*, No. 278, February 1976, p. 73.

8 René Depestre declared his allegiance to what he called 'Aragon's decisive lessons' and 'a new awareness of realism in poetry'. See *Les lettres Francaises*, No. 573, June 1975. Reprinted in *Optique*, No. 18, August 1955, pp. 46–50.

9 Glissant's views on the importance of landscape in literature, and in particular the shaping force of pastoral in European literature as opposed to the untamed landscape in the Caribbean imagination, are explained in an interview with Wolfgang Bader published under the title 'Poétique antillaise, poétique de la relation' in *Komparatistische Hefte*, Nos. 9–10, 1984, pp. 92–3.

10 *Soleil de la conscience*, p. 19.

11 *L'intention poétique*, pp. 143–4.

12 See interview published in *Cahiers Césairiens* No. 1, Spring 1974, p. 6, where Césaire refers to volcanic imagery.

13 Christophe Campos, 'Poetry and the Collective Experience' in *French Literature and its Background*, ed. John Cruickshank, Oxford: Oxford University Press, 1970, p. 148.

14 Gerald Moore, 'Leopold Sédar Senghor' in *A Celebration of Black and African Writing*, Zaria: Ahmadu Bello University Press, 1975, p. 108.

15 Octavio Paz, *The Bow and the Lyre*, Austin: University of Texas Press, 1973, pp. 254–5.

16 Roger Little, *Saint-John Perse*, London: The Athlone Press, 1973, pp. 93–4.

17 'Saint-John Perse et les Antillais', p. 70.

18 *L'intention poétique*, p. 121.

19 Derek Walcott, 'The Muse of History' in *Carifesta Forum*, ed. John Hearne, Kingston: Institute of Jamaica, 1976, p. 123. Another Caribbean writer who admired Perse was Alejo Carpentier. See 'Saint-John Perse, urbi et orbi' in *Chroniques*, Paris: Gallimard, 1983, pp. 485–9.

20 *Soleil de la conscience*, p. 41.
21 Saint-John Perse, *Exil* in *Eloges*, Paris: Gallimard, 1960, p. 1.
22 *Soleil de la conscience*, p. 41.
23 *Soleil de la conscience*, p. 17.
24 *L'intention poétique*, p. 49.
25 Jean-Pierre Richard, *Onze études sur la poésie moderne*, Paris: Seuil, 1964, p. 36.
26 *Le discours antillais*, pp. 228, 230.
27 Jean Paris, *Anthologie de la poésie nouvelle*, Monaco: Rocher, p. 50.
28 Beverley Ormerod, 'Beyond Negritude: Some Aspects of the Work of Edouard Glissant', *Savacou*, Nos. 11–12, 1975, p. 42.
29 *Soleil de la conscience*, p. 34.
30 *Les Indes*, 1956, reprinted Paris: Seuil, 1965, p. 123. Page numbers in the text are taken from this edition.
31 *Un champ d'îles* in *Les Indes*, Paris: Seuil, 1965, p. 28. Page numbers in the text are taken from this edition.
32 *Soleil de la conscience*, p. 22.
33 *L'intention poétique*, p. 48.
34 *Soleil de la conscience*, p. 54.
35 *Soleil de la conscience*, p. 54.
36 *L'intention poétique*, p. 48.
37 *Un champ d'îles*, p. 12.
38 *Un champ d'îles*, p. 13.
39 *Soleil de la conscience*, p. 3.
40 *Un champ d'îles*, p. 20.
41 *Soleil de la conscience*, p. 43.
42 *Soleil de la conscience*, p. 24.
43 *Soleil de la conscience*, p. 23.
44 *Soleil de la conscience*, p. 24.
45 Saint-John Perse, *Exil*, p. 155.
46 *La terre inquiète*, reprinted in *Les Indes*, Paris: Seuil, 1965, p. 56.
47 *La terre inquiète*, Paris: Dragon, 1954, p. 1.
48 *La terre inquiète*, p. 64.
49 *La terre inquiète*, p. 59.
50 *La terre inquiète*, p. 64.
51 *Les Indes*, p. 119.
52 *Soleil de la conscience*, p. 69.
53 Because of a general tendency to treat reality in an indirect manner, erotic images are rare in Glissant's work. However, in *Les Indes* the rape of the Indies provokes graphic images of sexual domination, for example 'Ne soyez pas mystérieuse, à ce point de cacher les merveilles de votre corps/Je veux descendre en vous aussi loin que la vie peut permettre' ('Do not be mysterious to the

point of concealing the wonders of your body/I want to go down into you as far as life will allow me,' p. 93.

54 Picon, *Panorama de la nouvelle littérature francaise*, p. 243.

55 Roger Toumson in 'Les écrivains afro-antillais et la réécriture' (*Europe*, No. 612, April 1980) seems to misread Glissant's relationship to Perse. He allows the issue of race to cloud his reading of both poets, when it comes to the figures of Columbus and Crusoe.

56 *Les Indes*, p. 123.

57 *Les Indes*, p. 128.

58 *Les Indes*, p. 129.

59 *L'intention poétique*, p. 187.

60 *Soleil de la conscience*, p. 70.

3. NOVELS OF TIME AND SPACE

1 See 'Le romancier noir et son peuple', *Présence Africaine*, No. 16, October–November 1957, pp. 26–31. In these 'notes towards a lecture' Glissant expresses the view that true freedom for the black novelist lay beyond 'revendication' and in the exploration of 'la réalité dans ses moindres replis' (p. 31). The image of folds or coils ('replis') is central to Glissant's theory of the Baroque and informs the meandering, unpredictable flow of the river in *La Lézarde*.

2 Richard, *Onze études sur la poésie moderne*, pp. 63–64.

3 *Le sel noir*, 1959 reprinted Paris: Gallimard, 1983, p. 69. Salt is so closely related to knowledge in this work that one feels that if it were an essay it would have been called 'Le sel de la conscience'. The enigmatic image of black salt is obviously more appropriate for poetry.

4 *Le sel noir*, 1983 edition, p. 72.

5 *Le sang rivé*, Paris: Présence Africaine, 1961, p. 9.

6 A poem such as 'Eléments' contains a reference to the serpent image of *Soleil de la conscience*: 'Toi serpente et labourée! Moi, écume de tes pas' ('You snakelike and furrowed! I, foam in your wake'). 'L'arbre mort et vivant' evokes *Un champ d'îles*.

7 *Le sang rivé*, p. 19.

8 *Le sang rivé*, p. 32.

9 *Le sang rivé*, p. 25.

10 *Le sang rivé*, p. 17.

11 *Présence Africaine*, No. 22, October–November 1958, p. 118.

12 Beverley Ormerod, *An Introduction to the French Caribbean Novel*, London: Heinemann, 1985, p. 39.

13 *La Lézarde*, Paris: Seuil, 1958, p. 224. Page numbers in the text are taken from this edition.

14 *L'intention poétique*, p. 205.

15 *Le discours antillais*, p. 198.

16 *Le discours antillais*, p. 199.

17 *L'intention poétique*, p. 187.

18 Bernadette Cailler, *Conquérants de la nuit nue*, Tubingen: Gunter Narr, 1988, p. 160.

19 *Le discours antillais*, p. 152. In *Le quatrième siècle* (p. 255), when Mathieu is forced to face the complexity of the past and reject his early identification with the heroes of Westerns shown at El Paraiso. Glissant clearly focuses on the Western as a New World phenomenon which distorts history and human relationships. Again, in *L'intention poétique* (p. 175) he refers to the simplifying violence of the Western.

20 Ormerod, *An Introduction to the French Caribbean Novel*, p. 39.

21 Richard Burton, 'Comment peut-on être Martiniquais? The recent work of Edouard Glissant', *The Modern Language Review*, Vol. 79, No. 2, April 1984, p. 305.

22 Recent novels by Patrick Chamoiseau (*Chronique de sept misères*) and Raphael Confiant (*Le nègre et l'amiral*) indicate this intense interest in Martinique's enforced self-sufficiency during the war years.

23 Even the best critics can succumb to this temptation of seeing Thael as a saviour. In a clear and full treatment of the novel, Beverley Ormerod likens Thael to Roumain's hero. See *An Introduction to the French Caribbean Novel*, p. 44.

24 Jacques André, *Caraibales*, Paris: Ed. Caribéennes, 1981, p. 161.

25 Perhaps Thael and Garin's descent along the river can be likened to the mock combat of the *laghia*, a traditional Martiniquan dance in which two partners go through the motions of a fight without touching each other.

26 The end of *La Lézarde* is strongly reminiscent of a similar scene in Djuna Barnes's *Nightwood* where the character, Robin, is attacked by a dog. Glissant expressed great admiration for Barnes's novel in *Les lettres nouvelles*, Vol. 5, No. 55, Dec. 1957.

27 Burton, 'Comment peut-on être Martiniquais?', p. 304.

28 *Poétique de la relation*, p. 86.

29 *Poétique de la relation*, p. 71.

30 *L'intention poétique*, p. 175.

31 Cailler, *Conquérants de la nuit nue*, p. 115.

32 *Le discours antillais*, p. 148.

33 *L'intention poétique*, p. 175.

34 *Poétique de la relation*, p. 86.
35 *L'intention poétique*, p. 182.
36 *Poétique de la relation*, p. 80.
37 *Poétique de la relation*, p. 89.
38 Patrick Chamoiseau, Raphael Confiant, *Lettres créoles*, Paris: Hatier, 1991, p. 36.
39 *Lettres créoles*, p. 62. This comment does bring to mind the victory of the *representant* in *La Lézarde* as he stands in the dark, before his public, in a circle of torches.
40 *L'intention poétique*, p. 179.
41 *Le quatrième siècle*, Paris: Seuil, 1964, p. 17. Page numbers in the text are taken from this edition. In her article on the figure of the 'quimboiseur', Simone Henry-Valmore mentions Glissant's view of the inexorable degeneracy of this figure over time because he has been stripped of his cultural function. See 'Une figure de l'imaginaire antillais: Le quimboiseur' in *Les temps modernes*, April–May 1983, Nos. 441–2, p. 2093.
42 The Martiniquan identification of time with disaster is discussed in *Le discours antillais*, p. 131.
43 The prevalence of this image of the whirlwind is also evident in other writers admired by Glissant. In Alejo Carpentier's *Kingdom of this World* a 'great green wind blowing from the ocean' brings the story to an end. In Márquez's *One Hundred Years of Solitude* Macondo becomes a 'whirlwind of dust and rubble'. Jacques Stephen Alexis similarly invokes the 'Vieux Vent Caribe' in his *Romancéro aux étoiles*, as does Aimé Césaire at the end of the *Cahier*.
44 In 1963 Glissant wrote but never published a play *Rêve de ce qui fut la tragédie d'Askia* which focuses on the beginnings of this rivalry.
45 Cailler, *Conquérants de la nuit nue*, p. 114.
46 *Le discours antillais*, p. 285, n. 5.
47 It is also Garin the assassin's sign in *La Lézarde*.

4. WRITING THE 'REAL COUNTRY'

1 Quoted in Susan Frutkin, *Aimé Césaire, Black between Worlds*, Miami: Centre for Advanced International Studies, University of Miami, 1973.
2 *L'intention poétique*, Paris: Seuil, 1969, p. 190. Page numbers in the text are taken from this edition.
3 Ormerod, *An Introduction to the French Caribbean Novel*, p. 38.
4 Beatrice Stith Clark, 'IME Revisited: Lectures by Edouard Glissant on Socio-cultural Realities in the Francophone Antilles', *World Literature Today*, Vol. 63, No. 4, Autumn 1989, pp. 599–605.

5 For a good discussion of the Martiniquan intellectual's response to Assimilation, see Richard Burton, 'Between the Particular and the Universal: Dilemmas of the Martinican Intellectual' in *Intellectuals in the Twentieth Century Caribbean*, Vol. 2, ed. Alistair Hennessy, London: Macmillan, 1992, pp. 186–210.

6 Cf. *Poésie et connaissance* in *Aimé Césaire: L'homme et l'oeuvre*, ed. Kesteloot and Kotchy, Paris: Présence Africaine, 1973. In general Glissant's rereading of some of the poets who are claimed as ancestors by the negritude poets is revealing. For instance for Senghor, Perse and Claudel are prophets of cultural wholeness and universal synthesis. The logocentric belief in the ordering and ordaining word is criticized by Glissant as a dangerous illusion.

7 Césaire himself was aware of the danger of either extreme, as could be seen in his *Lettre à Maurice Thorez* (Paris: Présence Africaine, 1967), but remained ideologically incapable of providing a solution.

8 Glissant's later theoretical formulations (*Antillanité* and creolisation) already exist in embryonic form of these early reflections on Caribbean culture. The 1980s and 1990s would produce more elaborate, oracular versions.

9 *Malemort*, Paris: Seuil, 1975, p. 231. Page numbers in the text are taken from this edition.

10 *Monsieur Toussaint*, Paris: Seuil, 1961. Page numbers in the text are taken from this edition.

11 'Théâtre, conscience du peuple', *Acoma*, No. 2, July 1971, p. 42.

12 'Théâtre, conscience du peuple', pp. 42–43.

13 'Théâtre, conscience du peuple', p. 58.

14 Communion with the dead and ancestral spirits is an important part of Haitian folk belief. Toussaint's conversations with the dead show the persistence of peasant beliefs in someone who is also a product of Europe's Age of Enlightenment.

15 Juris Silenieks, Introduction to English translation of *Monsieur Toussaint*, Washington, D.C.: Three Continents Press, 1981, p. 12.

16 *Le sel noir, Le sang rivé, Boises*, Paris: Gallimard, 1983, p. 151. Page numbers for *Boises* in the text are taken from this collection.

17 See *Acoma*, No. 3, February 1972, p. 7.

18 *Malemort*, Paris: Seuil, 1975, pp. 213–14.

19 Frederick Ivor Case, *The Crisis of Identity*, Sherbrooke: Naaman, 1985, p. 27.

20 Willy Alante-Lima, '*Malemort*' (Review) *Présence Africaine*, No. 97, 1976, pp. 178–82.

21 Bernabé, Chamoiseau and Confiant, *Eloge de la Créolité*, p. 23.

22 Patrick Chamoiseau, 'En témoignage d'une volupté', *Carbet*, No. 10, December 1990, p. 144.

23 Bernadette Cailler in *Conquérants de la nuit nue* (p. 108) categorises *Malemort* as 'hors genre' because of its intensely poetic nature and its complex narrative structure.

24 'Langue et multilinguisme dans l'expression des nations modernes', *Les études francaises dans le monde*, Montreal, AUPELF 1972, pp. 10–15.

25 'Langue et multilinguisme dans l'expression des nations modernes', p. 38.

26 'Langue et multilinguisme dans l'expression des nations modernes', p. 37.

27 *Le discours antillais*, p. 237.

28 For Mikhail Bakhtin's concepts of heteroglossia and dialogization as distinguishing characteristics of the novel, see his essay 'Discourse in the Novel' in *The Dialogic Imagination* tr. C. Emerson and M. Holquist, Austin: University of Texas Press, 1981.

29 *Acoma*, Nos. 4–5, April 1973, p. 20.

30 See 'Le noir et le langage' in Frantz Fanon's *Peau noire masques blancs*, Paris: Seuil, 1952, pp. 33–52.

31 *Acoma*, Nos. 4–5, April 1972, p. 67.

32 *Le discours antillais*, p. 485.

33 *Le discours antillais*, p. 15.

34 Elinor Miller, 'Narrative Techniques in Edouard Glissant's *Malemort*', *The French Review*, Vol. 53, No. 2, December 1979, pp. 224–31.

35 There is a brief analysis of the 'nous' narrator in Cailler, *Conquérants de la nuit nue*, pp. 163–4.

36 *Le discours antillais*, p. 14.

37 *Antilla*, No. 473, February 1992, pp. 29–33.

38 Bernabé, Chamoiseau and Confiant, *Eloge de la Créolité*, p. 23.

5. TOWARDS A THEORY OF *ANTILLANITE*

1 *La case du commandeur*, Paris: Seuil, 1981. Page numbers in the text are taken from this edition.

2 *Le discours antillais*, Paris: Seuil, 1981. Page numbers in the text are taken from this edition.

3 Cailler, *Conquérants de la nuit nue*, p. 176.

4 Jacques Cellard in *Le Monde*, No. 11365, Aug. 1981.

5 Barbara Webb, in *Myth and History in Caribbean Fiction* (Amherst: University of Massachusetts Press, 1992), emphasizes Mycéa's superiority over male characters, seeing her as an example of

Glissant's 'critique of male notions of mastery and control' (p. 124).

6 See my article 'Le roman de Nous', *Carbet*, No. 10, December 1990, pp. 21–31.

7 Cailler, *Conquérants de la nuit nue*, p. 54.

8 Beverley Ormerod, 'Discourse and Dispossession: Edouard Glissant's image of contemporary Martinique', *Caribbean Quarterly*, Vol. 27, No. 4, 1981, p. 6.

9 Ormerod, 'Discourse and Dispossession', p. 9.

10 Cailler, *Conquérants de la nuit nue*, p. 126.

11 This image of the concentrated opacity of the rock may well go back to Saint-John Perse. See the analysis of mineral metamorphosis in Perse's poetry in Richard, *Onze études sur la poésie moderne*, pp. 62–3.

12 Jacques André in his review of *La case du commandeur* makes the point that it is not surprising that women have this special access to a counter-poetics because men are 'accomplices of the prevailing order, reason and the universal' (*Présence Africaine*, No. 21–2, 1982, p. 429).

13 The quiet strength of women may be more pronounced in later novels, but even in *La Lézarde* Glissant observes that 'elles dépassent l'homme par la tranquille certitude qui est en elles, par une douce obstination' ('they outstrip men because of the quiet self-assurance within them, because of a gentle determination', p. 75).

14 The tendency of critics is to view the writing of this period as extraordinarily pessimistic. See Richard Burton, 'Comment peut-on être Martiniquais? The recent work of Edouard Glissant, *Modern Language Review*, Vol. 79, No. 2, April 1984, p. 311, and Case, *The Crisis of Identity*, pp. 130–1.

15 The term *Antillanité*, coined by Glissant, appears in discussions of his position as early as 1970. For instance, Jacques Corzani in 'Guadeloupe et Martinique: la difficile voie de la Négritude et l'Antillanité (*Présence Africaine*, No. 76, 1970) seems to defend negritude as an idea that still has a role to play and sees *Antillanité* as seductive but premature (p. 41).

16 The idea of a network of floating roots raised here is given further formulation in the idea of 'identité-rhizome' of *Poétique de la relation*.

17 The apparent similarities between the Caribbean and the Mediterranean are the seaborne nature of their histories, the confluence of European, Oriental and African cultures and the balmy nature of their climates. Both Alejo Carpentier (*Explosion in a Cathedral*, 1962) and Jacques Stephen Alexis ('Du realisme merveilleux des Haitiens', 1956) have emphasized these parallels.

18 Glissant sees the hoarding of ideas and the need for intellectual authority as an example of the pathological dimension of the Martiniquan personality. This manifestation of lived delirium is raised in *Le discours antillais* (pp. 379–80) where Glissant argues that knowledge becomes a possession for investment.

19 Derek Walcott develops this idea in 'The Muse of History' in *Is Massa Day Dead?*, ed. Orde Coombs (New York: Anchor Press, 1974).

20 Claude Lévi-Strauss, *The Savage Mind*, Chicago: The University of Chicago Press, 1966, p. 257.

6. A POETICS OF CHAOS

1 See Glissant's comments on Césairean negritude and Fanon's theories of revolution, in the interview with Wolfgang Bader in *Komparatistische Hefte*, No. 9–10, 1984, and on the practice of 'généralisation' in his 'Ouverture pour un dialogue' in *CARE*, No. 10, April 1983.

2 This almost seems a direct response to Fanon's assertion in *Peau noire, masques blancs* (1952) that because of the pathological nature of Martiniquan society 'Le Noir n'a pas de résistance ontologique' (p. 109).

3 Interview in *CARE*, No. 10, April 1983, p. 22.

4 *Pays rêvé, pays réel*, Paris: Seuil, 1985, p. 104. Page numbers in the text are taken from this edition.

5 *Mahagony*, Paris: Seuil, 1987, p. 184. Page numbers in the text are taken from this edition.

6 'Lam, l'envol et la réunion', *CARE*, 1983, p. 15.

7 'Lam, l'envol et la réunion', p. 14.

8 Interview with Priska Degras and Bernard Magnier, in *Notre librairie*, No. 74, 1984, p. 18.

9 Interview with Degras and Magnier, p. 18.

10 This section appears in the special edition of *CARE* dedicated to Glissant in 1983. There are some variations on the final text.

11 The excerpt that is in *CARE* contains the lines:

> Tu es Ata-Eli et tu es Laoka
> L'épouse qui s'assied au coin de tout
> silence. (p. 93)

> You are Ata-Eli and you are Laoka
> The spouse who sits by the corner of
> silence.

These had been dropped from the published version.

12 Interview with Degras and Magnier, p. 19.

13 Juris Silenieks, 'Pays rêvé, pays réel', *World Literature Today*, Vol. 63, No. 4, Autumn 1989, p. 635.

14 The island itself appears at times as the product of this difficult exchange between the unknown and the sayable, 'un bouquet de laves fusant de ces deux mers – la Caraïbe opale et l'Océan couleur de roches' ('a spray of lava bursting from these two seas – the opal Caribbean and the rock dark ocean', p. 31).

15 An interesting parallel in Caribbean literature is that of the Cuban novel, *Biografía de un Cimarron* ('Biography of a Runaway') by Miguel Barnet (1966). In this work Esteban Montejo, the subject, 'runs away' from the author and reaches beyond his role as native informant to turn the biography into an autobiography.

16 *Poétique de la relation*, Paris: Gallimard, 1990. Page numbers in the text are taken from this edition.

17 See *World Literature Today*, Vol. 63, No. 4, 1989, p. 560.

18 The beach at Diamant is enormously important to Glissant's later work. Diamond Rock itself may well explain the prevalence of images of rocks. It may also be a newer manifestation of the sand bar in *La Lézarde*.

19 For a good discussion of political and cultural developments in contemporary Martinique, see Richard Burton, 'Towards 1992: political–cultural assimilation and opposition in contemporary Martinique', *French Cultural Studies* 3, 1992, pp. 61–86.

20 In 1992 a book of short poems entitled *Fastes* (Toronto: Editions du Gref) was published by Glissant. Another novel, *Tout-monde* (Paris: Gallimard) appeared in 1993.

21 Derek Walcott, *Omeros*, New York: Farrar, Straus, Giroux, 1990, p. 325.

Bibliography

WORKS BY EDOUARD GLISSANT

PUBLISHED BOOKS

Un champ d'îles, Paris: Dragon 1953.

La terre inquiète, Paris: Dragon 1954.

Les Indes: poème de l'une et l'autre terre, Paris: Seuil, 1956.

Soleil de la conscience, Paris: Seuil, 1956.

La Lézarde, Paris: Seuil, 1958.

Le sel noir, Paris: Seuil, 1959.

Le sang rivé, Paris: Présence Africaine, 1961.

Monsieur Toussaint, Paris: Seuil, 1961.

Poèmes, Paris: Seuil, 1963.

Le quatrième siècle, Paris: Seuil, 1964.

L'intention poétique, Paris: Seuil, 1969.

Malemort, Paris: Seuil, 1975.

Boises, Fort-de-France: Acoma, 1979.

Monsieur Toussaint: version scénique, Fort-de France: Acoma, 1978.

La case du commandeur, Paris: Seuil, 1981.

Le discours antillais, Paris: Seuil, 1981.

Pays rêvé, pays réel, Paris: Seuil, 1985.

Mahagony, Paris: Seuil, 1987.

Poétique de la relation, Paris: Gallimard, 1990.

Fastes, Toronto: Gref, 1992.

Tout-monde, Paris: Gallimard, 1993.

ENGLISH TRANSLATIONS

The Ripening, tr. J. Michael Dash, London: Heinemann, 1985.

Monsieur Toussaint, tr. Joseph Foster and Barbara Franklin, Washington D.C.: Three Continents Press, 1981.

Caribbean Discourse, tr. J. Michael Dash, Charlottesville: University of Virginia Press, 1989.

The Indies, tr. Dominique O'Neill and followed by the original, Toronto: Gref, 1992.

SELECTED ARTICLES, TALKS AND MISCELLANEOUS PIECES

'Segalen, Segalen!', *Les lettres nouvelles*, Vol. 3, No. 32, 1955, pp. 626–33.
'Aimé Césaire et la découverte du monde', *Les lettres nouvelles*, Vol. 4, No. 34, 1956, pp. 44–54.
'Alejo Carpentier et "l'Autre Amérique"', *Critique*, No. 105, February 1956, pp. 113–19.
'Michel Leiris ethnographe', *Les lettres nouvelles*, Vol. 4, No. 43, 1956, pp. 609–21.
'Le romancier noir et son peuple. Notes pour une conférence', *Présence Africaine*, No. 16, October–November 1957, pp. 26–31.
'*L'Arbre de la nuit* par Djuna Barnes', *Les lettres nouvelles*, Vol. 5, No. 55, December 1957, p. 795.
'Structures de groupes et tensions de groupes en Martinique', *Acoma*, No. 1, April 1971, pp. 31–43.
'Introduction à une étude des fondements socio-historiques du déséquilibre mental', *Acoma*, No. 1, April 1971, pp. 78–93.
'Théâtre, conscience du peuple', *Acoma*, No. 2, July 1971, pp. 41–59.
'Langue et multilinguisme dans l'expression des nations modernes', *Les études francaises dans le monde*, Montreal, AUPELF 1972, pp. 10–15.
'Action culturelle et pratique politique: propositions de base', *Acoma*, Nos. 4–5, April 1973, pp. 16–20.
'Sur le délire verbal: introduction à une étude du délire verbal "coutumier" comme signifiant de la situation en Martinique', *Acoma*, Nos. 4–5, April 1973, pp. 49–68.
'Note sur une pré-enquête: le cas Suffrin', *Acoma*, Nos. 4–5, April 1973, pp. 84–92.
'Poétique et inconscient martiniquais', in *Identité culturelle et Francophonie dans les Amériques*, ed. E. Snyder and A. Valdmann, Quebec: Université Laval, 1976, pp. 236–44.
'Saint-John Perse et les Antillais', *La nouvelle revue Francaise*, No. 278, February 1976, pp. 68–74.
'La vocation de comprendre l'autre', *Le Courrier de l'UNESCO*, Vol. 34, December 1981, pp. 32–35.
'Lam, l'envol et la réunion', *CARE*, No. 10, April 1983, pp. 14–15.
'Ouverture pour un dialogue', *CARE*, No. 10, April 1983, pp. 94–5.
'Bâtir la tour', *Le Courrier de l'UNESCO*, Vol. 26, No. 7, July 1983, pp. 8–9.

'Brève philosophie d'un baroque mondial', *Le Courrier de l'UNESCO*, Vol. 40, No. 9, September 1987, pp. 18–19.

'Saint-John Perse: l'errance enracinée', preface to *Pour Saint-John Perse: études et essais pour le Centenaire de Perse*, Paris: l'Harmattan, 1988, pp. 13–17.

'Un marqueur de paroles', preface to *Chronique des sept misères* by Patrick Chamoiseau, Paris: Gallimard, 1988, pp. 3–6.

'René Char', *Le Courrier de l'UNESCO*, Vol. 41, No. 6, June 1988, p. 33.

'La Caraïbe, les Amériques et la Poétique de la relation', *CELACEF Bulletin*, Vol. 3, Nos. 1–2, 1989, pp. 2–14.

'Discours de Glendon', in *Discours*, compiled by Alain Baudot, Toronto: Gref, 1990, pp. 11–18.

SELECTED INTERVIEWS

Brossat, Alain and Maragnes, Daniel, 'Entretien avec Edouard Glissant', *Les Antilles dans l'impasse*, Paris: l'Harmattan, 1981, pp. 89–101.

Roget, Wilbert, 'Littérature, conscience nationale, écriture aux Antilles: entretien avec Edouard Glissant', *CLA Journal*, Vol. 30 No. 3, March 1981, pp. 304–20.

'Entretien avec Glissant', *CARE*, No. 10, April 1983, pp. 17–25.

Degras, Priska and Magnier, Bernard, 'Edouard Glissant, préfacier d'une littérature future', *Notre librairie*, No. 74, 1984, pp. 14–20.

Bader, Wolfgang, 'Poétique antillaise, poétique de la relation', *Komparatistische Hefte*, Nos. 9–10, 1984, pp. 83–100.

'La poétique d'Edouard Glissant', *Antilla*, No. 416, January 1991, pp. 29–32.

Dash, J. Michael, 'Interview with Edouard Glissant', *Caribbean Review of Books*, No. 5, August 1992, pp. 17–19.

Gauvin, Lise, 'L'imaginaire des langues: entretien avec Edouard Glissant', *Etudes Francaises*, Vol. 27, Nos. 2–3, 1993, pp. 11–22.

WORKS ABOUT GLISSANT

Alante-Lima, Willy, review of *Malemort*, *Présence Africaine*, no. 97, 1976, pp. 178–82.

André, Jacques, *Caraibales*, Paris: Ed. Caribéennes, 1981.

'Le renversement de Senglis', *CARE*, No. 10, April 1983, pp. 31–51.

Baudot, Alain, 'Edouard Glissant: A Poet in search of his Landscape', *World Literature Today*, Vol. 63, No. 4, 1989, pp. 583–8.

'Bibliographie des écrits de Glissant', *Discours de Glendon*, Toronto: Gref, 1990, pp. 19–62.

'*Bibliographie* annotée d'Edouard Glissant', Toronto: Gref, 1993.

Bernabé, Jean, Chamoiseau, Patrick and Confiant, Raphael, *Eloge de la Créolité*, Paris: Gallimard, 1989.

Berque, Jacques, Preface to *Le sel noir*, Paris: Gallimard, 1983, pp. 7–18.

Burton, Richard, 'Comment peut-on être Martiniquais? The recent Work of Edouard Glissant', *The Modern Language Review*, Vol. 79, No. 2, April 1984, pp. 301–12.

'Towards 1992: Political–Cultural Assimilation and Opposition in contemporary Martinique', *French Cultural Studies*, 3, 1992, pp. 61–86.

Cailler, Bernadette, 'Un itinéraire poétique: Edouard Glissant et l'anti-Anabase', *Présence Francophone*, No. 19, 1979, pp. 107–32.

Conquérants de la nuit nue: Edouard Glissant et l'H(h)istoire antillaise, Tubingen: Gunter Narr, 1988.

'Edouard Glissant: A Creative Critic', *World Literature Today*, Vol. 63, No. 4, 1989, pp. 589–92.

'Creolization versus Francophone', *L'Héritage de Caliban*, Pointe à Pitre: Jasor, 1992, pp. 49–62.

Case, Frederick Ivor, 'The Novels of Edouard Glissant', *Black Images*, Vol. 2, Nos. 3–4, 1973, pp. 3–12, 47.

The Crisis of Identity: Studies in the Martiniquan and Guadeloupean Novel, Sherbrooke: Naaman, 1985.

'Edouard Glissant and the Poetics of Cultural Marginalisation', *World Literature Today*, Vol. 63, No. 4, 1989, pp. 593–8.

Chamoiseau, Patrick, 'En témoignage d'une volupté', *Carbet*, No. 10, December 1990, pp. 143–52.

Chamoiseau, Patrick and Confiant, Raphael, *Lettres créoles*, Paris: Hatier, 1991.

Chassagne, Raymond, 'Edouard Glissant, homme de rupture et témoin caribéen', *Conjonction*, No. 148, July 1980, pp. 63–7.

Clark, Beatrice, 'IME Revisited: Lectures by Edouard Glissant on Socio-cultural Realities in the Francophone Antilles', *World Literature Today*, Vol. 63, No. 4, 1989, pp. 599–605.

Confiant, Raphael, 'Ko fanm, pawol nonm adan *La case du commandeur*', *Carbet*, No. 10, December 1990, pp. 51–6.

Corzani, Jack, 'Guadeloupe et Martinique: la difficile voie de la Négritude et l'Antillanité', *Présence Africaine*, No. 76, 1970, pp. 16–42.

Coursil, Jacques, 'Le travail du poétique et sa lecture', *Carbet*, No. 10, December 1990, pp. 65–79.

Crosta, Suzanne, *Le marronnage créateur*, Quebec: GRELCA, 1991.

Damato, Diva, 'The Poetics of the Dispossessed', *World Literature Today*, Vol. 63, No. 4, 1989, pp. 606–8.

Dash, J. Michael, Introduction to *The Ripening*, London: Heinemann, 1985.

Introduction to *Caribbean Discourse*, Charlottesville: University of Virginia Press, 1989.

'Writing the Body: Edouard Glissant's Poetics of Re-membering', *World Literature Today*, Vol. 63, No. 4, 1989, pp. 609–12.

'Le roman de nous', *Carbet*, No. 10, December 1990, pp. 21–31.

'Drunken Boats on a Sea of Stories', *JWIL*, Vol. 5, Nos. 1–2, August 1992, pp. 121–4.

Degras, Priska, 'Name of the Fathers, History of the Name', *World Literature Today*, Vol. 63, No. 4, 1989, pp. 613–19.

'Se nommer soi-même', *Carbet*, No. 10, December 1990, pp. 57–64.

'Glissant 80', *Notre librairie*, No. 104, 1991.

Ducornet, Guy, 'Edouard Glissant and the Problem of Time', *Black Images*, Vol. 2, Nos. 3–4, 1973, pp. 13–16.

Ebion, Roger, 'Mahagony, quelle langue', *Carbet*, No. 10, December 1990, pp. 117–41.

Hurbon, Laennec, 'Naissance de deux revues caribéennes', *Présence Africaine*, No. 80, 1971, pp. 177–9.

Knight, Vere, 'The Novel as History Rewritten', *Black Images*, Vol. 3, No. 1, 1974, pp. 64–79.

Laplaine, Jean, '*La Lézarde* ou la naissance nécessaire et balbutiante d'une littérature', *CARE*, No. 10, 1983, pp. 56–70.

Lucrèce, André, 'Paysage, mesure et démesure dans la poésie de Glissant', *Carbet*, No. 10, December 1990, pp. 81–8.

Miller, Elinor, 'Narrative Techniques in Edouard Glissant's *Malemort*', *The French Review*, Vol. 53, No. 2, December 1979, pp. 224–31.

Mortimer, Mildred, 'Conquest and Resistance in Edouard Glissant's poetry', *L'esprit créateur*, Vol. 32, No. 2, Summer 1992, pp. 65–76.

Ntonfo, André, *L'homme et identité dans le roman des Antilles et Guyane Francaises*, Sherbrooke: Namaan, 1982.

Ormerod, Beverley, 'Beyond Negritude: Some Aspects of the Work of Edouard Glissant', *Savacou*, Nos. 11–12, 1975, pp. 39–45.

'Discourse and Dispossession: Edouard Glissant's image of contemporary Martinique', *Caribbean Quarterly*, Vol. 27, No. 4, 1981, pp. 1–12.

An Introduction to the French Caribbean Novel, London: Heinemann, 1985.

'La notion d'Antillanité chez Glissant', in *Negritude et Antillanité*, Kensington: New South Wales University Press, 1982.

Pépin, Ernest, 'Le personnage romanesque dans l'oeuvre de Glissant', *Carbet*, No. 10, December 1990, pp. 89–99.

Pestre de Almeida, Lilian, 'Fastes, une poétique érudite et ensouchée entre l'écrit et l'oral', *Antilla*, No. 520, 1993, pp. 28–31.

Praeger, Michele, 'Edouard Glissant: Towards a Literature of Orality', *Callaloo*, Vol. 15, No. 1, 1992, pp. 41–8.

Racine, Daniel, 'The Antilleanity of Edouard Glissant', *World Literature Today*, Vol. 63, No. 4, 1989, pp. 620–5.

Radford, Daniel, *Edouard Glissant*, Paris: Seghers, 1982.

Roget, Wilbert, 'Land and Myth in the Writings of Edouard Glissant', *World Literature Today*, Vol. 63, No. 4, 1989, pp. 626–31.

Silenieks, Juris, 'Glissant's Prophetic Vision of the Past', *African Literature Today*, No. 11, 1980, pp. 161–8.

Introduction to *Monsieur Toussaint*, Washington D.C.: Three Continents Press, 1982, pp. 5–15.

'The Maroon Figure in Caribbean Francophone Prose', in *Voices from Under*, ed. W. Luis, Westport Conn.: Greenwood Press, 1984.

'The Martinican Chronotope in Edouard Glissant's Oeuvre', *World Literature Today*, Vol. 63, No. 4, 1989, pp. 632–6.

Toumson, Roger, 'Les écrivains afro-antillais et la réécriture', *Europe*, No. 612, April 1980.

Ugah, Adah, 'La mer et la quête de soi: une lecture bachelardienne des romans de Glissant', *Présence Africaine*, No. 132, 1984, pp. 108–25.

Webb, Barbara J., *Myth and History in Caribbean Fiction*, Amherst: University of Massachusetts Press, 1992.

Wynter, Sylvia, 'Beyond the World of Man: Glissant and the New Discourse of the Antilles', *World Literature Today*, Vol. 63, No. 4, 1989, pp. 637–47.

Yerro, Phillippe-Alain, 'La trace de Gani', *Carbet*, No. 10, December 1990, pp. 101–15.

Index